The Lost Road

A Search for the Soul of the West

Other Books by Sean J. McGrath

The Early Heidegger and Medieval Philosophy
ISBN-10: 0813214718

Heidegger: A (Very) Critical Introduction
ISBN-10: 0802860079

The Dark Ground of Spirit: Schelling and the Unconscious
ISBN-10: 0415492122

Thinking Nature: An Essay in Negative Ecology
ISBN-10: 1474449271

The Philosophical Foundations of the Late Schelling: The Turn to the Positive
ISBN-10: 139951119X

Political Eschatology
ISBN-10: 1666738093

The Lost Road

A Search for the Soul of the West

Sean J. McGrath

CHRISTIAN ALTERNATIVE BOOKS

Winchester, UK
Washington, USA

First published by Christian Alternative Books, 2025
Christian Alternative Books is an imprint of Collective Ink, Ltd.
Unit 11, Shepperton House, 89
Shepperton Road, London, N1 3DF
office@collectiveinkbooks.com
www.collectiveinkbooks.com
www.christian-alternative.com

For distributor details and how to order please visit the 'Ordering' section on our website.

ISBN: 978 1 80341 273 3
978 1 80341 274 0 (ebook)
Library of Congress Control Number: 2024904835

A CIP catalogue record for this book is available from the British Library.

Design: Lapiz Digital Services

UK: Printed and bound by CPI Group (UK) Ltd, Croydon, CR0 4YY
US: Printed and bound by Thomson-Shore, 7300 West Joy Road, Dexter, MI 48130

Contents

For Esther, who met me on the road and stayed with me.

In time, we shall have the whole Christian Church in our unconscious.

C.G. Jung

Preface

Writing a book is a bit like raising a child. One nurtures the child in order to set her free on her own course as an adult, without any idea of where she will go, what she will do in the world, and whom she will meet along the way. Nevertheless, an author should have some sense of to whom he is speaking or, at least, to whom he imagines he is speaking.

I completed this book in broad outlines ten years ago. It was first conceived as a popular book in the history of Western religious philosophy. My target audience was ordinary people who shared my cultural background (Western, secular, post-Christendom) with a desire for spiritual life but without a church, either because they can no longer believe in the forms of religion in which they were raised, or, ever more commonly, because they have never set foot in a church. I wanted to write a book on religion for de-churched Westerners.

I had as material the transcript of an undergraduate lecture course in philosophy I had given at Memorial University of Newfoundland in 2010. The course was called "Introduction to Western Spirituality." It was more or less a survey of Greek philosophy, Jewish and Christian theology, and psychoanalysis simplified for beginners. The basic idea was that the secular West was no accident or defection from religion but the product of the synthesis of Greek thinking and Hebrew faith. The unraveling of Christendom in the early modern period was the end of one era of religion and the beginning of another. I had not yet read Gauchet's defense of the same thesis (Gauchet 1999). My point of access was German philosophy, C.G. Jung, and the twentieth-century Christian writers who had more or less guided me my whole life (G.K. Chesterton, C.S. Lewis, Thomas Merton, Charles Williams, Nicholas Berdeyaev). I pursued the thesis with the students that our secular age is still religious in its way and lives from its religious roots in Plato, the Bible, and medieval spirituality.

The students liked the course but it was clear to me that the transcript did not quite hang together as a book. During a sabbatical in Sri Lanka in 2014, I revised the whole thing by including, upon the insistence of my wife, biographical details and personal reflections. The biographical narrative gave the manuscript unity, for it was in my life that these seemingly heterogenous things—existentialism, the Buddha, Greek philosophy, the New Testament, Christian monasticism, C.G. Jung—had become one. Writing in the early mornings in an office on the second floor of a house we rented in Kandy, with a bank of windows open to the jungle, which at dawn, was resonant with the noise of animals, I became more inspired. I wrote *my* story for those who, like me, still harbor a hope that there is something more to life than the sugar rush of a new Apple gadget, an "exotic" trip curated by AirBnB, or a new pair of designer jeans. I wrote to make a case for Western religion as a living tradition that is as relevant today as it was 800 or 2000 years ago. The irony was not lost on me that this apology for the West was being written in the heart of the East, in the center of the island of the former colony of Ceylon, where the Pali canon, the oldest Buddhist scriptures were preserved and still studied. I wrote of the Christ in the mornings; in the afternoons I visited the ancient stone buddhas—some several stories high—that are scattered throughout the jungles of Sri Lanka.

I was conscious that I was fighting against the current. No one I knew wanted this book. To do something toward securing a reception for the book, I needed to correct two misconceptions. First, I needed to make the case for an authentically contemplative Western tradition originating in the fusion of the horizons of Athens and Jerusalem in orthodox Christianity and persisting through the transformations the Christian tradition underwent from the Latin Middle Ages to early modernity. Westerners and post-Christian seekers continue to choose to believe that the East has found and sheltered that which was lost to us long ago, the secret to genuine spiritual life, the divine truth behind the play of illusions that is the world. While I would never dissuade anyone from undertaking such a quest, I wanted to suggest that the West has its own contemplative tradition and its recovery might prove even more effective as an antidote to nihilism than the journey to the East.

Second, I needed to tackle the elephant in the room, the chief historical-political effect of the Western tradition, which is lustily alive and growing: consumerism. I needed to concede to the critics of the West that consumerism genuinely belongs to the Western tradition, but not as its logical outcome; rather as its perversion, as the anti-Christ belongs to the biblical revelation (without the Christ he would not appear; see Rev. 19–20). One must recognize the true in the false if the false is to be known as false, the true twisted and turned upside down. As is the case with the anti-Christ of the Bible, the false has its role to play. It makes the true all the more sharply distinct and undeniable and forces a decision, for the one, or the other.

Contrary to popular misconception, consumerism is not a form of materialism. Rather, it is a form of spirituality—a false spirituality, to be sure, one that promises what it does not give, namely freedom, transcendence, and love, but a spirituality nonetheless. Consumerism works because it appeals to all aspects of human desire, both to what is lowest in us—the craving for pleasure, recognition, and power—and to what is highest in us: the drive toward the good. Consumerism is not an expression of a universal human desire. It is not merely another manifestation of age-old human ignorance and greed. It has its history. If consumerism enjoys such success in Asia, it is not because it is native to the great spiritual cultures of China, Japan, and India—quite the contrary. Its success in these countries has more or less obliterated their once-great philosophical and religious traditions.

I revisited the manuscript periodically over the past decade and struggled with how to better integrate the biographic and didactic elements. In preparing for publication with Collective Ink, I struck upon the solution. The two themes, the biographical and the historical, constitute two parts of a whole. The two parts can be read separately, but they were written together, the one intended as a commentary on the other. My model became Augustine's *Confessions*. The first nine books of the *Confessions* are biographical, an account of Augustine's conversion; the last four books are didactic, four inter-connected treatises, on memory, time, creation, and Genesis, which function as a theological meditation on Augustine's conversion story. So too is Part Two of this book a theological meditation on Part One.

With Augustine as my model, I have only included those aspects of my life that are necessary to explain the occasion for a particular insight or for the discovery of the contemporary relevance of some aspect of the Western tradition. The *Confessions* is not an autobiography; neither is *The Lost Road*. This book is a personal testament to a path of discovery, not an authoritative study of Western philosophy and religion or contemplative Christianity.[1]

It came out of my life, and I struggled to render every sentence of it true to that life. Like the child come of age who heads out alone into the world, I let it go trusting that it will find its friends.

1 October 2023
The Hermitage at Burnt Head, Conception Bay, Newfoundland

Endnotes

1. For readers seeking something more authoritative on these matters than this present book offers, I can still recommend Copleston's *History of Philosophy* (1946–1975)—a classic academic resource that I, like many professors, use

regularly in my teaching. For the history of Christian spirituality and theology, there are too many places to turn, with each historian having his or her peculiar agenda. If scholarship on Christian mysticism is wanted, the place to turn is Bernard McGinn's seven-volume series, *The Presence of God: A History of Western Christian Mysticism* (see volume one, McGinn 1991). Early in my search, C.S. Lewis helped me overcome certain rationalistic, twentieth-century prejudices that prevented me for a while from taking my first steps along the road. See especially his magnificent little book, *Mere Christianity* (Lewis 1952), and his quirky spiritual autobiography, *Surprised by Joy* (Lewis 1955). Crucial to my re-discovery of my Catholic theological heritage were Rosemary Haughton's *The Catholic Thing* (Haughton 1979), Thomas Merton's *Seven Storey Mountain* (Merton 1948), Peter Brown's *Saint Augustine* (Brown 1969), and G.K. Chesterton's *Orthodoxy* (Chesterton 1908), *St. Thomas Aquinas* (Chesterton 1933), and *St. Francis* (Chesterton 1923). Discovering Nikos Kazantzakis's works, *The Last Temptation of Christ* (Kazantzakis 1960; forget the movie) and *Saint Francis* (Kazantzakis 1962), was pivotal for me. Anyone struggling with Nietzsche's critique of Christianity, as I once did, will benefit from reading Kazantzakis. On the New Testament, I devoured C.H. Dodd's *The Meaning of Paul for Today* (Dodd 1920) and Daniel-Rops's *Jesus and His Times* (Daniel-Rops 1960). Both are dated in terms of New Testament scholarship but remain incomparably more inspiring than most of what is published today. Without Dostoevsky's novels, especially *Crime and Punishment*, *The Idiot*, and *Brothers Karamazov*, I would never have found my way to the road.

Acknowledgments

I gratefully acknowledge Memorial University of Newfoundland for the financial assistance that supported bringing this book into publication. I would also like to acknowledge Christina Galego, editor par excellence and critical interlocutor, who helped me with the first draft of the book. My thanks go to everyone who has ever cared enough about me to help me on my path. I would like especially to mention Sharon Doyle and Tessa Bielecki, my spiritual mothers and my first guides into the *mystici corporis Christi*. But above all, I thank my twin sister, Sheilagh McGrath (1966–2002), who first showed me the way and continues to.

Part One

My Search for Truth

"It's a toss-up when you decide to leave the beaten track. Many are called, few are chosen."

W. Somerset Maugham

Chapter One

How I Found the Road

Himalaya

When I was twenty years old, I took a semester off from school and traveled. I was struggling through an English degree at the University of Ottawa at the time. I shelved my books and bought a pair of sturdy Italian hiking boots, a backpack, and a plane ticket to India. It was 1987, and traveling then, as I say on occasion to my students, was still possible. One could get lost. I went East with no clear plan to return. I carried with me an already well-read copy of Lonely Planet India, a little leather journal my grandmother had given me on departure, and a money belt stuffed with 3,000 US dollars—my entire savings after a year of mind-numbing bureaucratic drudgery in a government office.

I had grown up in Ottawa, one of six kids, and had more or less happily occupied my teenage years, skipping school, skateboarding, and watching mob movies. Then, at eighteen, something happened that changed me and set me on the lost road, which is the theme of this book. My twenty-year-old first cousin, whom I loved like the brother I never had, was found hanging from a tree. John had bought a one-way bus ticket from his suburban home in Montreal to a small town in Ontario where, one afternoon, he walked into a patch of woods at the side of a road, climbed a tree in his bare feet (his shoes placed neatly at the trunk), and hanged himself from a length of rope he had purchased that day in a hardware store.

We talked incessantly about why he did it. But none of the offered explanations helped me understand. What shook me to the core was not the possible reasons for his decision, which we will never know, but the fact of the decision itself. John had taken his life.

Until that moment, I had not thought of my life, the world as I found it, as a limited whole, as Wittgenstein once put it. I had never really considered it as *one thing*.

My life is divided into two distinct and incommensurate periods: before and after John's death. For better or worse, John made me a philosopher. My intellectual and spiritual journey began with his death. In the pain and sorrow of it, I began to question. Because my intellectual path began in personal tragedy, philosophy could never be for me a merely academic discipline. It may disguise itself as such in order to secure a place in the knowledge industry, as I have disguised myself as a professor for the past two decades, but it really does not belong there. Compared, say, to history or physics, philosophy has little knowledge to disseminate. Philosophy is the practice of reflecting on life as such, of distancing oneself from it (to the extent that one can) in the interest of radically questioning it. What is life? Is it a good thing? There is something essentially human about the capacity to ask this question. It may be the single trait that most distinguishes us from other creatures. Existential reflection might just as readily be considered an imperfection as a virtue. It may be evidence of the dignity and greatness of the human being. But this capacity is also the source of the distinctive way that humans suffer.

John's death was all the more painful and puzzling, given his cheerful, happy-go-lucky disposition. John was no morbid teenager but a merry prankster, always laughing and finding humor in whatever situation he was in. His was not the type of carefully rehearsed clowning that can be so annoying, the trickery of one who is always a step ahead of the conversation, strategically plotting his next moves. John's humor was spontaneous, a direct expression of genuine mirth. And he was kind. He was a deeply personal young man who looked you in the eye and recognized your presence. He seemed to take the pressures of his upbringing in his stride, effortlessly acquiring the grades in school that were expected of him. He was no jock, but he played football and basketball well. More interesting to me (I was resolutely unenthused by sports), John had an encyclopedic knowledge of the golden age of rock music. I learned from him the essential bands of the sixties (the Who, the Zombies, the Animals), which I would then further research in secondhand record stores at home.

But at the age of twenty, John stepped back from his life, considered it as such, and concluded that it was not good. What went through his mind as he climbed the tree? Whatever else he believed, he thought that life was not worth the effort it was demanding of him. He believed this with a conviction that overrode his instinct for self-preservation. What did he expect would happen afterward? Did he fear the judgment of the God of Catholicism, traditionally understood to be so severe that suicides would be buried outside church grounds? Or did he expect nothingness? How can one expect nothingness?

Something had given way beneath me that I had, until then, regarded as solid ground. I found myself suspended over an abyss. I could not speak about it with my friends. I tried once, and the result was devastating. They shrugged it off and rolled another joint. And yet nothing was more important to me; nothing occupied my thoughts more. After John died, I no longer laughed at things as I had. The teenage sneer left me, and a pensive sadness took its place. I no longer fitted in.

I began to read, to really read, as though my life depended on it. The books were not particularly scholarly—Herman Hesse novels, mid-twentieth-century travel logs of British sojourners to Tibet, popular introductions to Zen. I was drawn to stories of men who traveled East searching for wisdom, men who could no longer tolerate the lies of the West. The thought that somewhere, hidden from modernity in the highest mountains of the world, an order of spiritual beings existed, as they had for thousands of years, safeguarding the secret to human happiness, entranced me. This fantasy (for that is all it was, as I was to find out) freed up limitless stores of energy in my soul that had lain dormant since my birth, the breakthrough energy, the power to will one thing. It gave me the resolve to break with everything I knew, to throw caution to the wind and risk it all. I pinned a huge, detailed map of India on my wall and studied it daily. I worked in a government office in my spare time and saved every penny for a year. I dreamed about the spiritual breakthrough I would make in the Himalayas at the feet of a lama who had selected me for special training. I would make the breakthrough for John, the breakthrough he couldn't make. I would do what he tried to do but by the wrong means, to liberate myself from suffering. I would expose the lie that had entrapped him and which also held me and my generation captive.

In the distance that opened between my peers and me, I became a wandering Buddhist. I held myself aloof from my friends. I still partied with them, but more than not, left early or talked of nothing but India and the wisdom of the East until I became a bore to them. I was deliberately following in the footsteps of Larry Darrell, the hero of Somerset Maugham's *The Razor's Edge*. Traumatized by his experiences in the trenches of the First World War and disgusted by the mindless hedonism of the roaring twenties, he travels to India to train at the feet of a guru. After years, he returns to America, to find his old friends middle-aged, neurotic, and miserable. Larry becomes a magic, healing presence among them, a messianic figure whose stillness, depth, and sheer goodness are inscrutable to others. He changes everyone who comes in contact with him. Like Larry, I would find the truth that would set me and others free.

It was not clear to me then why I felt so sure that the answer to the question would be found in the East. It was probably because the lamas of the mountains of northern India, Nepal, and Tibet, were about as far from my familiar world as could be imagined. I was going to the ends of the earth to find the pearl of great price, the one Jesus says the merchant is willing to sell all he has to purchase (Matt. 13: 45–46).

One thing seemed clear to me at the time: the answer to the great matter could not be found in the tradition in which I had been raised, Irish Catholicism. My family was perfunctorily churchgoing, even devout when appropriate, but without much reflection. No one talked of spirituality. I heard nothing much about the saints and certainly nothing at all about Christian mysticism. As a teenager, I found the religion of my home to be mechanical and full of absurd inventions that seemed to me to be designed to make people feel better about their sad lives. It seemed that Western religion, which I identified with my local parish experience, did not ask the question that John had brought to the forefront of my attention. I was wrong about that, as I was about most things then, but my misconception of the situation was powerfully productive. My conviction drove me away from the bourgeois comforts of my family home, from the partying and pleasures of young adulthood in middle-class North America circa 1987.

I backpacked to the sacred sites associated with Buddhism: Lumbini, on the border of Nepal, where the Buddha was born; Bodh Gaya, where he was enlightened sitting under a great Banyan tree that is still there; and Benares, where he taught the Four Noble Truths. I traveled with a pack stuffed with cheap Indian paperbacks on Eastern spirituality: *Foundations of Tibetan Mysticism*, *Hermit in the Himalayas*, and a copy of Thomas Merton's *Asian Journal*, which I had pinched from my best friend's father's bookshelf. I trekked to remote monasteries in the Himalayas and attended every religious ceremony I could. I practiced meditation everywhere, in my budget hotel room in Kathmandu, in a tent by the side of trekking trails through high mountain passes, or under the stars seated on the sand in the Thar desert that stretches between India and Pakistan.

I did not find the Buddha, at least not the Buddha I was looking for. But I found my desire for God, which has guided me ever since, like a star in the night sky.

I also found beauty. I found nature. I found my love for wilderness. The first mountains I ever saw were the Himalayas, the abode of the gods in Hindu mythology. These sacred heights, soaring 20,000 feet into the azure blue Himalayan sky, shall remain forever for me a symbol of infinity. One looks up and sees, at first, nothing but an immeasurably high wall of rock, snow, and ice. The immensity of these mountains cannot be described: one must experience it first-hand. As the eyes become adjusted to the saturated scene, one notices details: countless spires and crags, hidden valleys, and inaccessible dark caves high up in the side of granite walls. Suddenly a small avalanche appears high up, a waterfall of snow tumbling thousands of feet with a distant road. Beyond, one discerns further peaks and unseen landscapes, uninhabitable to us but the home of snow leopards and other spirit creatures. I could not get enough of it. I followed local guides through the mountain passes and stayed in huts I rented for a few dollars a night from the poor mountain people. If I was lucky, a pack mule carried my gear. Most of the time, I shouldered my heavy pack, climbing, always climbing. It was in the Himalayas that I learned that a human being is never more human than when he climbs. We should remain forever climbers. The one-pointedness, the fusion of physical and psychological effort, the strain that issues naturally into a forgetful trance, as the now of each step placed ahead of the last overtakes the mind. And the people of those mountains! Elfin children with leathery skin dressed in dark homespun clothes, watching over goats and sheep. Gaunt young men, sinewy and strong as oxen, ready to help me get to wherever I was going. People living in small stone shelters perched on the edge of steep ravines thick with cedars. And everywhere, little shrines, painted white, sparkling in the blinding sunlight and the thin mountain air, housing perhaps a Buddha surrounded by candles and the remains of incense sticks or a Shiva lingam.

After a month in the mountains, I descended to the plains and funneled alongside thousands of other train passengers into the great cities of northern India: Delhi, Varanasi, Calcutta. I saw for the first time in my life what poverty looks like: lepers waving rotting stumps in my face, heaps of reeking trash on street corners crawling with rats and children picking through it, hoards of people pressing in on me everywhere—a great mass of humanity in excess of all proportion, of all possibility of love. Who could care for such a multitude? They all seemed to demand care so desperately. Who could satisfy such infinite need? If it could not be satisfied, why did it exist?

Before I got on the plane home five months later, I had a few things that I wanted to give away: a woolen blanket and a huge unopened jar of peanut butter that I had brought with me because I believed stupidly that I would not be able to eat the local food. I decided to take my humble offerings directly to one of the bigger slums in Delhi, which I had looked at often from a distance. Slums have a fortress-like quality: the tin roofs and cardboard walls mound up around each other, forming an almost impenetrable ramshackle wall concealing the life of the community inside. I wanted to see inside. I did not realize that even a slum has its sense of itself, possessing as much dignity and self-respect in its way as a gated community in the US. It had not occurred to me that, without an invitation, I would be trespassing. I walked in through a narrow opening and into a labyrinth of shacks. Garbage was everywhere. Children peered at me from the darkened doorways of huts leaning in every direction. Mangy dogs sniffed about in the gutter.

I was only a few steps in when I was confronted by a young man with a fierce look on his face. "Mister," he said sternly.

"You should not be here. Go." He was right, of course. I had no right to be there, voyeuristically gaping at others' suffering. I passed him the blanket and dropped the jar of peanut butter into the arms of the tiny, wide-eyed girl who was watching our exchange. Her thin arms coiled around the jar like a sea anemone. She did not know what it was, but she saw that it was big and bright and new and from the West. She turned and ran home with it.

The degree of human misery I encountered exceeded anything I had previously imagined. It was not the mysticism of India that impressed me but the crushing poverty of the masses. Still, there was mysterious serenity amongst the poor. I saw it in the faces of the beggars, young and old, an inner freedom from their situation, a lightness that seemed to take everything in its stride. Was their religion at work in this, stressing, as it did, Shiva's ritual dance of death and rebirth? Did recognizing the circularity of life enable the average believer to approach suffering and death with lightness? Or was it that the caste system, with its rigid social determinism, alleviated them of the anxiety of upward mobility? Everyone, according to the law of karma, is exactly where they should be.

When I returned to my privileged home in Canada, I was an atheist. What I found in the East, however different from anything I had seen before, struck me as no more authentic than what I knew back home. Princely monks in red robes lorded it over the peasants who supported them. When I approached them for spiritual advice, they asked me for money. The *sadhus* with dreadlocks and painted bodies hung around the Hindu temples avoiding work. Young Indians treated me like a king from a land of promise. On the trails and in the budget hotels, I jostled with droves of other Westerners backpacking through Asia with the same Lonely Planet guidebooks.

Now that I reflect, thirty-five years later, it strikes me that Buddhism taught me something crucial. This path I was on, this search for the truth that transforms, I had to walk alone. Five centuries before Christ, Siddhartha Gautama, the historical Buddha, renounced his princely lifestyle along with the conventions of Brahmanism and the ancient religion of the Vedas and resolved to find the truth for himself. Nothing short of a personal experience of reality, he believed, could count as truth. No one could save him. No ritual passed down through countless generations was of any use to him. He needed to learn the secret of life, death, and liberation for himself. He had nothing to help him in this search other than his intellect, his will, and his experience.

I felt decidedly unenlightened upon my return and sunk into the worst depressions I have ever known. I could not resume my old life but had yet to find a replacement. When I wasn't studying, I spent my time roaming around the national parks of Ontario, Quebec, and Newfoundland with a large disobedient Golden Retriever named Ben. But I had made a significant advance since returning from India. I knew what I had to do: I would dedicate what abilities and energies I had to the question John had put before me. I would ask with my whole existence whether life as such was any good. I would ask what the question itself meant. What was life such that I could question it? What was "the good" that I demanded of life, as John had? Buddhism taught me that no one could answer this question for me. Later I would learn that my inner resources were woefully inadequate, that without what Christians call "grace," and Shin Buddhists call "other-power," nothing genuinely spiritual takes hold. But I would only come to this understanding by first believing that I could, indeed that I must, proceed on my own.

Buddhism, or more generally India, taught me a second thing, perhaps even more important. It taught me that I would not find the answer in a distant land. Wherever I went, I brought myself with me and my land and my culture. I could no more leave these than I could step out of my skin. The answer, if there was one, would have to come from home.

At the age of 20, I realized that I could not become a Buddhist without disowning my tradition, Roman Catholicism—which I scarcely understood, for I had never really looked into it. I was moved by T.S. Eliot's writings about his own failed journey to the East. After completing a dissertation at Harvard on Buddhist philosophy and writing *The Waste Land* (his most Buddhist poem), Eliot made an about-face and converted to Anglicanism. He felt that he could not become a Buddhist without abandoning his Western identity. And this he was not ready to do. Since my experience so closely matched his, I quote him at length.

> Two years spent in the study of Sanskrit ... left me in a state of enlightened mystification. A good half of the effort of understanding what the Indian philosophers were after—and their subtleties make most of the great European philosophers look like schoolboys—lay in trying to erase from my mind all the categories and kinds of distinction common to European philosophy from the time of the Greeks. My previous and concomitant study of European philosophy was hardly better than an obstacle ... My only hope of really penetrating to the heart of that mystery would lie in forgetting how to think and feel as an American or a European: which, for practical as well as sentimental reasons, I did not wish to do. (Eliot 1934, 40–41)

I felt something like this when I was 20 years old. I would only add that, from the perspective of middle age, it seems to me that we can never really forget "how to think and feel as an American or a European." It was not that I did not want to surrender my spiritual heritage for "practical as well as sentimental reasons." It was rather than I could not. Raised by devout Catholic parents,

I knew just enough about it to know that I did not know enough about it to make such a decision. My European spiritual ancestry was like the bedrock of my soul: I was standing on it but had never examined it. And yet it was immovably there all the same. With the best of intentions, I could not become a Buddhist then, and even less so now. My ideals collided with the factual reality of my historically situated soul. We might be able to bring unconscious cultural assumptions into consciousness through study and reflection, critiquing and refining them over time—and I have dedicated myself to little else in the past thirty-five years—but we will never succeed in totally uprooting them.

Tradition is the vehicle for understanding. Because cultural presuppositions are always relative and finite, they can never be the only way—but without them, there is no way.

I spent my twenties investing myself in Western philosophical and theological traditions. First, I immersed myself in the study of philosophy; theology would come later. My days and nights were spent in the company of Aristotle, Kant, Kierkegaard, Spinoza, Hegel, and Husserl. My obsessive approach to study caught the attention of some of my teachers. For the first time in my life, I was at the top of my class. But the academic achievement was not what I was after. Scholarships and academic posts were not part of the razor's edge that I sought. Academic philosophy, however useful it was to me then, struck me as a compromise with a world whose value I was putting into question.

One situation in particular summed up for me the problem with university studies. I was particularly taken by the lectures of a certain professor whose specialization was modern European philosophy. I was not unaware that I had become something of a favorite student of his, although we scarcely knew each other and rarely talked. He read my papers and graded them. I would pour over his handwritten comments and read them repeatedly, looking for hints between the lines indicating which direction I should take in my life. Instead, I would find things like, "Your account of the synthetic judgment a priori is spot on." Or, less flattering, "Hegel's notion of mediation seems to be eluding you." I felt as though we were communicating in code; I wrote papers summarizing the ideas of the philosophers we studied but searching in them for the truth of my life, he scribbled terse responses not about what was most important but about something else—related to but not *it*.

The moment came when it was time to speak to him. I asked him if I could meet with him during his office hours. We had met before on occasion to discuss such things as the synthetic judgment a priori and Hegel's notion of mediation. He expected further talk of this sort. When I sat in his cramped book-lined office and faced his question, "What did you want to see me about?" my heart pounded in my chest. I felt like I was asking a girl out on a date (a skill I have never mastered). But the thing was too important, and so I plunged ahead. "Would it be all right," I proceeded cautiously, "if we met occasionally to talk?" He hesitated, looking startled and uncomfortable. In that hesitation, the game was up. I saw instantly that he was not the one to talk to, that there was nothing I could talk to him about aside from the synthetic judgment a priori. So I beat a retreat. "What exactly did you have in mind?" he asked awkwardly. "Oh, philosophical problems that come up in class," I lied. He was visibly relieved.

I left his office and, within a matter of months, left the university. I would return five years later to pursue the degrees and distinctions necessary for a university career. But I no longer expected truth from academic philosophy. I returned to gain a livelihood.

The Buddha Leads Me to the Christ

At 20 years old, I realized with a steadily growing despair that my life was a series of lies. At the center of it all was the lie of consumerism: the deception cultivated through advertisement, social attitudes, and that nebulous cloud of unstated cultural assumptions which Hegel called "ethical life," that my future was an infinite horizon of possibilities for self-construction through shopping, travel and accumulated, exotic experiences. I could no longer pretend that I had not been living based on this assumption. The consumer lie was not someone else's problem, someone else's self-deception. It was my problem. I was not different from my contemporaries. I, too, lived in faith that my self could be endlessly varied and steadily improved through shopping, recreation, and experimenting with sex and drugs. Disgusted by my self and the age in which I was condemned to live, I turned away from the world and fled to the wilderness.

I started in the Himalayas and finished three years later in the woods of Nova Scotia, with many detours through the Rocky Mountains, the lakes and rivers of Northern Ontario, and the barrens of Newfoundland. I hiked, climbed, and paddled into the wild wherever I could find it, always with a backpack full of books. I was not only traveling externally; I had begun the inner quest, the search for my true self, and I was no longer interested in associating with anyone who did not know what that meant. I started in Kashmir, Ladakh, and Nepal. A profound spiritual awakening motivated this pivotal turn to the East. The Buddha appeared to me in the darkest moments of my youth like a beacon in a stormy sea, calling me to leave the safe and the familiar and to seek the path of wisdom, whatever the risk. I read everything I could get my hands on that spoke to this call.

Convinced for no particularly good scholarly reasons that authentic Buddhism had gone north into Tibet, I headed directly to the mountains, where photos of monasteries clinging to the sides of cliffs surrounded by the highest peaks in the world enraptured me with hope. The symbolism of climbing, physical climbing, was necessary to me. I needed to physically express what I was internally undertaking, an ascent into the truth that required leaving most of humanity below in the valleys and the lowlands of ignorance and craving.

A glow of transcendence emanated from the symbol of the Buddha wherever I encountered it. At first, the meeting was through books. I had never been much of a student, but now I started to read. Hesse's *Siddhartha* and Kerouac's *Dharma Bums* caught me up to speed with the counter-culture, for I soon discovered, much to my annoyance, that I was not the first to head East in search of the self. I also gobbled up travel diaries, especially those that led into Tibet: *The Way of the White Clouds, Seven Years in Tibet,* and *The Asian Journals of Thomas Merton.* I began a meditation practice.

The Buddha inspired in me an indescribable hunger for truth. When I got to India, I was delirious with excitement to be in a culture where art and architecture were shaped by the figure. At first, I felt the Buddha's presence in dark and smoky Tibetan monasteries draped with multicolored mandalas of the five celestial buddhas who have always existed and whose *dharmakaya* radiates through the ten realms. I remember feeling it with particular force in a remote monastery in the mountains of Ladakh, standing before a two-story high statue of Avalokiteśvara, the Bodhisattva of infinite compassion. But there were countless other small temples and stupas adorned with statues of the figure. I soaked it up like medicine. Whenever I looked upon the serene figure of the seated Buddha, eyes half-closed in meditation, a gentle smile on his lips, my soul ascended above the pain of the world. The junk culture of my middle-class North American upbringing receded from view, and I stood entranced by the possibility of liberation.

It was not a thought that gripped me so much as a feeling. The metaphysics of Buddhism, the jargon of the eightfold path and the mechanics of karma left me cold. Still, I was transfixed by a vague but powerful feeling that there was more to life than met the eye, an intimation of a depth dimension to existence, of which I knew nothing but which the Buddha had penetrated. I could follow him if I chose to. All that was needed was a single act of renunciation. All I had to do was say No to the world.

Several months into my trip, the buzz wore off, and I bottomed out in despair. In an ashram in Bodh Gaya in Northern India, eating a vegetarian lunch with a group of Westerners on a silent retreat, I crashed against a psychological limitation as real as a physical fact. I had just checked in for my one-month retreat and had been shown to my room by a kindly monk in a saffron robe. I looked around the dining hall at the earnest faces of the other retreatants and felt the seriousness of the place. They looked a lot like me: scruffy young Westerners, tripping around Asia, trekking in the mountains and sleeping in budget hotels, looking for something they could not find at home. Here, certainly, I could find fellow companions.

But that is not what happened. Instead, the opposite happened. I fell out of love with the Buddha as quickly as I had fallen in love with him. I lost faith in the Dharma, if I had ever had it. The mirror that the group held before me startled me into a painful, humiliating awakening. The whole thing—not the others but me, my thing, my "quest" for the Buddha—stank of self-deceit. To this day, I cannot quite explain my reaction. Without finishing my lunch, I suddenly stood up and, without a word to anyone, walked out the door and left.

I was not afraid of silence or religious commitment—on the contrary. I had already made my decision to live for the truth and to give everything that was needed to achieve it. But the symbol of the Buddha was only playing on the surface of my imagination. It was an ideological fantasy, in Jung's terms, a projection and a symptom of repression. The Buddha did not grip me in the depths of my psyche, not enough for me to find the resolve to cut the rope. Something was alien about the whole business. There was no path for me in the East, only a possibility that was not mine.

I fled the world, but not into a Buddhist monastery or an ashram. I headed as deep into the woods as I could get. Asia was already mapped and explored and crowded. But there was still wilderness back home, a vast wilderness free of automobiles, billboards, and shopping malls. There were mountains that had not been climbed, unmanaged forests, and long waterways that opened up to me alone in a canoe and led me away from the noise and madness of modern life. Thoreau in my pocket, I sought simplicity and elemental existence in a life roaming the wilds of Canada.

When I wasn't canoeing, hiking, and camping, I studied philosophy with an intensity that surprised even me. What was real in my experience? What was true in what I had learned from my parents, my teachers, and my culture? Did God exist? If yes, then what was required of me? If not, then what? Why should I continue living as though life were inherently meaningful and satisfying? Nothing was more important to me than these questions.

I was reading all the existentialism I could get my hands on: Kafka, Sartre, Camus and especially Dostoevsky. I discovered Dostoevsky's *Crime and Punishment* in a used book sale in Calcutta. I remember the moment vividly. It was a dusty open-air book market put on by a Soviet publishing house near the station where the train on which I was traveling had made a brief stop. It was January 1988. I no longer remember the name of the town. Images of the ordinary Indian chaos of beggars, hawkers, cows, and masses of people pushing in every direction come back to me. Most of the books were of no interest to me, but I needed something to read on the long train journeys to which I was subjecting myself.

I knew nothing about Dostoevsky, and I do not remember what thought prompted me to buy the book. Perhaps it was the only novel on the table. At first, I was hooked by the existential dilemma of the protagonist, Raskolnikov, with whom I immediately identified. If God did not exist, then everything was permitted, Raskolnikov reasoned. Morality was merely a method of socially controlling the masses. The great ones, the honest ones, the ones who know that there is no God, and therefore no good or evil, could live with the vertigo of nothingness and assert their own will on the world with impunity. History would reward them even if their contemporaries did not.

Raskolnikov conducts an experiment on himself to see if he is one of the great ones or one of the sheep. He murders his pawnbroker and her daughter with an axe to see if he is up for the truth. Can he live beyond the social conventions of good and evil? The rest of the novel describes in excruciating psychological detail the unraveling of his personality under the weight of his inextirpable, guilty conscience.

I could not put the book down. I was more shocked by Raskolnikov's encounter with the Christ than I was by the murder. The prostitute, Sonya, whose life is a pathetic series of misfortunes and injustices driving her ever deeper into self-degradation, implores Raskolnikov to turn himself in and teaches him the Gospel of mercy, forgiveness, and resurrection. One encounter earlier in the book stood out for me. Raskolnikov, the atheist, interrogates Sonya about her faith.

> "And what does God do for you?" he asked, probing her further.
>
> "Be silent! Don't ask! You don't deserve!" she cried suddenly looking sternly and wrathfully at him. "That's it, that's it," he repeated to himself.
>
> "He does everything," she whispered quickly, looking down again.
>
> "That's the way out! That's the explanation," he decided scrutinizing her with eager curiosity, with a new, strange, almost morbid feeling. He gazed at that pale, thin, irregular, angular little face, those soft blue eyes,

> which could flash with such fire, such stern energy, that little body still shaking with indignation and anger—and it all seemed to him more and more strange, almost impossible. (Dostoevsky 1914, 295)

Nothing about the injustice and hopelessness of Sonya's situation justifies her faith, but neither could any cruelty or misery of life take it from her. Christ had called her and would redeem her in the end. Raskolnikov is converted by the apparent irrationality of her witness. Reason has led him to violence, nihilism, and madness. But perhaps there was something beyond reason? And at the moment that I read this, in some very secret place of my soul not even known to myself, I too was converted. There was no power within me for self-transformation. I could not reason myself into truth. I could not meditate my way to enlightenment. Salvation came from without, or it would not come at all.

Dostoevsky's point, which he hammers home in all his great novels, is that Christ's power is most visible from a pit. The debauched and self-mutilated, the sinners who know they are sinners and persist in their sin, they know. They can see Christ for who he is. Like the thief on the cross in the Gospel of Luke who recognizes the divinity of Jesus as they both writhe in death agony, only the dejected, the ones without earthly hope, the ones without possibility, only they know who he is.

From then on, I no longer followed the Buddha of my fantasies. I had given up on the path of self-transformation, which is not a good interpretation of Buddhism, but it was mine at the time.

A year or so after my return to Canada, when I was finishing up my BA in philosophy, I was told by a family friend about the group of hermit monks living in the woods of Nova Scotia with whom I would spend the next five years of my life. The friend passed me a book by the group's founder, a Carmelite monk named William McNamara. I read it with fascination. Here was something new, a secret lying in plain sight, the Gospel of contemplative, mystical Christianity. McNamara's claim was that Christianity had become effete and culturally insignificant because we had forsaken the mystical heart of the Gospel. God had become man so that man could become God, the Greek Fathers had taught.

Gradually the figure of the Buddha began to shrink in significance for me while the Jewish Messiah and crucified savior filled my life. And unlike the Buddha, who had no foothold in my childhood or my cultural experience, Jesus was someone whom I once knew. The one I had been looking for was the one I had always known. My childhood devotion returned to me in a flood of feeling but now matured, tested by doubt. My love for him and desire to follow him crystallized and could no longer be ignored. I made a decision, the decision I could not make for the Buddha, and became a disciple of the Christ.

When I entered the Carmelite monastery, I knew next to nothing about contemplative Christianity or Western spirituality. I could quote passages from the Upanishads and knew the distinctions among the major traditions of Buddhism. I was all over modern philosophy, from Descartes to Nietzsche, but I had never heard of Plotinus and his formative influence on the Church Fathers. I had never read Augustine or Aquinas. I knew Saint Paul only because I had grown up listening to passages of his letters read at church. I did not know what these letters meant, or who they had been written for.

The monastery was a second childhood and a second education, this time into the forgotten traditions of Western spirituality. I learned that Western spirituality is the product of a creative historical fusion of Greek philosophy and the Jewish-Christian Bible. Paul's letters were not sent into a cultural vacuum. They were written by a Jewish convert to Christianity who had been educated among Pharisees. They were addressed to well-educated and, in some cases, highly cultured citizens of the Roman Empire. Many of Paul's followers would have been familiar with the teachings of the great Hellenistic schools of philosophy: Stoicism, Neoplatonism, and Epicureanism. Some of them would have been involved in the Greek mystery religions, the cults of Dionysus and Mithras, with their promises of esoteric knowledge through mystical union with the god or goddess. Many of these extra-biblical presuppositions of his audience were taken into consideration by Paul and, over time, were integrated into the Western tradition.

Christianity is not purebred but a hybrid of various heterogeneous cultural elements current in Southern Europe and Asia Minor in the first three centuries of the Church. These diverse elements cannot be extracted from the thing. There is no pristine Gospel that preceded its interpretation by Greek thinkers. The Gospel is a fusion of opposites and is most alive in the tension between them. It is, above all, a fusion of two very different ancient attitudes to life, death, and the afterlife, the Jewish view, and the Greek. The Jews emphasized the body, the earth, and life in time with all its paradoxes; the Greeks emphasized the mind, eternity, and the spiritual world beyond the body. The Christ unites both as he unites the human and the divine.

To my delight, I discovered that philosophy, to which I was addicted by now, was an essential part of the Christian tradition. It was to be supplemented and expanded by the Bible, but it was no less philosophy for that. Philosophy was the product of "natural reason." The Bible, by contrast, was God's revelation. The two were not in conflict but related as the reasoning of the human creature to the revelation of the divine Creator. We may not know the divine in its essence, but every truth we think and everything good that we do expresses something of the divine reality.

Equally important was my initiation into the philosophical and theological world of the Latin Middle Ages, the era of Christendom, which is, to this day, one of the periods of the history of ideas that is least understood. "Everything we think," Jung said, "is the fruit of the Middle Ages and indeed of the Christian Middle Ages."[1] He does not exaggerate. Medieval Europeans lived in a Christian universe; modern Westerners continue to live in the same universe but unconsciously. I could not find faith in the Buddha because I needed to first address this unconscious Christianity in myself.

A Second Childhood

Between the ages of twenty-three and twenty-eight, the shape and direction of my life was decided. I dropped out of the world, as Timothy Leary advised his hippie followers to do. But I did not "tune in" or "turn on." I did something decidedly unhip. I joined a Roman Catholic religious order. I became a monk.

Religious orders are special institutions within the Roman Catholic universe. They do not belong to the parish system, with its hierarchy of laity organized into churches presided over by local pastors overseen by regional bishops. The orders are relatively independent of these administrative structures and are, in some instances, answerable directly to the Pope alone. Existing on a special dispensation from the Vatican dating back to the original fifth-century Rule of Saint Benedict, religious orders are independent havens of spirituality, communities of men and women who band together under a founding vision or charismatic leader for the sake of living a communal Christian life and fulfilling their understanding of the Gospel's call to perfection. The orders of the Roman Catholic Church fall into two broad categories: active and contemplative. The active orders follow the *vita activa* and pursue Christian perfection through the service of others: the poor, the sick, and the uneducated. The best-known active order is the Franciscans. Think of Saint

Francis and his band of disciples in brown robes wandering the streets of Italian cities in the Middle Ages, caring for lepers and the poor, and you will get the idea. The contemplative orders follow "the higher life," the *vita contemplativa,* dedicating themselves to prayer and the liturgy, which they enact tirelessly in the solitude of a cloister, which is often set apart from the world in a rural area or a wilderness.

Contemplative orders practice solitude, regarding prayer as their chief work and restricting communal life to the liturgy and some shared meals. They might take vows of silence, speaking or singing only in liturgical prayer. The Church, with its strong Neoplatonic undercurrent, has always held that the *vita contemplativa* is the higher of the two styles of religious life, just as the contemplation of God is higher than any good work we might do here on earth. The assumption is that since the destiny of every human being is life with God, contemplation is to be regarded as the highest act of the human being and the perfection of all human potential.

The Church teaches that God calls us to serve, and the ultimate service is to contemplate the divine, which is the life of the angels and saints in heaven. All Christians shall experience the truth of God in the *visio beatifica,* the vision of God granted to the saved after death, as taught by Paul: "For now we see through a glass, darkly; but then face to face: now I know in part; but then shall I know even as also I am known" (1 Cor. 13:12). Some men and women, it is believed, are called by God to practice the contemplation of God here on earth, to begin to live the heavenly life now. The Church has always treasured these vocations and protected them through the institutions of contemplative orders, communities of monks, nuns, and priests who segregate themselves from society to create the ideal conditions for contemplation. These conditions are assumed to be (1) solitude; (2) simplicity, that is, voluntary poverty; and (3) community, a society of friends who share the same desire and protect each other's contemplation.

In the vast literature on this subject, the story of Martha and Mary from the Gospel of Luke is cited often. In it, Jesus visits two sisters in their home: a care-worn woman, Martha, and her more spontaneous and intuitive sister, Mary. As Jesus sits in the house with Mary at his feet, listening to every word he says, Martha bustles frenetically in the kitchen, preparing food for their guest. Exasperated, she complains to Jesus: "Lord, don't you care that my sister has left me to do the work by myself? Tell her to help me!" "Martha, Martha," Jesus answers, "you are worried and upset about many things, but few things are needed—or indeed only one. Mary has chosen what is better, and it will not be taken away from her" (Luke 10:38–42). The contemplative orders pursue the one thing necessary, the Church argues, and should not be begrudged for not participating in the more practical work essential for creating a Christian society.

I joined an offshoot of the Discalced Carmelites, the order founded by the great sixteenth-century Spanish mystics Saint Teresa of Avila and Saint John of the Cross. The Carmelites date back to the eleventh century when certain Crusader knights chose to stay behind in Palestine and live as hermits on Mount Carmel, the biblical site where the prophet Elijah was carried to heaven on a fiery chariot.

The group I joined was returning to the "primitive Carmelite ideal" and living a contemplative life in the wilderness. They had two monasteries at the time I entered the order. I started at Nova Nada, a hermitage on the site of a century-old hunting and fishing lodge in the woods of Nova Scotia. Later, I would move to their monastery in the Sangre de Cristo mountains of southwest Colorado, which was the older of the two foundations and was called simply Nada. The word *nada* means "nothing." It is John of the Cross's term for the path to union with God.

We must let go of everything, any concept or image of God that might have once consoled us.

Nova Nada was an oasis of solitude amid tall white pines on an uninhabited lake seven miles from the nearest community. The hunting and fishing lodge, which dated back to the early twentieth century, had been laboriously converted by the monks into a dozen buildings: a large main communal house on a forested hill, an octagonal chapel, and an adjoining library on the shore of the lake, and a collection of hermitages scattered throughout the woods, ranging from small dark and draughty log cabins to modern solar-heated eco-retreats.

In short, I left the university and entered the Middle Ages. The five years I spent as a brother with the Discalced Carmelite Hermits were among the most formative years of my life. Even if I wanted to reject everything I believed then, I could never shake off the habits I acquired in the monastery, above all, the pleasure in manual work, the love of solitude, and the need for community life to balance it. But most important to the story I wish to tell, I discovered in the monastery how far the West has fallen from its spiritual roots, which lie in the contemplative culture kept alive in monasteries.

While monasticism expresses a universal pattern in human civilization, the motivation behind Western monasticism differs in an important way from other well-known forms of monasticism, in particular, from Buddhist monasticism. The Christian monk is not trying to liberate himself or others from a world that is considered to be mostly or perhaps entirely illusory. He is not trying to achieve a higher state of consciousness. Enlightenment is not the aim. Rather, the Christian monk is responding to a call from God to more deeply revere and cultivate his humanity. This always entails a deeper reverence and care for nature. The Christian monk is endeavoring to rise to the occasion of God becoming incarnate in natural history. Once God has become man, we no longer need to transcend nature or our humanity to reach the divine; quite the contrary. We need to rather cherish, affirm, and develop what is most human and natural in us.

The Carmelite Hermits spent half of their time totally alone, and the other half engaged in communal activities: liturgy, work, and common meals. My day started at 5 a.m. with *lectio divina* in my hermitage, stoking the fire in the wood stove. *Lectio divina* is the ancient practice of spiritual reading. One reads slowly and with concentration, stopping when inspired by the text and savoring what insights might come. While the traditional text for this monastic practice is scripture—and I certainly discovered my love for scripture in those days, regularly working through the Pentateuch (the first five books of the Hebrew Bible) and the New Testament—I was encouraged to read widely. Sometimes it was Thomas Aquinas, sometimes Dostoevsky, and often it was philosophy or psychology of religion—the point was to follow the inspiration. The emphasis was not on the *what* but on the *how*. When one reads with a spiritual attitude, any text can be suitable for practice.

At 6 a.m., the bell would ring through the woods, and the monks would gather in the chapel for Lauds, the recitation of the psalms, followed by half an hour of silent meditation. Our meditation practices were as varied as our reading habits. Christian meditation is far less focused on technique than Yoga or Zen. This is no accident. It is indicative of fundamentally different understandings of what is needed for spiritual growth. Meditation in contemplative Christianity is always only a means to an end, not a technique for attaining higher consciousness, and never an end in itself. The end is prayer, which is always God's work in us, not the result of a method.

In those days, I preferred to sit half lotus on the floor. I had learned the Eastern Orthodox practice of the Jesus Prayer, the repetition of the words of the blind man on the roadside calling out to Jesus when he hears him passing by, "Lord Jesus Christ, Son of the Living God, have mercy on me, a sinner" (Luke 18:

38), which the Hesychasts of the Orthodox tradition developed into a kind of Christian Yoga. One repeats the phrase silently, in rhythm with one's inhalation and exhalation, until the words sink into the heart and continue perpetually and without effort. One starts by twenty minutes of repetition, extending it bit by bit until the mantra becomes a constant background of one's thoughts and activities. In this way, the Christian learns to pray "without ceasing ... in all circumstances," as Paul advises (1 Thess. 5: 16–18). The phrase itself says everything that needs to be said. It names the Christ as the living presence in the soul of the one who prays, "the image of the invisible God" (1 Col. 15). It positions the soul correctly in relation to this one and only Word of the Father through whom all things have come to be (John 1: 3). The soul is not identical to God, but the one who cries out in desperate need of divine redemption. The one who prays the Jesus Prayer says, I need you, I cannot do this, I cannot redeem myself, and I long for your redemption. To know this in one's heart is to feel the first effects of the Christ's redemptive act.

On Wednesday and Friday mornings, it was Mass at 6 a.m. The liturgy would be stripped down to the barest essentials—no songs, no homily, no noisy "signs of peace" or jokes from the pulpit. After the readings, we sat in silence for twenty minutes. At the end of that period of meditation, the priest stood up and raised the patina holding the offertory bread, intoning the words of consecration: "Blessed are you, lord of all creation, through your goodness we have this bread to offer. Fruit of the Earth, work of human hands, it will become for us the bread of life." The symbols of the ancient liturgy profiled against the contemplative silence became luminous with sense. In that quiet lakeside chapel, the Mass never ceased to blow my mind.

I had an hour or two to myself after morning prayer and would usually spend it in the woods or paddling on the lake. The workday began at 9 a.m. and ended at 4 p.m., with an hour of silence followed by Vespers (more recitation of the psalms and silent meditation). Work for me meant getting dirty: cutting and stacking firewood, building hermitages, or maintaining and repairing them. By 4, I was exhausted and filthy. From May to October, I took a solitary swim at the end of the workday. I had my secret pond, which I could access easily by mountain bike. Slipping naked into the cool dark water after a day of outdoor labor and feeling the dirt lift away was nothing short of a baptism. I did it as often as I could.

The work week finished with a common meal on Friday and the Eucharist on Sunday morning, followed by recreation with the community, volleyball in the summer, cross-country skiing or ice skating in the winter. We were hermits, to be sure, but a more lively human community I have not known before or since. We were united in a sustained effort to grow in love. The monastery, according to the ancient Benedictine rule, is a school of charity. Solitude is for the sake of living together more deliberately, deeply, and generously. We were not friends and likely would never have spent any time together had we met each other in some other situation. But what we shared in common—our commitment to the Christ, whom we believed in more than we believed in ourselves or our projects and goals—made us a family.

By far, the highlight of my week was the celebration of Benediction. This liturgy is almost forgotten today. It culminates in the blessing of the congregation with the exposed Eucharist raised by the priest in a golden monstrance. We celebrated it every Saturday night and followed it with an all-night silent vigil. In the rite of Benediction, the congregants do not consume the Eucharist; they worship it. To understand why, one needs to remember that the Eucharist in Roman Catholic, Eastern Orthodox, and Lutheran theology is much more than a symbol; it is the physical continuation of the incarnation. The divine descent into matter, which comes to a certain kind of climax in Jesus (but in fact began with creation), continues the altar of every church that subscribes to the doctrine of the real presence. The Mass, then, is not only a commemoration of the Last Supper but a repetition of the infinite and cosmological act of God becoming human.

I was the "thurifer," the monk who carries the incense burner or "thurible" and incenses the altar and the host. I can still smell the frankincense rising around me in rings of fragrant smoke. I knelt before the literal presence in time and space of the incarnate God in the form of a piece of consecrated bread. "Let all mortal flesh keep silent, and with fear and trembling stand," we chanted, in words written in Greek in the fourth century. "Ponder nothing earthly minded, for with blessing in his hand. Christ, our God, to earth descending, comes our homage to command." I swung the thurible, which rattled on its chain and sent up wreaths of frankincense before the priest enrobed in the "humeral veil," a special golden vestment used only in this ritual. He held the monstrance high for all to see. Kneeling in the smoke gazing upward at the Christ present in the Eucharist, I would feel the doubts and fears of daily life dissipate and the undeniable radiance of divine presence: God present before me, I present in God, the world present through me, with me, and in me. I was praying for the world, and the world, without knowing it, depended upon me at every instant to do so.

The priest made the sign of the cross with the raised monstrance. With one voice, the kneeling monks responded in plainchant:

Tantum ergo Sacramentum
Veneremur cernui:
Et antiquum documentum
Novo cedat ritui:
Præstet fides supplementum
Sensuum defectui.

This hymn, written by Thomas Aquinas, speaks directly to the paradox of the whole affair of the Eucharist, which is nothing less than the paradox of Christianity itself. "Let us greatly venerate the sacrament with heads bowed / And let the ancient practice give way to the new rite / Let faith make up for the failure of the senses."

The liturgy of Benediction is the same wherever it is still practiced. Imagine it, however, happening in an off-grid chapel in a forest by a dark lake at 7:30 p.m. on Saturday evening. The nearest other human community is a small town seven miles away. Miles of dense forest surrounds the chapel. The occasional hoot of an owl or the yap of a coyote sounds through the trees. The stars twinkle above the black line of woods on the horizon. The chapel is lit with candles, and the little community of monks prepares for their all-night vigil. After the Benediction, the Eucharist remains exposed on the altar. For every hour of the night, one monk remains present in silent prayer before the incarnate God.

We would sign up for our hour and set our alarm clocks to rise. Walking through the woods to the candle-lit chapel with the Christ waiting for me on the altar was an indescribable experience of mystery, dedication, and divine power. The hymns from the liturgy would resound in my soul:

King of kings, yet born of Mary,
As of old on earth he stood,
Lord of lords, in human vesture,
In the body and the blood;
He will give to all the faithful
His own self for heavenly food.
At his feet the six-winged seraph,
Cherubim, with sleepless eye,
Veil their faces to the presence,
As with ceaseless voice they cry:
Alleluia, Alleluia,
Alleluia, Lord Most High!

Then there were the weeks of solitude. They always began the same way for me. After the intensity of a communal week, with all of the interaction and togetherness, I would be mildly repelled by solitude, usually exhausted and a bit down. By the end of the week, the situation would have reversed itself. Silence and solitude would have opened up, ushering me into a universe of mystery and meaning. Only hermits and solitaries know the immense spaciousness of time. Once the noise of the mind quiets down, and the agenda simplifies, one feels time expanding. Suddenly, there is time for everything and a time for everything. There is time for a long walk in the woods, for an evening with a book of poetry, for a visit with a trillium. There is time for working deeply, self-forgetfully, and restoratively, stacking wood or writing. There is time for resting and the inner work of constantly re-orienting oneself to the truth. During these long expansive bouts of solitude, my soul would steadily synch with all the other quiet spirits around me, the spirits of the trees, of the loons, of the coyotes and bears. My prayer would flow spontaneously from my open heart, and my every breath would become a dialogue with God. I would dedicate whole mornings to meditation and reading, then push off in a canoe for the afternoon and evening, perhaps sleeping out in a tent with the monastery dogs snuggled beside me. At the end of the week of solitude, I would dread returning to the community. I knew that this silent communion had to be shattered by the ordinary and necessary activities of common life.

Shortly after I arrived at the monastery, I began to meet regularly with my spiritual director, Sharon, a fair-haired Celt from Cape Breton with a brilliant mind and a passion for truth that matched my own. She was in her forties when we met. We had an indissoluble bond from the moment we laid eyes on each other. She seemed to me someone with special access to mysteries—a climber of spiritual heights most admire from a distance. I trusted her without reservation and spoke to her of all my doubts and hopes and my frustrations. She could lighten my heart in days of depression with a single word. I would never have stayed for five years without her support, encouragement, and friendship.

I was the wild one of the order, a kid as excited by the wilderness as I was by Catholic mysticism. The woods and water were, for me, the body of God, the direct expression of the mind of the Creator. I was convinced that I could experience something of divine infinity in the pathless forests, the tangled wetlands, the shining lakes and rivers of North America as it appeared before the Europeans settled it and still does today in neglected or protected corners. I carried Thoreau's *Walden* everywhere I went and read it as though it were sacred scripture. I memorized whole passages of it, reciting them as if they were psalms: "I went to the woods because I wished to live deliberately, to front only the essential facts of life, and see if I could not learn what it had to teach, and not, when I came to die, discover that I had not lived" (Thoreau 2004, 90). Like Thoreau, I could not get enough wilderness. Three days to myself with a canoe full of camping gear was, for me, a religious experience.

But I had spent enough time alone in the woods to know that strange things happen to a monk without a community. The first monasteries were founded in the deserts of Egypt to moderate the asceticism of the "white martyrs," the early Christian hermits who had fled the city to escape bourgeois Constantinian Christianity. The desert fathers, as they are called, were susceptible to bouts of madness. One sat naked in swamps, allowing the flies to feed on him. Another installed himself on a pole twenty feet above the ground for weeks on end. Others starved themselves and roamed the fields grazing on grass like cattle. The monastic rule was designed to grant these God-crazed souls the solitude they needed within a communal structure that tempered their excesses and counteracted the psychosis that seems latent in the human being. Most importantly, the monastery gave the hermit a communal arena to practice charity. By deferring to his brethren in all things, the monk overcame, by the grace of God, his self-centeredness, what Christians call sin and psychoanalysts, narcissism.

Before entering the order, I experimented with long periods of isolation in the wilderness. One day, during a six-week sojourn on the remote and largely uninhabited south coast of Newfoundland, I found myself as tormented by my thoughts as Saint Anthony had been tormented by the demons that tested his faith when he lived alone for a year in a cave in Egypt. I could not master my mind, as the Buddhists I was reading at the time enjoined me to do, nor could I escape it. I shot up from the desk I had been sitting at trying to write and bolted out the cabin door, shouting like a madman. My companion, Ben, a large, disobedient Golden Retriever, chased after me in great agitation. In a desperate bid to flee myself, I tore up the hill behind the cabin, through the woods, and into the barrens that rose behind them. And yet, how could I flee myself? It was a contradiction and weighed upon me like a death sentence.

I did not yet know that the only way out—so simple and yet so hard—was to relate oneself to another, to put the interest of the other before one's desires, to make the other oneself. According to Christian mysticism, interpersonal relation is the only way to freedom from the natural narcissism of the soul, which will suffocate the soul if not relieved. I ran uphill following a stream that gushed through the rock until it crashed into the sea, seeking the source of my pain as though the torrent were my soul. I ran until I could go no further and flung myself, exhausted, on the hot granite baking in the spring sunshine. I lay on my back, panting, staring into the blue sky. Ben sniffed at me with his great lovable head hanging over my face. But Ben was not the other I needed. I needed another person to talk to, and not just anyone. I needed to talk to someone who knew from experience what I was so desperately seeking, someone who could understand, really understand, the urgency of the question my dead cousin had put to me. Why live? Why not, rather, die?

Sharon was the one. I knew it immediately. She unraveled the tangled knot of my nascent spiritual life and affirmed what was coming to birth there. She gave me a new language for my inner struggles, a sublime word that elevated what I was going through into a sphere of light and truth. She called it "a vocation." I surrendered to her benevolence completely. She was for me what the ancient Celts called an *anam cara*, a friend of my soul. I trusted her absolutely. If she had commanded me to retreat naked into the woods and fast for a week, I would have done it without hesitation. But Sharon placed no such demands on me. For the most part, she endeavored to moderate my zeal and taught me that true asceticism was not about practices of self-mortification but about giving oneself in communal life.

It was in the monastery that I discovered my love for the Bible, a love which I have never lost. I would read from the Pentateuch (the first five books of the Hebrew Bible) daily as part of my *lectio divina* or practice of spiritual reading (a central part of the monastic rule). I did not worry much about the historical veracity of the stories which are attributed to Moses; I let their meaning seep into my soul. I understood them to be myths in the proper sense of the term, ancient symbolic stories, passed down orally long before they were written down, narratives which constitute the identity of a people. The symbolic meaning of the stories, read with faith, lit up my path. If I could not understand everything I read there, I let myself sink into the unfathomable depths of their symbolic significance. I saw myself in Noah, Abraham, and Isaac, and especially in the prophets, following the inconceivable Yahweh into the desert where he would speak to my heart (Hosea 2:16). I was Elijah, Jonah, and Isaiah, a God-intoxicated man.

I approached the New Testament differently than I did the Old Testament. The style of these writings is quite different from the books of the Hebrew Bible. The writing is far more fragmentary. The authors of the texts are neither aiming at writing founding myths for a nation nor at giving eyewitness historical accounts. The goal is to announce the Christ event, an event which occurred in the historical Jesus, but which also exceeds him. The Christ event occurs in the lives of Peter, Mary, John, Paul, Stephen, Barnabas, Phoebe, etc. The list goes on through history, right to the present day. The New Testament is not so much reporting a past event as identifying an ongoing irruption of God in our midst.

When I was preparing for my final profession at Nada, I took a six-week retreat among the Trappists of Snowmass, Colorado. Saint Benedict's Abbey is nested high up in a mountain valley near Aspen. Nearby was luxury skiing but Snowmass might as well have been in a different century. The valley was ringed by high mountains. On one side was the jet-setting world, on the other, the ancient way of Benedictine monasticism, essentially unchanged for a thousand years. The Trappists belong to the Cistercian order, a Benedictine reform movement that began in the eleventh century. The Trappists or Cistercians demanded a deeper solitude and a stricter observation of the Benedictine rule than the great cloisters of medieval Europe practiced at the time. The medieval monasteries had grown wealthy and powerful under feudalism. The Trappists called for a return to the simple life, to voluntary poverty, and to contemplation.

Saint Benedict's Abbey in Snowmass consisted of two four-story gabled brick buildings converging on a large church with a bell tower in the center of a valley of hay fields ringed by snow-capped mountains. My retreat started in January, shortly after Christmas. The fields were buried under several feet of snow. The monks accepted me as one of their own and gave me a wooden stall in the choir, where I assembled with them seven times a day to sing the psalms in solemn plainchant. My days at Snowmass floated serenely on undulating waves of Gregorian chant. This music has not ceased in the West for fifteen hundred years. The words are the very words Jesus would have spoken in the synagogues of Galilee, the psalms of King David.

In the mornings, after Vigils, Lauds, and Mass (a three-hour liturgical start to the day that began shortly after 4 a.m.), I had free rein of their library. I read deeply: the Church Fathers, Thomas Aquinas, but also the religious psychology of C.G. Jung, which helped me immensely make sense of my tempestuous 27-year-old soul. I worked afternoons in the carpentry shop and retired with the monks at 8 p.m. after Vespers. Every day was exactly like the previous day and created the feeling of eternity.

Each day, we met in the dark before dawn for the first service of the day, Vigils, the brothers filing into the church, which was lit at this time by candlelight alone. No one spoke or interacted. We silently took our seats as one of the brothers turned on a small lamp and opened the Bible. At this point in the liturgical year, the cycle of biblical readings reboots, and begins again at the beginning, with the book of Genesis. "In the beginning, God created heaven and Earth." I listened to every word as if hearing it for the first time.

This thought, that the world and all it contains was created freely by a personal God in an act of glorious self-expression—a God who is not part of creation and does not appear in it—swept me off my feet in amazement. We look up to heaven, or within the soul, and hope to catch a glimpse of the transcendent Creator, but God is no more imaginable for us than the author of a novel is imaginable on the basis of one of its characters. The idea of absolute personal transcendence transported me into what an anonymous medieval monk described as "the cloud of unknowing." Abandoning all my concepts and images of God, I sat still in the presence of the mystery.

A year after the Snowmass retreat, I left the monastic life for reasons that I am still unraveling. It was not an easy decision. To put it somewhat vaguely, I wanted the world. I wanted to know what there was to learn from a society that I had turned my back on at a young age. I longed for a more formal study of philosophy and theology than was possible in the monastery. I wanted to go to graduate school and get a PhD in Philosophy. But like all big decisions, my leaving of the monastery is not reducible to these reasons. It felt necessary at the time; something that had to happen. I was not *choosing* to leave; I was being sent out. The same inner voice that had brought me to Nova Nada was now commanding me to leave. I left heartbroken, tears streaming down my face, for I loved my monastic life and wanted to stay. But the contemplative life is not about doing what you want, it is about wanting to do what you must.

I Turn Back to the World

I decided that if I was going to go back to the world, I would go big. I wanted to suffer the full intensity of modernity. I would be as deliberately and resolutely modern and urban as I had been deliberately and resolutely primitive and wild five years earlier. I moved to downtown Toronto and enrolled at the University of Toronto, where I would spend the next seven years of my life studying philosophy and theology.

I was only 28 when I arrived in Toronto, but I felt older. I was a different person than the one who had disappeared five years before. I had new eyes. The world was rushing headlong as it always had. It was the mid-nineties, the height of the American Empire, and everyone had one thing on their mind: to make as much money as possible. I remember watching the young men and women in suits rushing up and down the concrete canyons of downtown Toronto. I watched them in amazement, thinking to myself, why are they rushing? Where are they going? When I arrived, I had no driver's license, no bank card, and fifteen dollars in my pocket (my entire fortune). But I had no worries about money. I was following Jesus, who advised his disciples not to worry about what they would eat and what they would wear, for the Father would look after them. The disciple is poor but free and cared for, as the sparrows in the sky are free and the lilies in the field are clothed in beauty.

It is one of the ironies of the canonical vow of poverty that the one who takes it is granted what is most desired by those who pursue wealth: freedom from anxiety over money. I had scarcely touched the stuff for five years. Not that the order was rich—far from it. We had grim monthly meetings with the accountant of the community, who reminded us that we were as ever on the verge of bankruptcy. But security was not what we were after. We wanted only what we needed to buy enough brown rice and beans to keep us all alive, to fuel our four-wheel drive vehicles (essential for getting to town), our chainsaws, and the gas generator that ran our power tools. I wore donated clothes when I was not in habit, ate what was offered me, and lived in a variety of one-room huts heated by wood stoves.

When I stumbled onto the bustling streets of Toronto and jostled with the well-heeled men and women yammering into cell phones and rushing to their next urgent meeting, I was like Perceval at King Arthur's court, a total naïf who, precisely because he is naïve, can see what is going on around him with a clarity that eludes those who are closest to it. I saw a civilization in disavowal of its spiritual heritage. Consumerism was a sophisticated lie that could no longer trick me. My eyes were washed clear by five years of monastic practice, and the Western way of life came into sharp focus as a set of empty rituals to which people sacrificed their lives. In the place of the one satisfying desire, which is the desire for God that cannot be satisfied in this life, consumerism substituted fleeting pleasures, and the incessant work of attending to the thousand little cravings constantly kept alive by advertisement.

I dutifully acquired my proofs of legitimacy: a driver's license, a bank card, a student loan, a position in a graduate program, and even a girlfriend. But I felt, for the first few years, as though I was playing a role, merely pretending that I thought all of these achievements were important.

Initially, I tried to bring as much of my monastic training to my new life at the University of Toronto as possible. I could not imagine living without two hours of prayer and meditation daily. It went badly. The perfunctory services of the parish churches I attended were a weak substitute for the mind-altering liturgies of the monastery.

This effort to carry forward into the world the life I had lived in the monastery went on for some time until the day I found myself in a wealthy parish in Vernon, British Columbia. I had been tree planting in the summers to pay for my education, applying some of the outdoor skills and work ethic I had learned in the monastery to the business of earning a living. While I tried to invest as much dignity into this menial work as I could, fully subscribing for a time to the bohemian eco-subculture that pervades tree-planting communities, I could not conceal from myself the unpleasant fact that I was a cog in a capitalist wheel, working at the bottom of a hierarchy at the top of which sat a CEO far removed from the violence of the clear-cuts he was fattening on. I was no eco-warrior; I was an obedient worker. I awoke before the others to sit in my tent at dawn and read the battered breviary I had brought with me from the monastery. I attended Mass when I could, when we were not camping in a remote location.

It was on one of these occasions when my tree-planting tribe was quartered in a seedy motel in Vernon that the contradiction I was trying to live became undeniable. The church was the kind of wealthy modern Catholic parish I had attended as a child, moderately well attended by preppy families and presided over by a sleepy priest moralizing the scriptures. I dutifully recited the responses, sang along, and offered my hand pleasantly in the sign of peace to those around me.

After the service, I walked back to the motel. The walk was about thirty minutes and took me through the suburbs of upper-middle-class Vernon: sprawling bungalows with two-car garages on generously watered lawns. By the time it was over, I was no longer a Catholic. "Why am I looking for something that is not there?" I asked myself. The monastic church and the parish church were two different universes, two parallel lines that never touched. There was nothing for me in the routines of parish life. I would eventually find my way back to the Church, but I shall never forget the emptiness I felt on that hot summer day in suburban BC. When religion becomes mechanical and uncontemplative, it is, in fact, ideology, as Marx described it. People go for the same reason they might attend a country club: to convince themselves that they are who they think they are and that their socio-economic identity is the truth. The atheist rightly names it thus and calls for its abolition.

In the following years, I acquired my professional credentials as an academic philosopher and theologian. I mastered philosophical theology and the history of Christianity, giving myself with particular intensity to the study of Protestant theology (something I had heard nothing about in the monastery). I published the papers and books necessary for academic advancement and presented my work in posh hotels at conferences all over North America and Europe. In everything I wrote and said, I remained a Christian philosopher.

I now teach young people what I once searched for. Not that I have any wisdom of my own. But I have the wisdom of the West to offer, in books, some of which I have written myself. I do not for a moment confuse books about the love of wisdom ("philosophy") with the real thing. I spend my springs and summers in an off-grid cabin that I built on the north shore of Conception Bay in Newfoundland, and there I am most myself.

There I am still a monk practicing the contemplative art of being human. During the academic year, I try as best as I can to be attentive to the deep spiritual hunger that attracts young people to the study of philosophy and religion. I want to give them more than my teachers gave me, more than training in speaking and writing as an academic. Still, it is difficult to subvert the academic structure. However essential the discussions that occur in my classes—and everything comes up, love, suffering, death, God, nothingness—I still feel constrained by the institutional setting. At the end of the day, I need to give the student a grade, and for that, the student needs to give me a performance of academic competence. The class, which begins with everything on the table, always finishes on a somewhat tragic note, for I must "grade" the student.

Shortly after graduating from the University of Toronto, I fell in love. Esther grew up in a lighthouse on the southern shore of the Avalon Peninsula of Newfoundland. Her father was a well-known artist and a close friend of my father. We had met years before when we were both in our twenties. I will never forget first meeting her. There was something fairylike about her: petite, dark eyes, bewitching smile. She wore a long black skirt. Her blond hair cascaded to her waist. We both remember the moment as love at first sight. At the same time, the attraction forced me to make the decision that had been on my mind for some time. Would I leave the world? Esther was offering me a way in. I was not ready. The monastery called.

When we met again by chance years later, it felt as though we were picking up where we left off. Monasticism and graduate school were behind me; a career in academia lay before me. Esther had returned to Newfoundland after many years of living in British Columbia. She was working as an artist. We fell in love again or rather fell back into the love that had never died between us. We were engaged within a year.

Together we conceived a boy, Ethan. My son has been my greatest spiritual teacher. I have learned far more from him than anyone else. The greatest obstacle to spiritual growth is narcissism; children are the only solution I know of. They break natural narcissism in a way that no spiritual practice can. Indeed, spiritual practices can have the opposite effect and consolidate narcissism, even if they are intended to break it. Children have no interest in protecting their parents' "me" time. My memories of raising Ethan are full of moments when the bright-eyed blond-haired boy looks up at me at my desk and insists that I put down my books, get on the floor, and play.

When it came time to educate Ethan, there was no question in my mind. He would be educated Catholic. A formed religious imagination is far better than no religious formation. At least the child raised religious has something to consider when the time comes, as it must, to make up his or her mind on the ultimate questions. To raise Ethan Catholic, I needed to bring him to church. And so I found myself back in the pew. At first, it was only at Easter and Christmas. And then I discovered that despite the bad homilies, I needed liturgy. I needed the ancient symbols. They freed me from my overly reflective mind. I did not have to sort everything out for myself. It was enough to hold up a symbol, a genuine religious symbol, like the Eucharist, which can maintain the coincidence of opposites that human reason cannot tolerate: matter and spirit; human and divine; sinner and saved. I cannot explain these things, but I do not need to. The Church thinks them collectively down through the ages and includes me in the thinking.

When they asked the American writer Walker Percy why he was a Catholic, he answered, "What else is there?" I see his point. Spirituality without religion too quickly becomes another consumer product. We uproot texts and traditions and arrange them to suit our inclinations and prejudices. Religion is far more demanding, and far less tolerant of our prejudices.

Still, I identify with much that goes on outside of Catholicism because much of it strikes me as authentically Christian. Contemporary Catholicism is as much a product of the Reformation as is Protestantism. It is one Church broken up into countless pieces.

The era of the churches as we have known them, with their hierarchy of priests and bishops at the hub of a functional Christian lay community, is a thing of the past. However, I do not believe that Christianity has died with the demise of its institutions. It is changing forms, as it has many times before. Christianity is migrating into new styles of communal life. It is most vital in experimental countercultural communities like Nova Nada. And it seems plain to me that it is not yet finished with us in the West. Either the Church is what it has always claimed to be, the presence of Christ in the world, which shall persist until the end of time, or it is not. If it is over, it is manifestly not what it claimed to be and we ought not mourn its passing. And if it is indeed the presence of Christ in history, it is not over. It is only changing form, as it has countless times in the past, and we must be vigilant not to miss the new form it is taking.

Endnotes

1. C.G. Jung in an address given in 1934 (Jung 1970: 341). The passage continues: "Our whole science, everything that passes through our head, has inevitably gone through this history. The latter [the Christian Middle Ages] lives in us and has left its stamp upon us for all time and will always form a vital layer of our psyche, just like any phylogenetic traces in our body ... The Christian *Weltanschauung* is therefore a psychological fact, which does not allow any further rationalization; it is something which has happened, which is present."

"Open your eyes, and the whole world is full of God."

Jacob Boehme

Chapter Two

The Art of Being Human

Contemplative Being in the World

On the surface, monasticism is bound up with rules and rituals. A monk lives a regulated life. He awakens at a fixed hour, prays at the same time every day, works with his brothers for the same allotted period every day, and eats and sleeps when the "rule of life" (which is binding on all in the monastery) prescribes that he should. These rules are not the end, but a means. The end is contemplation. Every minute in the monk's daily life is regulated by the Rule, ordered for him so that he can free his mind from minor concerns and be available to God's presence in everything he does. He does not need to fuss over what he will do in the morning. He does not need to decide what he will wear, whether he will meditate that day, what his work will be, or whether he will take a holiday instead. All these decisions are already made for him. The rule prescribes what he will do and when he will do it.

My teacher, William McNamara, defined Christian monasticism as the art of being human. He taught us that the monastery is a school of contemplation, as the tradition has always maintained. The contemplative, McNamara said, is not a special kind of person. Rather, everybody is a special kind of contemplative (McNamara 1967; 1976; 1983). The monk is not trying to transcend his humanity. Trying to transcend humanity would mean fleeing the site of God's descent into creation. God enters humanity in Christ to redeem us. To go beyond humanity would be to leave the place where God comes to meet us. "The Glory of God is man fully alive," the second-century Bishop Irenaeus writes.[1] Christian monastic practices are so many ways of cultivating a contemplative way of being in the world on the assumption that to become God, we must become more, not less, human.

The essentials of monasticism are thus, in principle, compatible with a secular, contemplative life in the world. A *contemplative* life in the world—this is no small achievement. The world does not value contemplation and leaves little space for it. From adolescence to old age, we are told that the goal of life is to get what you want, to assert your will on the world, and to take from it what you desire and thereby achieve your happiness. Contemplative life is based on surrender and letting life take the lead. Self-will is the obstacle to peace. Let go of your agenda and enter the real world, which mercifully does not revolve around you. In every tradition, contemplation is counter cultural. The contemplative goes against the grain of the world. But her resistance to the logic of the world is not dramatic. It is not eye-catching or sexy. Rather, contemplative resistance is so subtle as to be imperceptible to others. The contemplative does not necessarily look any different than anyone else. She dresses the same, works as hard as anyone, has similar ordinary human needs (food, shelter, and love), and relaxes like others. She is not strange, "mystical," or other-worldly in the least.

As it is practiced in the Christian monastic tradition, contemplation does not require special techniques of meditation or challenging spiritual exercises. It only requires attention, a quiet mind, free of self-obsessive patterns of thinking, and attuned to reality. The monastic rules, discipline, voluntary poverty, obedience, and chastity are only the means for supporting the cultivation of contemplative attention. None of these rules and regulations are necessary because none of them can guarantee that contemplation will occur. This is why monasteries are full of failed contemplatives, neurotics, and people hiding from life. At the end of the day, contemplation is an intimately personal act of attunement to reality that no one can do for you. The contemplative receives every moment of his day as a gift from the divine. He does not search for extraordinary "spiritual" experiences but finds divinity in the ordinary. Daily life—waking, eating, working, and recreating—is theophanic for the contemplative; all of it is a showing of God. The greatest teacher of Christian contemplation in the thirteenth century, Meister Eckhart, scandalized the nuns to whom he preached by insisting that if they believed that they were getting closer to God in church than they were in the kitchen, they were turning the divine into an object.[2] They were making an idol of God. The infinite is not a thing. "It" is everywhere and nowhere. No place, person, or activity can be closer or further from God than any other.[3]

This simplest of human acts proves elusive to most of us. For contemplation to occur, we need to stop the inner monologue, the incessant self-reflection, the anxious planning, and the obsessive reflection that occupies our minds most of the time. We must empty our hearts and minds and let God fill them with Godself. Eckhart spoke repeatedly of *Gelassenheit* as the breakthrough virtue. This German word is untranslatable. It is a noun built on the adjective *gelassen*—calm, serene, surrendered—from the verb *sich lassen,* to let something happen. *Gelassenheit* is the quality of letting be or letting-be-ness. To cultivate *Gelasseneheit* is to let go of agendas, plans, and self-will and let life lead you. It is not cynical or pessimistic. One does not let go in a defeatist way. Rather, one lets go trusting that the God who brought you into being shall lead you to the life you need.

Above all, we need to stop perpetuating the lie that the isolated ego is the center of the world. Most of our ordinary thoughts and feelings serve this false life. The contemplative ceases thinking this way and indulging these feelings. But it is not as though the contemplative thinks and feels nothing. Christian contemplation is intellectually and emotionally oriented in a particular way that makes it distinct from Buddhist contemplation, for example, or Islamic contemplation. The

Christian contemplative has her moments of insight, her "enlightenment experiences," and her moments of darkness. Sometimes contemplation is easy, and everywhere the contemplative looks, grace abounds. At other times, she pines for the smallest trace of the presence of God, who seems to have abandoned her. The story of the crucifixion and the resurrection of the Christ gives her the terms with which to express her suffering, her hope, and her joy. Whether enraptured by the divine presence or quietly persisting in the dark night of the soul, the contemplative Christian recognizes the source of the gift of life as self-giving, infinite goodness.

Contemplation is pure receptivity, a kind of holy passivity, and yet it paradoxically requires work. We must constantly correct our routine mental delusion, our habitual narcissism. We need to break with the fantasy of the solitary self, making its lonely way through the brief season of existence allotted to it by accident. We must stop deluding ourselves with the thought that we are in a zero-sum game with others and must become the architects of our lives, the outcomes of which depend entirely on us. Contemplation is not so much about doing something novel or extraordinary; it is rather about ceasing to do something repetitively ordinary. We need to get out of our own way. "All God wants of you is for you to go out of yourself ... and let God be within you" (Eckhart 2009, 13b: 110).

It is enough to pay attention to the moments of life as they open up before us. It is enough to pay attention to whatever is happening at any given moment: to the sunlight playing on the ceiling; to my child sitting at the breakfast table; to the cat crossing the path as I step out the door; to the student in my office. The universe is full of beauty, spontaneous activity, and life-giving movement. The contemplative Christian delights in ordinary life. She immerses herself fully and attentively in it. She sees divinity shining through the forms of this world, like light through a stained-glass window.

Our problem in the early twenty-first century is that we have lost direct access to the ordinary and basic material terms of planetary existence. We live technologically mediated lives. It is not that we do not have countless opportunities to appreciate the beauty of the real. But we have become addicted to the virtual. We prefer artificial environments to natural ones. After a day working online, we would rather spend our evenings streaming fantasy on TV than exploring reality. What most of us need to get our contemplative lives in motion is a renewed sensitivity to elemental nature: to earth, air, fire, and water. We need nature and constant reminders of our naturalness. We need simplicity, voluntary poverty, and participatory technology, i.e., the ordinary work that brings us back into our bodies. We need less stimulation and more self-discipline to enjoy the exquisite here and now of the everyday, what Zen calls *tathata,* suchness.

Nothing deepens my own inner experience of grace better than an afternoon stacking firewood. I realize that not everyone can heat their homes with wood. But on my North Atlantic island, wood is plentiful, and the weather is usually wet and cold. I spend a good part of my year gathering and storing fuel and kindling fires in my wood stove. It is not just a chore but a ritual act of attuning to the elemental. I stand before the sputtering fire in the early light of the winter morning. Its light and heat warm my face and hands. A spontaneous experience of reverence rises within me. Praise be to God for the cultivation of fire, without which humanity would have never evolved.

If the demands of life confine me to my apartment in Montreal, then I can still practice the discipline of the ordinary. Cooking the evening meal slowly and thoughtfully and enjoying it seated around the dining room table with my family grounds me in the real. I do not need extraordinary settings and starry-eyed gurus. All that I need lies ready to hand.

Contemplation, however, is not all light and bliss. To get to the real we must pass through the unreal. We must come face to face with our inner complicity with unreality. I suffered countless interior crises in the monastery.

Some days were so difficult that I could barely drag myself out of my hermitage to the chapel in the morning. My whole being was in rebellion against the life that was leading me deeper into God. I writhed and protested like one undergoing a painful medical procedure with an inadequate anesthetic. I wanted to flee. But I remained through grace rooted in place. My mind reeled, but faith burned all the brighter in my heart. I believed—through no special virtue of my own—that whatever it was I was going through would pass. Faith held me where my conviction failed. The rhythm of monastic life, the weekly round of prayer and work (*ora et labora*) allowed me to focus on eternity. Everything I was suffering was transitory; God alone was eternal. This is what my cousin John failed to grasp. It is the fatal error in judgment every suicide makes. The suicide assumes his experience of hopelessness and meaninglessness is definitive and final. He believes that things will never change for him. He could not be more mistaken.

Sometimes, I could not open my mouth to pray the psalms with the community. I would stand silent in the chapel during morning prayer, destructive emotions overwhelming me. My mind churned with negative thoughts. What was I doing there? Then one of the nuns would recite the great prayer of Teresa of Avila: "Let nothing disturb you, Let nothing frighten you, All things are passing away: God never changes." The despair would dissipate like morning mist in the rising sun.

The critics of Christianity believe that faith leads to a denigration of the world. This commonplace critique of faith originates in the writings of Friedrich Nietzsche, a deeply neurotic man who was traumatized by the perverse Christianity of his upbringing. It has now become a formula among atheists. The way to deepen our appreciation for this life, Nietzsche theorized in his delirium, is to cease believing in a better one. That sounds reasonable to many. And certainly, there is something destructive about preferring fantasy to reality. But faith has nothing to do with fantasy. Faith is a relationship with life so personal and intimate that it can scarcely be described. But the pattern it inscribes in the lives of believers is unmistakable. The person of faith is more, not less, engaged with the real. She is more, not less, present to those around her. She is more, not less, creative and productive. The person of faith can withstand any disappointment and personal defeat because she knows that nothing depends upon her.

This is one of the many paradoxes of contemplative Christianity: to see the divine *in* this life, we must first acknowledge that God is *beyond* everything we know and experience. Only by seeing how infinitely transcendent the divine truly is will we see everything around us in its light. God is beyond our comprehension and cannot be compared with anything that we know.

Faith is trusting in grace—an overused term that is almost meaningless to most. We might do well to use the language of other traditions. The Shin Buddhists call grace, "other power." When the Shin practitioner stops relying on "self-power," he makes the breakthrough he longs for. It is not his will to break through that brings it about. The moment he gets out of his own way, the power of the Bodhisattva's vow takes effect, and he is granted the peace of mind and compassion for others that eluded him in his efforts to enlighten himself.[4] In Christian language, faith never ceases to rely on God's goodness despite the obstacles in the self and the evils of this world. But faith is not optimism. The distinction between faith and optimism is crucial and almost always overlooked. The confusion between the two is at the root of Nietzsche's rejection of Christianity. What Nietzsche correctly discerned as destructive of life is the self-deluded refusal to accept it on its own terms. But repression and fantasy have nothing to do with genuine faith.

Faith does not *expect* things to turn out for the best. And yet it is tireless in its efforts to alleviate the sufferings of others. Faith knows that the good cannot be brought about by our efforts alone. And yet it gives itself without reserve to the work of building a better world. This paradoxical attitude of surrendering to what must be while spending oneself in the service of what should be is found throughout the contemplative Christian tradition. It is the secret to the inexhaustible energy of the saint. Saint Paul, Saint Francis, or in our own time, Dietrich Bonhoeffer and Simone Weil gave themselves entirely to the work of building the Kingdom of God. Bonhoeffer and Weil gave their lives for it.[5] There was nothing passive or "quietistic" about their Christianity. Each of them knew that the Kingdom would only come when God wills it. Nevertheless, they never gave up and spent themselves entirely in the work of love.

Faith does not distort our experience of reality, quite the reverse. Faith gives us the eyes to see what is truly real.

When I was a monk, I basked in the universe like a child in spring sunshine. I loved nature and could not get enough of it. I cherished the simple human activities of sustaining life on its most elemental terms. I had the habit of building cook fires wherever I went. I carried a battered pewter kettle in my pack, a package of tea, and set out on solitude days, either on foot or by canoe. I sometimes come across bears. I would stand still and look at them. They looked at me and backed away slowly or lumbered away into the underbrush.

I headed out in all weather: on the wettest, grayest days in October; in the deep freeze of January, when the frozen lakes would become open highways; in the early spring, when the water would rise and one could canoe easily between the lakes through channels that became covered with water lilies as the days grew warmer; or in the dog days of summer, when I could refresh myself from the heat at any time by stripping down and jumping into whatever lake or river was nearby.

I learned how to build fires in the wet winter weather typical of the east coast of Canada. If you have a sharp pocketknife, you can build one whenever or wherever you like. Carve the wet outer bark off a dead branch of a tree and whittle small strips from the dry interior until it accumulates into a little pile. This is enough to get a small flame started. Light the pile with a dry match. When the tiny flame appears, you must build on it slowly, not smother it with wet wood. You need to be ready for this with three little stacks of twigs, small, medium, and large, organized beforehand. Add the smallest pieces of wood first. Even the wettest piece of wood will light once the water steams off of it. Once the small ones dry out and light, add the larger ones. It is possible in this way to get a good blaze going within an hour, large enough to boil a steel kettle, which can be laid directly on the flame.

When time permitted—during solitude weeks, for example—I stayed out overnight. One day I found an island on a lake several miles from the monastery. It was reachable by canoe in a couple of hours of negotiating the channels connecting the lakes. In the summer, the channels were too shallow to paddle, but in the spring, the high water opened the whole area up. The lake was large, with many arms and hidden coves. The small island—no bigger than a two-story house—was situated in one of these hidden coves. It was circular, ringed by rocks that rose to a small hill crowned by eastern white pine, spruce, and yellow birch. I named the island "Innisfree" after my favorite Yeats poem. I told no one of my discovery but went there whenever I could to swim, read, and pray.

Early one spring, I paddled to Innisfree by canoe with two of the monastery dogs, who followed me everywhere, crammed into the front of the canoe. With the sharp ax I had taken with me, I built myself a tilt. This is a rudimentary Newfoundland shelter that one can assemble in a few hours. I felled and stripped a medium size spruce tree. I cut a log out of it, six inches in diameter and eight feet in length, and lashed it horizontally to two trees about six feet above the ground. I leaned freshly cut trees against it, boughs on, at about 45 degrees. I lay my sleeping bag on fresh boughs inside and built a roaring fire at the open end.

Lying in my sleeping bag with the dogs nestled tight against me for warmth, I gazed up at the stars twinkling in the night sky. I belonged to a cosmos that sparkled with meaning. Like Saint Francis, I knew that the sun was my brother, the moon my sister. I was created. I did not need to understand everything. How could I understand my Creator? I was not trying to fit the world into my head. Instead, I stretched myself out in it and enjoyed the display.

Faith and Reason

A popular misconception has it that reason is the enemy of religion. It is assumed that faith flourishes in ignorance and dies like a virus with the vaccine of "critical thinking." The historical record of Western religion demonstrates the falsity of this assumption. From Saint Paul to Karl Barth, the Christian tradition has been sustained by its intellectuals. In the Middle Ages and the early modern period until well into the nineteenth century, Christian intellectuals were at the forefront of developments, not only in theology but also in philosophy, politics, and science. A similar point can be made for Judaism, medieval Islam, and Mahayana Buddhism, which, each in their way, testify to the lively relationship between faith and reason, but it is particularly true of Christianity. Christianity is a book-based religion. One needs considerable knowledge of history, languages, and philosophy to assess it responsibly. This is not only because Christianity is rooted in historical events which took place 2000 years ago in the Middle East and which were recorded not only in the Bible but also in secular documents of the time. The central Christian doctrines, the Incarnation and the Trinity, simply cannot be understood, let alone believed, without careful metaphysical distinctions rooted in ancient Hebrew, Greek, and Roman thought. Even our period, dominated as it is by scientism, has its share of Christian thinkers.[6] It is enough to name a few modern Christian intellectuals to make the point. C.S. Lewis, Teilhard de Chardin, Paul Tillich, Karl Barth, Simone Weil, Edith Stein, and Rowan Williams stand out for me as exemplary modern men and women of intellect whose thinking was grounded in faith.

I have never experienced the so-called conflict between religion and reason, which is not to say I have never doubted or questioned what I believe. It was precisely *reason*—skepticism about what the world called true, questions that could not be answered by my teachers, and above all, tireless inquiry into myself—that led me to religion. And once firmly installed in the faith, I did not stop reasoning. My intellectual life became more intense, not less. I continued to question and reflect on everything. This is a puzzle that many contemporary academic philosophers do not grasp simply because they have never experienced it for themselves. It is possible to believe a religious doctrine with unswerving faith and, at the same time, question it radically. Indeed, it is only through constant interrogation and reflection that faith remains alive. Christian faith is not a static affair but a living dialogue with a long and complex tradition, and without critical reasoning skills and study, it dies.

In the early days of my conversion, the questions were basic and unavoidable; general questions concerning the human situation, which I turned over and over in my mind like Zen koans. If we cannot prove God's existence to anyone's satisfaction, can we refute objections to the possibility of God's existence? If God is good, why does evil exist? Why did God create the world if God knew it would fall? Other questions were more specific to Catholicism. How did the early Church justify the claim that Jesus was divine? Do other religions possess truth, and if they do, how are we to reconcile the contradictions they pose to Christianity? Why did the Church practice monasticism when Jesus did not? How did the simple accounts of the Last Supper become the complex symbolic ritual of the Mass? Even more urgent were questions related to the Bible. Could it be trusted as history? Did the Gospel writers make up stories to justify their religious beliefs, or was their religion a response to real experiences? What could we know about the Jesus of history? These questions churned in my mind as I worked in the woods or served at Mass or recited the psalms with the monks. They were not obstacles to my growth in faith but the life of it.

I entered the monastery with a BA in philosophy and an abiding interest in modern philosophy, especially Kant and existentialism. I read whenever I had free time and was encouraged to read widely and follow my inspiration. The monastery had a good enough library with an eclectic mix of theology, spirituality, and philosophy. I awoke every morning at least an hour before morning prayer to read by the light of an oil lamp.

In philosophy, the existentialists were my guide. Anyone who thinks faith is for intellectual lightweights should spend some time reading the Danish existentialist Soren Kierkegaard. Faith, Kierkegaard says, is not an intellectual conviction but an infinite passion, a passion that is rendered hotter and more intense by relentless intellectual critique. I was and remain convinced by Kierkegaard's critique of rationalistic religion. Rather than setting up reason as a simple support of faith, which is falsely assumed to rest on proofs for the existence of God, Kierkegaard argues that the relationship between faith and reason is much more profoundly dialectical. Faith and reason are indeed opposites, but not opposites that exclude each other, as scientism assumes. Rather, they are opposites that attract one another, like tumultuous lovers who fight viciously but cannot bear to be apart. Kierkegaard's central idea is that the "objective uncertainties" of philosophy and ethics are the very fuel of faith. What is true? What ought I to do? Where am I going? Philosophy can offer us no final answer to these questions. Indeed, it deprives us of intellectual certainty about all the answers already on the table. Faith, for Kierkegaard, is, above all, a decision, and reason decides nothing. It does not matter if the rest of humanity believes or does not believe. All the testimonies of all the saints and mystics of all time add up to nothing for the doubting mind. Reason can always find plausible grounds for doubting the whole thing. If I do not decide for faith—and the decision risks everything—then I am lost. I cannot ride on the faith of others. A camera crew set up outside the tomb of Jesus on the first Easter Sunday would not render faith any more logical. Weird things happen all the time: UFOs, spontaneous combustion, quantum indeterminacy. A resurrected man is no more undeniably God than a burning bush or a voice in the ear of an obsessed man living alone in the wilderness with a slim hold on sanity.

Reason for Kierkegaard is not given to us to lessen the demands of faith or to make religious doctrines easier to accept—exactly the reverse. Reason creates intellectual problems, not only in religion but also in cultural assumptions and prejudices. All of this intellectual turmoil renders the decision for or against God unavoidable. Reason corners the individual and demands of him a decision that it itself cannot make. As doubt turns from objective matters of science and public life to the religious problems that are so near to our hearts, the questions become so intimate that they can barely be articulated. What is the truth *for me*, the truth for which I am willing to die? For the religiously tormented individual, this question is anything but playful and disinterested. In the abyss of objective uncertainty opened up by relentlessly critical reasoning, faith does not die; it flourishes and sustains the thinker, not by solving the problems but by mysteriously allowing him to hold the course in spite of them.

Kierkegaard's model of faith is Abraham, the patriarch of Judaism, Christianity, and Islam, who believed, Kierkegaard writes, "because of the absurd" (Kierkegaard 1983: 35). Simultaneously told two seemingly incompatible things by God, that he would be the father of many nations and that he should sacrifice his son, Isaac, Abraham is plunged into a torment of self-doubt that he can share with no one.[7] The child Isaac was the fulfillment of a divine promise. Born to Abraham's elderly wife, Sarah, when she was beyond childbearing years, Isaac's birth was foretold by three angels (Gen. 22: 1–15) who promised Abraham that he would be the father of a multitude. How would he become the father of many nations if the son of the promise is slain? Kierkegaard examines Abraham on his long, lonely journey up Mount Moriah with Isaac to offer the sacrifice. As they climb, Isaac innocently asks his father, "Where is the animal for the sacrifice?" Abraham does not have the courage to tell him that he, Isaac, is the sacrifice. When they reach the top of the mountain, they prepare the altar, and Abraham is torn apart by self-doubt. But he does not hesitate and continues on his terrible path without pausing. "He bound his son Isaac and laid him on the altar, on top of the wood" (Gen. 22: 10). He raised the knife to slay his son. The inner monologue continues. What if he is wrong? What if the voice he heard was not the voice of God? How will God keep his promise without Isaac? And how could he, Abraham, sacrifice his own son? Is it not a violation of the ethical duty of a father to a son? Is it not a crime? Why would God demand such a thing of him? Was it really God who had spoken?

At the last minute, the Bible tells us an angel appears. "Do not lay a hand on the boy," the angel said. "Do not do anything to him. Now I know that you fear God, because you have not withheld from me your son" (Gen. 22: 12). The sacrifice was a test, and Abraham passed. God saw his faith;

the boy should live. A ram caught in the thorns nearby is sacrificed instead.

Kierkegaard does not spend much time with this happy ending. What interests him is the psychology of Abraham as he resolves to do the awful deed. He is driven to believe two things that seem to contradict each other: that his only and beloved son, Isaac, must die, and that God is good and will keep his promise and give him progeny. As Kierkegaard puts it, Abraham believes that Isaac will be given back to him even as he must die at his father's hand. He will be given back by virtue of the absurd. What Abraham sacrifices on Mount Moriah is not Isaac but his own sense of what is possible. And in the process, a deepening of what Kierkegaard calls "inwardness" occurs. Abraham can talk to no one about his struggle. He is driven into the innermost depths of his heart. He cannot even put his faith into coherent words. The whole thing is a tangle of contradiction. And yet he resolves to obey God rather than himself. In this resolve, this site of an irreducibly free decision to trust despite all the counter-evidence, Abraham enters into an "absolute relation to the absolute" (Kierkegaard 1983, 56).

It is no surprise that Kierkegaard has been misunderstood as an irrationalist. His point, however, is not that only absurdities can elicit faith. If this is what he means, one could have faith in anything. Kierkegaard's point, rather, is that in the ceaseless back and forth of faith and reason, reason plays many roles, sometimes seductive, like a lover who is not particularly committed; sometimes supportive, like a loving wife; and sometimes persecutory, like a demon. Faith is not irrational; it is an act of freedom. I am not free to believe or not to believe that 2+2=4. I am free, however, to believe or not to believe in God's existence. Faith is ultimately a matter of the heart, not the mind. In the decision for or against faith, we commit ourselves not only to a view of the world but also to a view of ourselves. The will, Kierkegaard says, goes beyond reason, and few of the great thinkers of the tradition, from Paul through Augustine to Aquinas, disagree. Faith is not the conclusion of a process of reflection but a superhuman virtue, planted in us by grace, nurtured in hiddenness, and growing in suffering. It grows quietly and secretly until it takes hold of you entirely and permeates your life. It orients your thoughts and decisions during the day and seeps into your dreams at night. Once you open your heart to faith, nothing is ever the same again.

It is difficult for me to locate the precise moment when the decision occurred for me. I remember returning from India, desperate and bereft of belief. I remember, shortly after my return standing beside my twin sister's wheelchair in the little hospital chapel where I would take her to mass, beginning to seriously question my skepticism. Sheilagh, of whom I shall say more in pages to come, was deprived of a normal life just as it was beginning. She was diagnosed with brain cancer and given a death sentence at the age of 16, a death that would be precipitated by a slow medical decline and loss of basic physical abilities. Something about her unflagging faith in the love of God for her, which grew more, not less intense as she declined physically, threw me off of the track I was on. Her quiet witness demanded that I think more deeply about these things, less speculatively and safely from a distance. Sheilagh's faith did not carry me—no one can believe for another. But it put my smug atheism into question.

Not long after this moment, I found myself in a hermitage in the woods at Nova Nada, immersing myself in biblical scholarship: Bornkamm, the Jerome Biblical Commentary, C.H. Dodd—the books piled up on my desk. I simply had to learn as much as I could about this religion in which I was raised and about which I knew so little. I could not hide from any questions or objections. I needed, above all, to come to terms with the strangest feature of Christianity, which renders it so different from Buddhism: its historical claim. Jesus's significance did not consist in his preaching an eternal wisdom that others had known and that you could experience for yourself. Had he only done this, he would have been a messenger and no more essential to the truth than the countless other messengers the world has known. No, Jesus *was* the message. His life, death, and resurrection were not allegories of eternal truths: they were singular events, witnessed by many, and for which the first Christians were willing to die. One could not follow Jesus without facing three historical claims: that Jesus lived two-thousand years ago in the Middle East, that he died in agony on a Roman cross, and that he was seen to rise from the dead three days later. A Christian must weigh the evidence for or against these claims. The evidence will not decide the issue, but it cannot be ignored because we deal here not with an eternal truth but with an event in our history. "If Christ has not been raised, our preaching is useless and so is your faith," Paul writes (1 Cor. 15:14). And just to be sure that we do not mistake resurrection for a metaphor—the spirit of Jesus living on in the community or something similarly easy to accept—Paul says, "He appeared to Cephas, and then to the Twelve. After that, he appeared to more than five hundred of the brothers and sisters at the same time, most of whom are still living, though some have fallen asleep. Then he appeared to James, then to all the apostles, and last of all he appeared to me also, as to one abnormally born" (1 Cor. 5:7). Paul's testimony to the resurrection of Christ is neither poetic nor indirect (and he is frequently both). Rather, he offers a falsifiable historical record of events and a list of witnesses. Some of the five hundred witnesses, he takes the trouble to add, are still alive and presumably could be consulted on the truth of the claim. Their testimony will not decide the issue, for what is at stake is not merely that a man rose from the dead—Lazarus was said to have been raised by Jesus (John 11: 1–46). Everything depends upon who this man was who rose from the dead and what his resurrection signifies for the world.

Everything hinges on your answer to the question he repeatedly put to his disciples, "But what about you?" Jesus asked. "Who do you say I am?" (Matt. 16: 15).

The history of Jesus's life and works, which is found only in the four Gospels, is admittedly full of holes. The resurrection accounts of the Gospels do not match each other. There are structural differences among the Gospels which indicate that these texts were edited to suit their audiences: Matthew wrote for Jews, Luke for Greeks, and John for contemplative Christians living in a community a century later. Matthew frames things differently than Luke, and John has stories unknown to the others. Mark, which might be the oldest Gospel, is missing key elements, notably the Sermon on the Mount. The oldest version ends with the empty tomb, not with the appearance of the resurrected Jesus to the apostles. Some Gospels include stories of his infancy; others seem to know nothing about Jesus's life prior to his encounter with John the Baptist by the River Jordan, when he was 30 years old. It is hard to deny that John puts words into Jesus's mouth. Not only the terms but the grammar of Jesus's discourses in the Gospel of John repeats the language of John's letters. With all of this "objective uncertainty," it is no wonder that the only thing that academic historians can agree on is that Jesus claimed to be the Messiah, was put to death on a cross by the Romans, and was believed to be resurrected by his followers, who were particularly difficult to politically suppress. The historical record doesn't prove the faith.

But neither does it prove the skeptics to be right. In the view of many skeptics, the whole thing was probably made up by the apostles. But the Gospels do not read like fiction. If the apostles made it up, why would they make themselves look so bad? They continually miss the point of Jesus's teachings and miracles. One of them betrays Jesus, and the other denies him as Jesus is led to his torture and death. They all doubt he has risen until he appears in a "closed room" with them. Even then, Thomas refuses to believe until he can put his fingers in the wounds made by the Roman nails. If the thing was made up, wouldn't one expect a better job of it? At the very least, couldn't these author-apostles write a more seamless narrative? The Gospels are fragmentary and choppy. They do not resemble Greek or Indian myths or the Hebrew fables in the Bible, which have satisfying narrative arcs. The Gospels are more like the conflicting accounts one gets from witnesses of a car accident. The writers of these strange books were either terrible poets, or they were not poets at all.

I studied these things in the monastery as though my life depended upon it. The other area of particular concern for me in those early days was comparative religion. Freshly returned from India, I simply could not accept that "there is no salvation outside the Church," as the Catholics once insisted (most of them don't anymore). More urgently, I was disturbed by the idea that sages living in caves in Asia who had never even heard the name of Jesus could have made breakthroughs to the truth and been revered as enlightenment masters. It seemed to me at the time that it should be all or nothing: with the Jesus community, we find wisdom and truth and the way that leads to life; outside that community, nothing but ignorance, falsehood, and death. But that is not the case. Not only is wisdom, truth, and life to be found in the teaching of Chuang Tzu, Nagarjuna, Rumi, and countless unnamed Shamans of North America; but the truths proclaimed by these non-Christian sages do not agree with the Gospel message. It would be preferable if, as the Sufis believed, all religions were one and said more or less the same thing. One might conclude this based on a superficial survey of comparative mysticism. However, this interpretation does not stand up to scholarly scrutiny. On the contrary, Buddhism and Christianity, to single out two chief contenders for me in my youth, say quite different things about the origin and end of human life and the meaning of suffering. My guides in this research were the twentieth-century Christian monks who turned East, Bede Griffith, John Main, and especially Thomas Merton. I never solved this puzzle, either. But wrestling with it was key to coming to understand exactly what it was that Christianity was about. I will say much more about this later in the book.

The monks encouraged these research projects of mine and even invited me to lecture on philosophy and theology on occasion. The first time I did so, I was living in a monastery in Colorado. The whole area, a stunning ridge at the base of a fourteen-thousand-foot mountain on the edge of a sprawling desert, had been donated by a rich philanthropist to a variety of religious contemplative communities in the interest of fostering inter-religious dialogue. Nada, the Carmelite hermitage, stood beside a Hindu temple and down the road from a Zen center. I befriended one of the Zen monks, a young man exactly my age, of Western descent and trained in Japan, who was studying to become a Zen priest. Osho Robert was very strict in his religious observance of the precepts of Zen and had little time for Christian theology. But he was as interested in me as I was in him. I would visit him in the Zendō, where he would instruct me in Zazen or seated meditation. He, in turn, visited me in the hermitage, always in his striking Zen attire. We had lively discussions about a range of topics. Most interesting to both of us was how, despite the extremely different sets of beliefs undergirding our practices, our lifestyles were remarkably close. Monasticism varies little from religion to religion: discipline in eating, drinking, studying, working, and playing; a regular schedule of meditation and ritual; a communal life of subordinating one's desires to the common good.

When Robert visited, we would talk about philosophy, something in which we had a common interest. His approach was anti-intellectual and pragmatic. In classic Zen fashion, he affirmed that reason is sometimes useful—if you needed to change a tire, for example. But the breakthrough to truth—*kensho*—is always a break from the confines of reason. I was much more Socratic. How could reason be unimportant, I objected, if the whole force and tension of a Zen koan come from the intellectual effort one puts into thinking about it? Surely reason has an essential role to play in the mystical life, even of Zen practitioners. We disagreed and delighted in our disagreement.

Robert attended the first lecture I gave at the monastery. It was on Plato's doctrine of forms and I put my whole self into it. I remember him sitting at the front of the room in his magnificent Zen robes, listening politely and believing none of it.

This story underscores something essential about the Western contemplative tradition. Inseparable from Western contemplation is the Western intellectual tradition. There is nothing rationalistic about contemplation, but there is no way into it without the intellect. The greatest contemplatives—Augustine, Aquinas, Cusa—are towering intellects and philosophers as well as contemplatives. To put it tersely, in terms that will need to be developed, Western spirituality might have a Jewish heart, a heart that "has its reasons which reason does not know," as Pascal put it (Pascal 1995, 158), but it has a Greek mind.

The Greeks insisted on the unity of the true, the good, and the beautiful. To know the truth was to live virtuously, and such a life was beautiful. Living beautifully meant to imitate the transcendent human form itself, the standard by which all things human were to be measured. This was the purpose of life, the reason for human existence: to be fortunate enough to be Greek and to have the moral sense to avail oneself of all that civilization had to offer, not in a crass and self-indulgent way, but for the sake of cultivating the self. A virtuous person was good at many kinds of activities and moderate in everything.

He gave himself equally to the perfection of the intellect as to the perfection of the body.

One night I was walking across "the bridge" at Nada, our Colorado monastery. I was accompanied by a young man my age who was studying theology at university. The bridge connected the small chapel, with its little wooden bell tower, to the main building and offered the best view of Kit Carson, the fourteen-thousand-foot mountain at the base of which the monastery lay. Kit Carson is crowned by a pitch of ragged ice-encrusted granite rising above forests of pine and cottonwood. As we walked, the view of the stars wheeling in the sky behind Kit Carson was superb. We were returning to our hermitages after evening prayer in the chapel. A feeling of inner quiet was on me, which was typical for me after meditation. I had made my profession a few months before and was now a novice in the order. I wore a sand-colored habit that ran to my sandals, belted by a heavy sash of leather. Lights from the hermitages scattered about the sand dunes twinkled in the valley below. Beyond lay the dark expanse of the San Juan, a high-altitude desert stretched between two mountain ranges, fragrant with sage and flowering cactus, inhabited by deer and rabbits, and as wide as Nova Scotia.

The retreatant was interested in pursuing the possibility that he, too, might have a vocation for this kind of life. He was frustrated by the formality of academic theology. "Isn't theology about holiness?" he asked. I was giving him what advice I could. As we looked up into the night sky, I told him that I thought the sense of life was obvious from the vantage point of the monastery. Here we devoted all of our attention to caring for the soul for the sake of being better able to care for everything else. This was the *true* philosophical life. We, not the academics, were the genuine followers of Socrates. And even if the theology that we believed turned out not to be the whole truth (a suspicion I had even then), even if we were living a myth, the life justified itself aesthetically. We were living beautifully.

The transition from philosophy student to Christian monk did not consist in assuming a life of solitary meditation, study, and prayer. I had already taken that on to some degree in India. What was much more challenging for me and much more enriching was entering a vibrant human community in the woods of Nova Scotia. Yet another paradox wrenched my thinking apart and liberated me from my habitual categories: the religious hermit, far from being an antisocial lone wolf, is the most related of all people. The monk is alone before God and, at the same time, one with his community.

Father William

McNamara became my spiritual master for five years, from the moment I met him when I was 23, on my first retreat to Nova Nada, to my last conversation with him when I left the order at 28. His teaching was not particularly original. It was drawn entirely from the Catholic Neoplatonic tradition of which he was a virtuoso rather than an innovator. He was a gifted preacher who knew his way backward and forwards in this tradition and spoke of it, not in a scholarly way, but much more directly, as though he was speaking of his own experience. McNamara's re-actualization of Christian Neoplatonism remains, to this day, the greatest influence on my religious thinking. The power of it drew me deep into the spirituality of the West, a spirituality that precedes Christianity by five centuries. The Christian Neoplatonic tradition does not begin with Jesus and Paul. It is not even original with Plato, for Plato references his predecessors, not only his teacher, Socrates, but the ones who taught him. If an origin of this tradition is to be named, the shadowy wandering pre-Socratic philosopher, who was a pagan mystic, Parmenides (fifth century BC, southern Italy), has the best claim for being its founder. And since the tradition from the beginning taught the mystical transformation of human erotic life through ascent from the body to the spirit, it is important to also remember that Parmenides had a female counterpart, an even more obscure figure, the high priestess of love, who Socrates quotes at length in Plato's dialogue the *Symposium*. Her name was Diotima of Mantinea.

The development of the pre-Christian Hellenistic mystical tradition in many ways paralleled the growth of Vedanta, which was happening simultaneously in Northern India. Both systems of thought describe how all things have emerged from unity and return to unity (*exitus et reditus*) through the contemplative practice of the sage. The universe for Neoplatonism emanates from the One, streams forth into time and diversity, and returns to unity through the contemplation of the philosopher-mystic. In Vedanta, the universe emerges spontaneously from Brahman, from undifferentiated, eternal unity into plurality and cyclical time, and returns to unity through the yoga of the Rishi. The parallels between these two great ancient religious philosophies are undeniable. It is not at all impossible that there was a connection between the Indus Valley civilization and the peoples of the Mediterranean. Ideas might have traveled back and forth along with the goods that we know were traded amongst Southeast Asian and European peoples. Or it may be that Neoplatonism and Vedanta are both expressions of a perennial philosophy, which is found everywhere, in Ancient China, for example, in medieval Islam, and in the shamanistic mythologies of pre-historical peoples. One thing, however, is clear. Monasticism has pre-Christian roots in both Greek Neoplatonism and Vedanta, if not in even older societies.[8]

McNamara had become a Carmelite when he was fourteen years old after a mystical experience swept him off his feet as he received Communion one day. When I met him, he was in his sixties, an awe-inspiring figure with a great gray beard and a twinkle in his eye. He wore the dark brown habit of the Discalced Carmelites, with a long wooden rosary swinging from his hip. In the early sixties, McNamara had received permission from his order to live as a hermit. He traveled to Rome during the Second Vatican Council to obtain Pope John the XXIII's approval for his idea to start a new monastic community in North America that would return to what Thomas Merton called "the primitive Carmelite ideal," something he discussed directly with Merton.[9]

The first Carmelites did not dwell together in a cloister but lived alone in huts on Mount Carmel in Palestine in the twelfth century, emulating the Hebrew prophet Elijah, who is alleged to have lived there as a hermit nine centuries before Christ and who was carried up to heaven in a chariot of fire (2 Kings 2–11). This ideal of ascending from solitude into heaven and directly encountering God is the mystical foundation and remains the charism of the Carmelite order. Some orders, like the Franciscans, were founded at the same time as the Carmelites to serve the poor. Others, like the Dominicans, were founded to preach and teach. The Carmelites were founded to pray. They were a medieval school of contemplative prayer.

The first Carmelite hermits were probably Crusaders who stayed behind in Palestine after the fighting stopped, hung up their swords, and took up a life of eremitical prayer, living alone in caves scattered around the peak of Mount Carmel. They were loosely organized according to the rule of Saint Albert, which was a revision of the Benedictine Rule and which they adopted when it became clear that they needed some modicum of structure if there were to be a community of hermits. Where Benedict's Rule is Byzantine in its detail, Albert's Rule is Zen-simple: a few pages prescribing a certain degree of communal activity as support for solitude and a certain amount of apostolic work (preaching, teaching, and serving the poor) as an outflow of solitary prayer.

By the time McNamara entered the Order of Discalced Carmelites (OCD) in the mid-twentieth century, the mystical-eremitical beginnings of the order were all but forgotten. Teresa of Avila and John of the Cross had reformed the order and, to some degree, restored it to its contemplative roots in the sixteenth century, founding the OCDs to which McNamara belonged. McNamara adored John of the Cross and spoke of him incessantly, but he wanted more than John's urban cloisters. He wanted to go back to the wilderness, to the desert and the mountains, and find the path to the divine ascent in nature, as did the first Carmelites. He received permission from his superiors and from Pope John XXIII to found a loosely structured community of hermits in the desert near Sedona, Arizona, in the sixties. They called themselves the Spiritual Life Institute. While publishing and preaching were central activities, the heart of the community was the effort to return to the original form of Carmelite life: loosely organized solitaries in the wilderness praying for the world. The institute would, in McNamara's words, "put contemplation back onto the roadmaps of the world." But it would be fed by far deeper springs than study and scholarship. Its mystical root would be the life of prayer of the desert hermit community.

In terms of his preaching, McNamara at first targeted the secular elite, the intellectuals, writers, and leftist policymakers. A journal was launched, and McNamara became a busy retreat director and public speaker. At the same time, he developed his growing charismatic power over the younger generation, the baby boomers, who came to hear him on Catholic campuses in the US, where he held student retreats. Some of these young people followed him and became his disciples.

The first community in Arizona was attached to the Chapel of the Holy Cross in Sedona, where McNamara was the pastor. The church is a superb modernist tower firing like a rocket out of the red cliff, stone, steel, and glass, faced with an enormous cross. McNamara's followers ran the retreat center, helped out with the publication, grew vegetables, and listened to him speak of things that were new to them. In long, sprawling homilies, he told them of the seven stages of the mystical union of John of the Cross, the bridal mysticism of Teresa of Avila, the mystical transformation of eros, and the contemplative ascent into God.

When encroaching suburbia pushed McNamara and his hermits out of Sedona, the group purchased a century-old hunting and fishing lodge on a remote lake in the wilderness of interior Nova Scotia, where McNamara founded a more structured religious community of Carmelite "apostolic hermits," with a rule of life, taking vows under the canonical oversight of the local bishop. Later a sister house was founded in the Sangre de Cristo mountains of Colorado. Irving Oil chased the monks out of Nova Scotia by clear-cutting the woods around the monastery in the late nineties—a horror I was spared (I left in 1995). The monks moved to Ireland, where they remain to this day.

Charismatic, approachable, comedic, and intellectually powerful, McNamara attracted a small but vibrant group of young people to his cause (male and female) who had the energy and the sheer physical power for the Herculean labor of transforming a hunting and fishing lodge into a monastery and living without electricity or running water through the long, wet east-coast winters. Other priests and religious joined, and soon the small movement grew into something much more identifiably Roman Catholic than what had started in the desert around Sedona. When I joined them, they were the darling of the local bishop, who ordained their priests and visited regularly.

When I first read his books, I was struck by how different McNamara's approach to Christianity was from anything else I had read. There was nothing of the pious sentimentality and affected meekness of modern Christian spiritual authors, literature which I, for the most part, despised. McNamara ripped into the "waist high" consumer culture, which he found un-erotic and coddled. He spared no words in his indictment of the contemporary Church, which he thought was infected by the "pretty poison" of secular humanism. In its place, he offered a robustly Christian humanism, God-centered and mystical and natural and earthy all at the same time.

For McNamara, Christianity is as heroic as anything Nietzsche ever dreamed of and as philosophical as anything produced by the Greeks. McNamara's Christianity is a religion for saints and sages, as virile as Homer and spiritually profound as Buddhism. But there is nothing syncretistic about his theology. McNamara regards Christianity as unquestionably true and superior to all other forms of religion, which it does not negate so much as sublate by giving them back their own truth claims in a higher form, supplemented, and fulfilled with the revelation of the Christ.

McNamara's writing was compelling, but it was nothing compared to his preaching. He would often preach for two hours at a time. This was not the sleep-inducing stuff that I endured on Sunday mornings with my family. McNamara could thunder like an Old Testament prophet, or wax lyrical like a Romantic poet, or fall suddenly into prolonged and pregnant silence. His preaching plunged me into depths of mystery and elevated me to heights of knowledge at the same time. Under his mentorship, Christianity, which I had taken for granted, opened up before me as a *terra incognito* of transcendent truths, extraordinary facts, and wild and wondrous characters.

I learned of the history of Christian mysticism and monasticism (for him, the same thing)—not only of the Benedictines and Carmelites but of the Celtic monks, whom McNamara idolized, those Dark Age madmen perched on inaccessible rocky outcrops in the North Atlantic. The Celtic monks could never find a site harsh and remote enough for their monasteries, where they wrote poems to their blond-haired Christ, whom they saluted as "the king of fair fame." The Roman Empire had not touched Ireland, and so the Celts were not burdened by the decadent hedonist-nihilist paganism of Southern Europe. They could engage the "principalities and powers" of nature, which Paul talked about (Eph. 6:12), without fear of sorcery or demons. Celtic Christianity blended seamlessly with the nature mysticism of pre-Christian Ireland. Like McNamara, the Celtic Christians were as happy in a moonlit glade of trees as they were in the little stone chapels they built all over Ireland.

Some of the Celtic saints even spoke like druids, invoking the protection of earth, air, fire, and water, marshalled by Christ "the Lord of the Elements," as does Saint Patrick in "the Deer's Cry" (so called because Patrick, escaping from aggressive wizards, turned himself into a deer as he sang it): "I arise today, through the strength of heaven; light of sun, brilliance of moon, splendour of fire, speed of lightning, swiftness of wind, depth of sea, stability of earth, firmness of rock ... Christ with me, Christ before me, Christ behind me, Christ in me, Christ beneath me, Christ above me."

I learned of the power and stability of the Benedictine tradition, the socio-political bedrock of European civilization. I have no doubt Benedictine monks will be there after our cities have crumbled into ruin. I learned also of the mendicant orders of the Middle Ages, the Franciscans and Dominicans, wandering poor through Europe and preaching the gospel of simplicity to a Church grown fat. When Arabs invaded Palestine and took it back from the Crusaders, the Carmelites reformed in Europe. The Pope, wary of introducing yet another religious innovation into the Church (he had just barely survived Francis), allowed them to start up only as mendicants like the Franciscans and Dominicans. Hence the medieval Carmelites in Europe were also wandering teachers and preachers, sounding the call to contemplation in all of the capitals of Europe.

As only an archetypal figure can, Father William (as we monks used to call him) became the focus of all my projections. I saw him as a warrior of truth like Columbanus, who left his native Ireland to brave the fury of the wild men inhabiting the forests of Northern Europe, and in so doing, bring Christ to the heathens. McNamara was also, for me, a love poet of the divine like Bernard of Clairvaux, who wrote his rhapsodic and sensual commentary on God's love for humankind, *The Sermon on the Song of Songs*, in a simple wooden Cistercian cloister in twelfth-century France. So too was McNamara, for me, a scholastic mystic like Meister Eckhart, who in the great gothic cathedral of Cologne in the fourteenth century preached the doctrine of God's place in the hidden center of the soul. He was a fearless religious reformer like his beloved John of the Cross, who in sixteenth-century Spain summoned the Carmelites back to their contemplative calling while writing his great mystical treatise of ascent to the divine through the negation of all that is creaturely. McNamara could be all of these things for me because he was never, for me, an ordinary man. He was the guru, the wizard, the wise old man. It was as though he had stepped directly out of medieval Europe into the woods of central Nova Scotia. I was smitten.

I was also understandably intimidated. Father William did not spend much time in community. He had a hermitage some distance apart from the rest of us. It was understood that at this stage of his life, he was called to a deeper solitude than the rest of us. But I caught his attention. Something about the intensity of my quest for the truth intrigued him, and he agreed to meet with me on occasion. I carefully prepared for these meetings with a list of questions that I desperately needed to ask him. These were questions that arose out of my intense study of modern philosophy and comparative religion in those years. What is human freedom? How is it possible, given the law of causality? How does Christ fit in with the mystics and sages of other religions? Is there revelation outside the Church? Why does God permit evil? These things kept me awake at night. Father William received my questions with good humor and endless patience. His answers were always fascinating, but most disarming for me was his presence and attention. He appeared to care deeply about me. And he gave me the impression that there was no intellectual puzzle too deep for the contemplative and no objection to the Gospel that could not be refuted.

We grew close. Father William became, for a time, my confessor. Meeting with him was the highlight of my week. In all of his interactions with the other monks and me, he was eminently personal. He was as attentive to me, a lowly novice and chief manual laborer (specialist in what we used to refer to as "grunt work"), as he was to the senior monks he relied on to run things. He was wholly present to the birds he liked to feed from his balcony as he was to the dogs we lived with. He loved everything about monasticism and was strict after a fashion, but never allowed the rule to stand in the way of love.

One day I was dropping off some mail to his hermitage in the afternoon. It was a solitude day, and we were expected to keep silent and avoid unnecessary contact with each other. His house was directly on the edge of the lake, deep in a copse of white pines. I was going to slip the mail between the doors as quietly as possible in order not to disturb the great man. As he heard the screen door creak, Father William came out. He had been sick—his health was always poor—and his voice was almost gone. But he wanted to say something to me. In a raspy voice, he said, "I want to thank you for granting me a religious experience yesterday morning." I stared at him in disbelief. What had *I* to teach *him*? "As I was reading my breviary, I caught sight of you canoeing into the mist with the two dogs." This was a regular activity for me on solitude Mondays when I was not expected to report for work. Ben, the Golden Retriever, at my feet, and Polo, the husky, perched on the gunnels in the bow like a masthead; we would disappear into the woods for a day and a night. "The sight of you and those dogs heading out into the morning was a vision of the wildness of God. And so I wanted to thank you for that. You must never lose this. Monasticism is important, but it is only a means. God is not tame. He is as wild and fearsome as a lion. And God loves nothing more than a wild and passionate heart." By founding religious communities of both men and women celibates, McNamara was trying something both ancient and daring. There are examples of such things in the long history of the Church. Contemporary Catholicism prefers to keep men and women celibates out of sight of each other for fear that proximity will lead to carnal sin. No doubt the Church knows what it is doing. However, there is something quaintly naïve about the assumption that single-sex communities are safe from illicit sexual encounters. The all-male communities I visited were hardly free of sex. Some of them were havens for homosexuality in a Church that refused to recognize the phenomenon. Eros was, in McNamara's view, not only good but essential to a healthy spiritual life. Celibate men and women ought to live erotically together without sleeping with one another. If disciplined and directed upwards instead of at each other, the erotic energy awakened between them could enliven the community and produce sanctity, as it had in the case of John of the Cross and Teresa of Avila, or Francis of Assisi and Clair—something like Christian Kundalini Yoga.

McNamara refused to fit neatly into either the conservative or the progressive camps that divide the Church. He would enrage the conservatives by saying the most outrageous things, "God is a bear," he would say, as cryptically as a Zen master breaking the head of the disciple with a koan. The theologians would sputter in protest about the importance of distinguishing metaphoric from analogous sense. McNamara would smile and stick obstinately by his proposition, "God is a bear." Or he would argue that the *Logos*, the second person of the Trinity, first became incarnate in the creation of the world. Conservative theologies, ever anxious of pantheistic confusions of God and nature, speak of the incarnation as a unique event that occurred in the figure of Jesus. McNamara was a devotee of the Cosmic Christ and a follower of Pierre Teilhard de Chardin, the Jesuit geologist who was silenced in the fifties for suggesting that the divine was far more material than we had previously suspected. Teilhard argued that evolution is an ascent toward consciousness that passes from primates through humanity to the Christ and continues through the history of the Church into modernity in a continuous upsurge toward what he calls "the Omega Point" (Teilhard de Chardin 2001). The Omega Point is God become "all in all," as Paul prophesies (1 Cor. 15: 28). But Teilhard's God does not float free above creation; rather, God is messily entangled in it. Like Teilhard, McNamara was uncomfortable with rigid separations between nature and supernature, matter and spirit. There were no gaps in McNamara's cosmology: nature was the supporting substructure of supernature (much as sexuality supported mystical eros). Spirit incarnates itself in all matter.

He never missed an opportunity to make fun of fussy piety and the monastic temptation to take religious observance too seriously, as though God was impressed by fasts and vigils. And yet no one was more intolerant of flabby self-indulgence. Himself an insomniac, McNamara urged us to sleep as little as possible. God was revealing Godself incessantly in the wonders of the natural world and in the depths of our souls, he said, but we were too often asleep when it occurred.

In the 1980s and '90s, when he was at his peak as a writer and preacher, McNamara displayed the subtlety of a great thinker, carefully heeding the fine lines that demarcate orthodoxy from heterodoxy. He had no time for the progressives in the Church, for guitar-playing Jesuits and feminist nuns bedecked with make-up and jewelry. Liberal Christianity was, in his judgment, wimpy, timid, and self-indulgent. His theology was often shocking but wholly orthodox, a blast of wind directly out of the ancient Church. Nevertheless, McNamara's theology of the Eucharist struck many conservatives as suspicious, if not outright heretical. We must not idolize the Eucharist, he taught. It is the focus of God's presence in the world, which is ubiquitous. Too many Catholics act as though God is present in the Eucharist but absent everywhere else in the material world. The Eucharist, in McNamara's view, is "the focus not the locus." We should concentrate our devotion to the divine in all matter, an indwelling of God in creation, which is especially revealed in the Mass. This reverence, this attentiveness to the divinity present here and now, should not be absent when we sweep the floor, cook dinner, or romp with the dogs.

McNamara's preferred term for a mystic was a "disciplined wild man," and his favorite example was Jesus himself. He called Jesus's theology (and his own) "earthy mysticism" because it did not indulge in spooky, otherworldly spirituality but emphasized the embodied and realistic quality of genuine faith. The earthy mystic is not the one who is aloof to the pleasures and pains of life but the one who suffers them more keenly than anyone else in her desire to participate in the redemptive suffering of Christ. She watches and reads everything, is sensitive and vulnerable to everything and everyone that crosses her path, weeps over the world but refuses herself the luxury of despair and is as likely to be buckling over with belly laughter as she is to be mourning with the marginalized. The earthy mystic takes God so seriously that she can take everything else, especially herself, lightheartedly.

The guru must die if the disciple is to grow, and McNamara had to die for me. The day came when I saw that Father William was not who I thought he was. My idea of McNamara and McNamara himself were two different people. I was no doubt beguiled in my relation to him by my own projections. I left the monastery in abject disillusionment and without a teacher. But the desire for God that McNamara evoked in me was no illusion. The history of mystical Christianity he mediated for me was not a projection. Without McNamara, I would think differently about everything.

The Hidden Life

Common to all monasticism, whether Christian or Buddhist, is a community set apart from the world. Monks live a common life, serving one another in a micro-society. They may not all like each other, but they remain bound together by an unwritten contract, a solemn agreement implicit in the vows they take, that the wisdom of the world is folly and that something immeasurably better than pleasure, wealth, and power can be gained in a community that sets itself apart and lives under a rule. The world teaches us to make something awesome of ourselves, to become somebody in the eyes of others, whether that means wealthier than most, more influential, or more sexually successful than others. Monks become nobodies for the sake of something deemed immeasurably higher and more worthwhile than pleasure, recognition, or power.

Contemplative community is a common goal of Buddhist and Christian monastics. One could also include Sufi communities and Hindu or Vedantic Ashrams as monastic forms of life that share the emphasis on building spiritual or non-worldly forms of community for the sake of fostering contemplation. What distinguishes the varieties of monasticism is the organizing spiritual principle of the monastic community, what Lacan calls, "the master signifier." Buddhists seek enlightenment, which consists in snuffing out ego-centric desire (Nirvana) and identification with Buddha-Mind. Sufis seek total non-dual surrender to Allah, a mystical ecstasy wherein the soul forgets itself completely and becomes one with the Creator. Vedantists seek *Moksha*, the enlightenment that consists in realizing that

Brahman is Atman or that God is the soul. Christian monks, while they on occasion speak of non-dual identity with God, are not seeking enlightenment or release from the body. They do not believe that the human being is fundamentally deluded, nor do they regard life in the body as something evil. How could the body be evil if Christ himself was fully human, that is, fully embodied? The search for enlightenment targets a divine essence that is distributed equally in all things but which the deluded mind cannot grasp. The essence is impersonal and can to some degree be realized through techniques of meditation. Christian monks, by contrast, have as their goal discipleship with the Christ. The aim is holiness, which means *personal* identification with the Christ. "Let the same mind be in you that was in Christ Jesus," Paul writes (Phil. 2 5). What exactly this means is subject to interpretation. For some, it means a non-dual union with the Christ. For others, it means becoming a second Christ, not so much disappearing into the Christ nature as repeating the pattern of self-sacrificial love that was manifest in Jesus. In all cases, however, the goal of Christian monasticism remains a profoundly personal connection between the soul of the monk and the Christ.

Discipleship at Nova Nada meant becoming your best, most spontaneous, personally engaged self. Father William taught us to love wildness, both in ourselves and in the world around us. The setting of the monastery, about as deep into the densely forested wilderness of central Nova Scotia as you could get, fostered the love of the wild. On occasion there were retreatants to pick up at the airport: lay people brave enough to live as a monk for a while. In the spring, the seven-mile dirt road to the nearest town turned into a river of deep mud. One could not walk it: you would sink to the knee. The only way to get through was in a four-wheel drive truck in low gear, revved high, which did not stop for anything. If you stopped, you would get stuck and would need to return by foot through the woods to the monastery to fetch the tractor to pull the truck out of the mud. Such rescues would take hours, so the pressure was on to fly through the mud as fast as possible, waves of brown sludge parting to both sides of the bouncing vehicle. Inside, everything was flying: groceries, luggage, and ashen-faced passengers. I enjoyed it perhaps a little too much. These wild trips were a welcome relief for me from the monotony of everyday duties.

We had no television, internet, or shopping to distract us and fill up our hours. The drudgery of the daily routine was the crucible that drove us out of ourselves. Outwardly, there was little variation in the order of the day. Wake up before dawn, read for an hour, pray and meditate, work, go for a walk, pray and meditate, read for another hour, sleep. Behind the scenes, in the hidden life of the hermitage, anything at all could be going on. Some went through major depressions. Others made breakthroughs to higher levels of prayer. Some were visited by saints. My prayer life was an exhilarating intellectual journey, full of discovery and surprise.

In solitude one quickly discovers that the chief enemy of the contemplative is his own mind. And the only way out of the torturous self-problematization that people mistake for the spiritual life is the not-self: the woods, the animals, the human companions. People who have never tried it assume that contemplation is self-absorbed or introspective. Only when all that is not the self becomes the focus of the spiritual life, only then does contemplation become real.

I had not forgotten my cousin's question and meditated often on despair, its causes, and its cures. I read as much as I could, in psychology and the history of philosophy and theology, looking always for the answer. I had not yet found it, although I had found what I believed at the time was the right direction to look—not Eastward but Westward, and not ordinary lay Christianity, but the mystical heart of the Church, which has been guarded and tended by countless monastics through the ages.

My views on philosophy, religion, and politics have changed in the years since I left the monastery. But on one point I have not wavered. I am as convinced as ever that everyone can have something of a contemplative practice as part of their daily routine. It can be as simple as fifteen minutes alone with a cup of coffee and an inspirational book before anyone else in the house awakens. If mornings are taken from you by duties and family, it could be twenty minutes of yoga in the late afternoon followed by a few minutes of meditation. If the days and nights are not yours to arrange as you wish, a candle lit in your bedroom at the end of the day and a moment of quiet reflection can be enough.

These exercises are not the point; the elevated state of mind that they evoke is. In our day-to-day grind, we habitually lock into a pattern that the Shin Buddhists describe as relying on self-power. A Christian would call the pattern unbelief. We plough through our day, assuming that everything depends upon us and revolves around us. This thought fills us with anxiety, with what Thoreau called "quiet desperation." Contemplative practice breaks the pattern. Contemplation ushers in moments of stillness when the inner monologue ceases. We lift our heads from our self-absorption and notice how wrong we are: nothing depends upon us; we are not the center of things. There is other power. We cannot of our own power even pray, McNamara taught. Prayer happens by God's good pleasure when the love that animates the universe floods our open hearts. God is always trying to get in. But we are usually too occupied with other things to notice. The best we can do is meditate and be ready for the moment when prayer happens.

If I were to name the one thing most needed for a contemplative life, it is not a meditation technique or a hermitage in the woods, or yoga. It is solitude. The word "monk" comes from the Greek *monas* or "one." The monk is the one who is alone. The community of monks protects the solitude of each of its members. But it is not only monks who need solitude; we all do. We all need a moment or two alone every day, to remember *that* we are, that we have been given being, and that the origin and destiny of being is a mystery. It is in such quiet moments that it becomes apparent that, far from a self-indulgent luxury, contemplation may be the most countercultural thing we can do. Our society has no tolerance for it. A desire for solitude is regarded as pathological. From the moment we rise to the moment we fall asleep, we are "on": texting, talking, buying, selling, planning, working, playing—whatever. "Man's unhappiness springs from one thing alone, his incapacity to stay quietly in one room," Pascal wrote in the seventeenth century (Pascal Pensées 1995: 44). Inscribed over the gate of Nova Nada on a wooden sign was a quote from Psalm 46: "Be still and know that I am God." I don't know how many times I walked by that sign and considered it. In it is condensed the secret of contemplation, the secret always known and always forgotten and always in need of re-discovery: first, stillness; then, in the stillness, recognition that there is other-power, and the proper name of this power is God.

Sometimes, not always, for God cannot be commanded, but sometimes, when we are alone and the mind quietens down, prayer happens. That is the whole mystery of monasticism, the whole point of the rules and the rituals and the communities in the wilderness. While we wait for prayer to happen, we meditate.

Meditation in a Western context is not all that different from the yoga and Zen practiced in the East. Some predominant forms of Western meditation, such as the Ignatian exercises, place emphasis on the imagination and acts of the mind—visually placing oneself in a biblical scene, for example. But an equally central part of the Christian tradition, especially the Carmelite tradition, is "the prayer of quiet," or "the practice of the presence of God." Referred to by Benedictines as "centering prayer" and rooted in mystical practices of Eastern Orthodoxy, here the monk no longer generates pious thoughts and feelings through acts of imagination, but endeavors to quiet the mind, to detach it from the parade of images and concepts that continually run through it, and be still in the presence of God, who is always present to us. Zen breathing exercises are more than appropriate and useful in this regard. I spent many hours seated on a cushion in half lotus on the floor of the chapel. Sometimes a mantra is used, a special phrase, silently repeated over and over again, as a way of focusing attention and drawing it back from the inevitable distractions that arise, the arbitrary images and concepts that emerge of their own accord the minute we try to sit quietly. "Lord, Jesus Christ, Son of the Living God, have mercy on me, a sinner," I would repeat, to the rhythm of my inhalation and exhalation—for an hour or more at a time.

When I returned to the world and entered graduate school, I did my best to maintain the basics of monastic life: early morning meditation, spiritual reading, and regular liturgy. It did not go well. There was no community to support me. Sunday Mass in the local parish was hardly a help. It was busy with families and noisy with a communal bustle that was hardly conducive to the stillness I sought. I longed for the early morning Masses in the monastery, when after reading the Gospel, and without a word of preaching, the priest would take his seat, and we would sit in silence for twenty minutes until the celebration of the Eucharist erupted in our midst like a communal revelation. From these contemplative experiences, I developed a deep love for the liturgy of the Church, which I still have today. I often feel that the contemplative lives of average churchgoing Christians would be greatly enriched if the priest simply read the liturgy at half the speed he usually does, allowing the ancient prayers to sink in. "Blessed are you, Oh Lord, God of creation. Through your goodness, we have this bread to offer, which Earth has given and human hands have made. It will become for us the bread of life." Say it like you mean it. Say it as though reciting poetry.

In the first years after leaving the monastery, I began to avoid Sunday Mass and instead attended the daily Masses in a downtown parish of Toronto. There might be only ten people there. The priest never preached. The ones who went—the elderly women saying their rosaries ("telling their beads"), the lonely single man finding reprieve from the indifference of the world outside, the solitary middle-aged woman starting her workday with a silent act of devotion—these quiet ones were not performing their "Sunday obligation." They were there because they needed a time and space where a human being could do that quintessentially human thing: sit still and pray.

Sheilagh

My greatest teacher in prayer was not Father William or any of the great authors on contemplation. It was my twin sister, Sheilagh, who died of a brain tumor at the age of 36. It was Sheilagh in particular who helped me recognize the power of weakness and so to understand the central message of the Gospels. Sheilagh showed me that Christianity had nothing much to do with self-transformation or scaling spiritual heights. It had everything to do with self-surrender and descending into the depths of humility, powerlessness, and weakness. Only there, where we no longer have anything of our own to boast of, does the power of God become effective. While we assume ourselves to be capable of divinity through our own power, God remains powerless to perfect us. God so loves our freedom that God will do nothing without our consent. Christ-nature is everywhere and in everything, and everywhere unseen and unheeded. We are too busy looking at ourselves to see it. Sheilagh was a master of surrender. She taught me the heroism, the courage, and the radical vulnerability of genuine prayer.

The human being has seemingly always fantasized about transcending humanity, climbing up to the divine by ascetic practices, mental training, philosophical insight, whatever, and leaving the messy human reality behind. I never felt worthy or enlightened, and always found myself incapable of self-perfection. Every effort to reform my life, every new regime of prayer, fasting, and meditation, would end in relapses into old patterns of depression, sloth, and distraction. Even as a monk, I was a sloppy ascetic. The Protestants rejected most of medieval Catholicism for overemphasizing "works," i.e., self-power, and forgetting the absolute necessity of grace. We will not be redeemed by our efforts but by grace alone (*sola gratia*). But it was not Protestantism that initially demonstrated to me the power of grace. It was Sheilagh. She showed me the futility of relying on myself.

When we were children, Sheilagh was slightly smaller than me, with the same blast of platinum blond hair that I had. She spoke little and tended to disappear into the chaos of our noisy home. With four older sisters in a constant state of war with each other, and a large Labrador Retriever galloping through the house, silence was a rare and under-appreciated phenomenon in my family home. The needs of the noisiest were met first. Sheilagh was always last in line.

I am often asked how it feels to be a twin. I never know what to answer. I came into being accompanied by another. I was never without a companion. I was nurtured and touched even before I set eyes on my mother. As a small boy, I felt like I had two mothers, for Sheilagh naturally mothered me. Not that she was more advanced or developed, but there was something about her that needed to give. After our teachers separated us at school (Sheilagh was always doing my work for me), we grew apart somewhat. But even when we were most distant from each other, in our teenage years, we were always connected on a deep and unconscious level.

Sheilagh's first illness, at nine years old, was caused by an infection in her leg as a result of a fall at school. The disease that followed weakened her left tibia to a brittle stick that broke three times consecutively over the course of a year. She experienced a depth of physical pain during this time that I have to this day never known. A large ungainly leg brace was installed, and Sheilagh was plucked from the stream of childhood and the games and sports of her peers. She entered a world of hospitals, specialists, and nurses, which she would inhabit for the rest of her life.

When the medical troubles were localized in her leg, Sheilagh could still enjoy a more or less normal life. After her diagnosis of a brain tumor in her sixteenth year (probably the effect of the leg disease), her life changed dramatically. She was given five years to live. Radiation treatment led to the complete loss of her hair. This was hard on her, a teenage girl on the threshold of young adulthood, but like everything that came her way, she learned to accept it, even laugh about it. She wore a wig of curly brown hair at school that the dog loved to steal at home, tearing through the halls of our house like a hound with a rabbit.

The radiation punched a hole in the tumor and relieved the pressure for a time. Sheilagh was able to finish high school. Graduating meant nothing to me. I never studied and barely attended classes. I used to boast that the number of days absent on my report card was higher than my average. But for Sheilagh, graduating was a monumental achievement. The slow-growing tumor besieged her with headaches and damaged her short-term memory, making it difficult for her to keep up. Sheilagh was as quiet as a mouse but had the will of a warrior. She did not make any noise about what she needed; she simply went silently about pursuing it. With fierce determination, she invented strategies for offsetting the deterioration of her memory and passed her exams.

This success was followed by further failures to advance academically. She was forced by her teachers to withdraw from college a few weeks into the first semester. She had always loved children and had enrolled in early childhood education at the local community college. One day, the dean and her teacher called her in and coldly told her she could not continue. Her disability made it impossible for her to keep up with the work.

This became a pattern: starting a program of study only to be forced to withdraw. Sheilagh refused to believe that she would not be able to do it. Even after her doctors explained to her, with that clinical indifference modern medicine has mastered, that her situation was one of slow and inevitable decline and that she would never be able to finish university, Sheilagh stubbornly refused to accept it. At the start of each new semester, which would invariably begin without her, she would sit at the edge of her bed studying the course calendar, the book a few inches from her nose (her eyesight was badly damaged), planning her return.

While I was searching for the Buddha in India, Sheilagh fell into a coma and came close to death. A storm of headaches, a collapse into unconsciousness, and suddenly her life was hanging from a thread again. I had to return home. When she regained consciousness, Sheilagh's vision, speech, and motor skills were even more deeply impaired and it became obvious to her that there would be no degrees or normal life.

She recovered somewhat but not to the level of health she had enjoyed before the collapse. She walked with a cane. Soon another setback would send her to the hospital paralyzed and unable to talk for the better part of a year. I visited her every day in the hospital that year, usually on my way home from university, where I was now studying philosophy. Her sight would not allow her to read, so I read to her. I read her the entirety of *The Lord of the Rings*. She had always been a devout Catholic. Now she began to go deeper into prayer than most of us ever will. We began to notice her making curious gestures with her right hand. When Sheilagh saw us watching this, she quickly stopped. I asked her what it was about. She explained in her slow drawl—all that she could manage at this stage—that it was a sign language she had invented in which she prayed. I can see her now, lying mute in her hospital bed, with her right hand signing at her side. She tried to hide this from the family because we did not like it. It scared us. We wanted her to stay with us.

She improved intermittently and would be home for a time, and then would slip yet again, needing hospitalization or medical intervention. The five-year mark passed. Somehow Sheilagh had found a way to live with the tumor. The doctors could not explain it.

Sheilagh spent her last decade as a resident in a chronic care facility in Ottawa. Any other young person would have found the institution unbearable. The halls smelled of urine and were loud with the bellowing of the Alzheimer's patients wheeling up and down in a pathetic search for family and friends they could no longer recognize even if they were fortunate enough to be visited by them. Amazingly, Sheilagh rose to the occasion and thrived there. She entertained visitors in her room with board games. A one-person cottage industry in the arts and crafts room, she slowly created her Christmas presents by hand. The Alzheimer's patients troubled her at first, but she came to understand that she was called to minister to them, befriend them, listen to them, or simply reach out and touch them.

On her last Christmas, for whatever reason (no medical explanation was given), the cranial pressure that had been impeding her over the years suddenly released. A clarity of speech and mobility such as she had not had for years returned to her. She seemed to be healed—although we all knew it was a momentary remission. She could walk without assistance. Her speech was clear. She was more awake and able to participate in ordinary family life. That Christmas, newly empowered, Sheilagh took girlish pride in herself. Her sisters dressed her in a black velvet dress for dinner, and she quietly considered her siblings gathered around the table, busy with all that she had missed out on—partners, children, and career. But at this stage, she was miles beyond envy and self-pity. Her gaze was the look of a Buddha watching the empty forms of the world rise and fall like lovely, shiny soap bubbles.

Like a brief break in the clouds releasing a flood of sunshine only to be followed by even darker skies, the moment of relief passed, and Sheilagh's decline was swift and inexorable. Early in 2002, the tumor, which had lain more or less dormant for years, began to grow again. Her body could not withstand any more radiation. Buried as deeply as it was, at the center of her brain, the tumor could not be operated on and slowly killed her.

There was little pain and no depression at the end. Sheilagh always accepted whatever was offered to her as a life. After twenty years of suffering and setbacks, she had wholly surrendered to the will of God which she believed in without reservation. Her gentle capacity to accept everything was inscrutable, as though she knew something the rest of us did not, that mobility, travel, education, and achievement were fine things, but not the most important thing, and that when they were taken away, nothing essential was lost. She knew that we are held by love and would pass into love.

On a day that we all silently dreaded but never discussed, we received the announcement from the doctors that this was it: she would not live the year. One always wonders how one will feel in such a situation. I can only say that I was surprised by how I felt—how we all felt. We let go of our private hopes and, through no power of our own, we accessed the peace in which Sheilagh spent her days, the peace of God, which Saint Paul said, "surpasses all understanding" (Phil. 4:7). We entered into an unspoken agreement with one another to meet Sheilagh in that place of serene acceptance, if only to say goodbye.

The months moved on towards the day of death. Sheilagh lost all power of movement, speech, and most of her vision. But something extraordinary happened. As her physical existence declined, her serenity increased. No longer able to express herself in word and gesture, crumpled in her wheelchair, she would look up at those who cared for her and smile silently.

In her thirty-sixth year, with the quiet resolve that accompanied everything she did, Sheilagh let the world go.

Sheilagh helped me to understand that prayer is always directed to a person, however imageless the prayer might be. The Zen practice of sitting and not thinking is excellent preparation for prayer, but it is not prayer. Prayer is a dialogue with the other power that lets all things be what they are. It is never forced but arises spontaneously in the attentive heart. The beginning of prayer is always attentiveness to reality, whatever it might be, whether it be good or bad, beautiful or ugly, joyous or painful. What kills prayer is self-reflection. Prayer goes best when the self forgets itself. It's a little like making love. If one pulls back at a certain moment of intimacy to think about the relationship, the thing is ruined.

My prayer life only took off when I dropped my intellectual objections to a personal God and recognized that I am not and have never been alone. Christ is the face that God revealed to me in my early life. I would not for a moment deny that God reveals different aspects of Godself to others: Krishna, Amita Buddha, Allah, and the Tao. But for me, these are all aspects of the one divine person who is the Second Person of the Trinity. When I think otherwise—for doubt remains in the ground of faith—I cease praying. When I begin to reflect on it, prayer stops. There are three activities that are not improved by reflection: jumping into cold water, making love, and prayer.

To pause in prayer and think, "Christ is just a symbol, there are others that could work equally well, and anyway symbols are not the thing itself" (thoughts that occur to me all the time) is to cease praying. As in romantic love, one has to give oneself entirely to one person, so unreservedly that one forgets that one has done so, if love is to get off the ground. The lover must let the beloved fill the space of care that is usually occupied by the self. And there can only be one beloved. One cannot love all potential partners equally without ceasing to love any one of them fully. The lover forgets the other possible lovers. They become nothing for him.

Resistance to prayer, to the whole idea of a personal God, is a big problem for intellectuals. Correctly assuming that God, if God exists, is infinite and so beyond all the categories by which we understand the things around us, intellectuals regard the idea of a personal God as naive and incoherent. It is so plainly a projection of ourselves unto the infinite, they assume. Far better to leave the divine as an impersonal inconceivable power if you must have divinity at all. Many intellectual critics of the Abrahamic traditions consequently show a preference for Asian traditions, where the talk is not about God the loving Father and Creator of all things but of an impersonal first principle, the Tao or Buddha Nature (although the great Taoist and Buddhist writers regard the first principle as neither personal nor impersonal). It is no doubt correct that infinity exceeds our comprehension. It is also true to conclude from this that our language about God is hopelessly inadequate to the divine reality. In the medieval monotheistic traditions, this has always been acknowledged. Hence "negative theology" is regarded as the pinnacle of the human quest for knowledge. When we arrive at the threshold of what we can know, we must practice what the Renaissance theologian Nicholas of Cusa called "learned ignorance" and recognize precisely *why* we cannot know what God is. The highest act of the theologian is not saying things of God but taking the predicates away. God is *not* good in any sense of the term that we can understand. God is *not* a person in any sense of the term that is correctly applied to human persons. Any reader of Thomas Aquinas knows that this position is perfectly orthodox.

But here is the rub: far worse than projecting the best things we know unto God—personality, relationality, the capacity to know and love—is reducing God to an impersonal force. A God who is a force that I can access and to some degree command through meditation is not above me at all. Such a God is lower than the human person, like gravity or inertia, not higher. To address God as a person is no doubt, from a certain conceptual standpoint, a shot in the dark, a speaking into the abyss, but it is far preferable to regarding God as a sub-personal force. More importantly, God reveals Godself in the Abrahamic scriptural traditions to be personal, if not a person in the way you and I are persons, at least capable of personalizing, of descending to our level to raise us to God's level.

We don't need to perfect ourselves, intellectually, spiritually, or morally, to enter into the God relation. God takes the initiative, and everything goes as it should. Intellectuals bristle at this idea, as I did originally when I fled Christianity and headed East. They habitually make the mistake of thinking that they know more about what is going on in themselves than they do. We do not even understand what it means to be a human person, let alone a divine person. Who are we to say that God cannot be personal? If we paid more attention to what we actually do rather than what we think, we would see that the personal factor in life—love—is what we most value and least understand. We might think that the universe is a meaningless accident, mindless forces all the way down, but we don't live out of that thought. Most of us, at least, whether atheist or believer, act as though the personal element in us, the part of us capable of love, is what is highest, most precious, and most worth cherishing.

It took me a while to shake the intellectual prejudice against a personal relation to God and to see that my objections were based on ignorance and to some degree arrogance. I preferred a divine force that pervades the natural world to an inconceivable origin and goal of everything. I would not allow my heart to spontaneously turn to the origin, the great mystery of being, as a child would, and cry, "Father." I choked the child's voice in me and said, "Grow up," failing to realize that wisdom, in all traditions, is childlike and spontaneous. Sheilagh's childlike faith in the loving Father of all things was a challenge to the young aspiring Buddhist that I was, a koan, a paradox that broke my assumptions. Her immovable faith was plainly authentic and born of immense silent suffering. It was also clearly life-giving and the source of her serenity and quiet power. I saw that with Sheilagh's faith, one could face any calamity life throws at you. Disease, injustice, even death.

Endnotes

1. *Gloria enim Dei vivens homo, vita autem hominis visio Dei.* Another translation runs: "For the glory of God is the living man, and the life of man is the vision of God." Irenaeus, *Adversus Haereses*, Book 4, ch. 20, section 7. The point is that God has come to meet us where we are, and, therefore, we should remain humbly rooted in our flawed humanity to receive the gift. It should be noted that this is also an argument of Protestant Christians against Christian monasticism. Genuinely Christian monks know the difference between the spiritual pride of the ascetic and the practice of preparing oneself for the reception of grace. They know that the monastery is a school of humility and charity and not a place for transcending humanity through

spiritual practices. Still, Protestant Christians are better at making this point than Catholics. See the superb collection of the spiritual writings of the greatest Protestant thinker of the twentieth century, Karl Barth (Barth 2022).

2. See Eckhart (2009, Sermon 13b: 110): "Indeed, if a man thinks he will get more of God by meditation, by devotion, by ecstasies, or by special infusion of grace than by the fireside or in the stable—that is nothing but taking God, wrapping a cloak round His head and shoving Him under a bench. For whoever seeks God in a special way gets the way and misses God, who lies hidden in it."
3. See Nicholas of Cusa's argument for why this must be the case in his *De Docta Ignorantia*, Book 1 (fifteenth century, Cusanus 1954). God, the infinite, is likened to an infinite circle, the circumference of which is everywhere and the center nowhere. The point is that infinity is not reached by piling up finite things. Every point in the universe is equally distant from the infinite, or, what amounts to the same thing, equally near.
4. In Mahayana mythology, the celestial Buddha, Amitabha, vows not to enter the pure land of enlightenment, which is his right and his karmic inheritance, while any sentient beings long for release from suffering but fail to achieve it. The power of Amitabha's compassion floods the universe and liberates every suffering being who calls upon him. Thus, enlightenment occurs not through the effort or "self-power" of the practitioner but through the "other power" of Amitabha. The Shin Buddhist gives up trying to enlighten himself and instead entrusts himself to Amitabha by a simple, unpretentious recitation of the *nembutsu* mantra: "I take refuge in Amita Buddha." On this sophisticated Buddhist psychology of what Christians call grace, see Watt (2016).

5. Dietrich Bonhoeffer (1906–1945) was a German Lutheran pastor, theologian, and anti-Nazi dissident. He was a founding member of the Confessing Church, the minority group of Protestant Christians who resisted the Nazis (by distinction from the majority of those who collaborated). He turned down an opportunity to continue his theological work safely in England during the war and returned to Germany to be with his suffering people. He became implicated in the plot to assassinate Hitler and was hung by the Nazis shortly before the end of the war. For more on Bonhoeffer, see Marsh (2014). Simone Weil (1909–1943) was a French laywoman and political activist who wrote extensively on mystical Christianity. She died of starvation because she refused to eat more than the rations allotted to those struggling in the French resistance. See Weil (2009).
6. "Scientism" refers to the belief that the most important philosophical and religious questions can be answered by natural science. It is a prejudice widespread among a certain class of Anglo-American philosophers, many of whom are in recoil from difficult religious upbringings and rare among genuine scientists.
7. Jews refer to the story of the binding of Isaac as the *Akedah*. It is described in the Book of Genesis Chapter 22.
8. The Siberian word "shaman" may be a variation on the Sanskrit word *sraman,* which means wandering monk. The etymology suggests that the first monks might have been pre-historic wandering holy men of Eurasia, the healers, and visionaries who painted the walls of caves with images of animal gods. The shaman dwells alone with the spirits to receive knowledge and power from the other side, which he or she could then share with the community. See Eliade (1964).

9. See Merton's essay, "The Primitive Carmelite Ideal," in Merton (1985). McNamara's correspondence with Merton is archived at The Thomas Merton Centre of Bellarmine University and can be consulted via the Centre's website: http://merton.org/Research/Correspondence/y1.aspx?id=1361.

"A mass of legend and literature has sprung from this single paradox; that the hands that had made the sun and the stars were too small to reach the huge heads of the cattle."

G.K. Chesterton

Chapter Three

The Christ Event

Paul Sets Me Straight

Early one winter morning at Nova Nada, an hour before dawn, with the ice frosting over the windowpane of the hermitage so that I could just barely make out the dark shapes of the trees on the edge of the clearing in which my little house sat, deep in snow, I lit my oil lamp and opened a book by the biblical scholar C.H. Dodd. The book was called *The Meaning of Paul for Today* (Dodd 1920). It had fallen into my hands the day before as I practiced a private ritual in the library, which I called "following the spirit." There were some dull things that I had to read for "formation," but for the most part, I was free to read what interested me. I spent many hours poking around the small but substantive library for the next thing that would inspire me. I came to learn that timing is everything in the spiritual life. A book that might have the most profound effect on me in the future could strike me as dry and uninteresting if I picked it up at the wrong time.

Knowing I needed something new, and not knowing what, I browsed the shelves, without deliberation or forethought, until a book caught my attention. It was a little like the old practice of opening the Bible randomly and reading the first thing your eyes landed upon as though it were a message directly from God. I returned to my hermitage with this undramatic looking little volume by C.H. Dodd, a faded paper cover with nothing but the title on it, tucked under my arm.

As I read, and the pink light of the rising sun appeared in the sky behind the black filigree of pine trees, scales fell from my eyes.

Dodd showed me that Paul speaks of God in terms that are neither wholly Jewish nor wholly Greek. Indeed, Paul speaks of God as no one before him had ever done, not even Jesus himself. For Paul, God is the superabundant love at the heart of the universe and this love is eminently personal. Everything began in love; everything will end with it.

What astonished me about Paul's letters, when I finally began to understand them, is that they are unconcerned with details of Jesus's life and teaching. Rather, Paul's focus is the cosmological significance of the Christ. For Paul, far more important than the eye-witness stories of the life and teaching of Jesus of Nazareth is the experience of the cosmic Christ. He is "the image of the invisible God, the firstborn of all creation," through whom all things are made (Col. 1:15), the one who pre-exists everything, in whom "the fullness of God was pleased to dwell" (Col. 1: 219). Christ is the "mystery hidden for ages" and now revealed in the church (Eph. 3: 9). God has "put all things under his feet and has made him the head over all things for the church, which is his body, the fullness of him who fills all in all" (Eph. 1:22). The believer will be given not only conviction but knowledge (*gnosis*) of Christ. "I pray that you may have the power to comprehend, with all the saints, what is the breadth and length and height and depth, and to know the love of Christ that surpasses knowledge, so that you may be filled with all the fullness of God" (Eph. 3:18–19).[1]

Paul understands Jesus to have come to reveal the primordial truth of "God's wisdom, secret and hidden, which God decreed before the ages for our Glory" (1 Cor. 2: 7). Sin introduced pain and death into creation. But love will be victorious. Any religious teaching in conflict with this bright and simple truth—for example, the legalism of the Pharisees—is, for Paul, *ipso facto* false. We cannot earn love; it is pure gift. We can only receive it, like a child receiving life from its parents. Nor can the truth of love be understood philosophically. Love is "what no eye has seen, nor ear heard, nor the human heart conceived" (1 Cor. 2: 9). The truth of love, so out of keeping with the wisdom of the world, can only be revealed. And it is revealed, according to Paul, in the crucified and risen Jesus.

The Christ event makes manifest "the weakness of God" (1 Cor. 1: 25). God humbles Godself before human freedom, allowing that freedom to twist and distort creation, for to prevent sin would have meant to abolish freedom. We could have been created determined to sing hosanna forever without deviation, just as flowers are made to blossom beneath the rays of the sun. Instead, God creates a universe in which praise can rise freely from the hearts of creatures.

Paul's God decides not to leave freedom to its doom. God intercedes in history so that the effects of sin would not be suffered by the sinner. But even this dramatic intercession is a display of weakness: the Christ comes not in glory but in lowliness, poverty, and failure. This is "the wisdom of God," to conquer sin by love, to overcome greed, violence, and power by humility.

That Paul's message is so difficult to fathom is an indication of how high above our intellects the revealed truth is. In Paul's view, we are not ready for reality. We need to be changed to be rendered capable of truth. "For now we see in a mirror dimly, but then face to face; now I know in part, but then I will know fully just as I also have been fully known" (1 Cor. 13: 12). The "then" refers to the general resurrection and the end of time. What we shall know on that last day is what the Christ knew on the Sunday morning when he stepped out of the tomb physically, superbly, alive: that suffering and death are unavoidable but "love never ends" (1 Cor. 13: 18).

This was, for me, the only true answer to my cousin John's question, the answer that overwhelms the question, making it appear tragically mistaken from the outset. "Is life good?" Paul showed me that the one who asks such a question is lost in what he calls "sin"—which is not moral wrongdoing, but a cosmic state of delusion, akin to *maya* in Buddhism, the veil of lies and self-deceptions which is the tragic inheritance of humankind. Such a questioner is not to be reprimanded but pitied. The only answer to the question, according to Paul, is not to deny the tragedy of life but to refuse to give it the last word. The answer is Christ crucified, the God-man whose death is an identification with all human suffering, even, or especially, John's despair. The resurrection overcomes sin and death and reveals that the answer to the problem of life is love.

Dodd's book is not particularly unique. If a little out of date, the scholarship is sound enough. The exegesis of the letters of Paul is insightful and at times profound. What was so dramatic for me was to think of Paul, the man, the last apostle, carrying this word of love into the Roman empire at the dawn of the Christian era. Here were the teachings of a man whose existence no one doubted, whose identity, even physical appearance, is confirmed by many sources.

Passages from the letters of Paul are read in droning tones from the pulpits of Christian churches everywhere. But we are rarely if ever given a glimpse of the passages in their context. Paul's letters are not abstract treatises. They are personal letters written by a Jewish man who was born on the southeast coast of what is now Turkey in the time of Jesus. Where Jesus is always inflating into a mythic symbol under the pressure of the sheer volume of art and literature dedicated to him, Paul remains solidly, immovably, historical. He traveled tirelessly through Asia Minor and Greece, preaching the Resurrection, until the Romans had him executed. The letters are addressed to real people, the members of the little rag-tag communities of men, women, wealthy landowners, poor craftsmen, free citizens, and slaves, which were the first churches. These groups were not allowed to meet publicly and had no official buildings.

Rather they met quietly in each other's homes, always in fear of the suspicion of their neighbors and the Roman intolerance for self-organizing communities, especially those that, like the Christians, practiced social customs, such as egalitarianism and common property, which challenged the values of the Empire. Paul's letters were written in answer to the theological questions of these first Christians. He attempted to answer these questions in terms they could understand.

At this time in the history of ancient Rome, many people were searching for a new religious orientation. The old religions were no longer gripping the hearts and minds of large segments of the population. The worship of the gods and goddesses of the mythological traditions had hardened into empty formalism. Many of the ruling class no longer believed in the traditional gods of Rome. At the same time, fascination with mystery religions and other esoteric traditions from Africa and the Middle East was on the rise. Paul's Christianity appealed to people who were looking for something new, especially those who felt there was something fundamentally mistaken or even deceptive about traditional Roman religion, which elevated the emperor to the status of a god.

Some of those who heard Paul preaching in the marketplace invited him to stay with them in their homes and tell them more. Paul would stay for as long as needed—two, three, four months, a year, maybe—preaching the good news of salvation from sin. If the mission was successful, everybody in the house would be converted—man, wife, children, servants, slaves.

His mission complete, Paul would leave the household and go on to another town. He left behind a few rules to follow, some prayers to recite, and a few simple rituals to practice, most notably the commemorative meal, the Eucharist, which repeated Jesus's words at the Last Supper and symbolically enacted, in the communal eating of bread and drinking of wine, identification with the body and blood of Christ.

The household thus became an *ecclesia,* which we translate as "church," which means simply "community," a center for the practice of the new way. The Christians would meet at the house on Sundays to discuss the teachings of Jesus—only preserved orally at this point—to pray the psalms together, and most especially to share the Eucharist. After he had moved on to another town, Paul would write letters to the household churches he had established to continue to instruct them, to answer their questions, and to correct misunderstandings that would emerge from time to time. These letters constitute the entire corpus of Paul's writings.

As churches became larger and more numerous, concern for the unity of Christian theology emerged, and the need to preserve a basic core of doctrine drove the Church into the construction of the hierarchy with which we are familiar today: the pyramid of a large stratum of lay believers, a middle layer of priests, and a narrow top layer of bishops, all under the singular authority of a pope, archbishop, or patriarch. But it is crucial to remember, especially now, when institutional Christianity in the West is in serious and seemingly irreversible decline, that the Church did not begin as it looks today. The Church can exist without priests and bishops, for thus did it begin. But it cannot continue without a living experience of the Christ who transforms suffering and reveals the boundless love of God.

Jesus was a prophetic figure, a speaker of parables and cryptic aphorisms; Paul is an intellectual and strives to rationally convince his audience of his often subtle points. He addresses the questions put to him and, like a good philosopher, comes up with some of his own. How do we know that love is the origin and end of everything? What does it mean that we will be resurrected? What ought we to do to grow in the knowledge of God? How does the revelation of the Christ relate to the religious experience of other religions? What about the truths of philosophy? In lucid, powerful terms, and not without a touch of poetry, Paul speaks directly to such concerns. I could even imagine Paul enjoying the act of writing them, carefully editing his letters for maximal rhetorical effect, some of which were theological treatises. The Letter to the Romans alone is over 7,000 words long. If I had doubted whether there was a place for my restless intellectual life in the Church, reading Paul dispelled my doubts. Whoever else he was, Paul was a thinker, a born philosopher humbled by the revelation of the personalizing God of Jesus Christ.

The other apostles could not make head or tail of his difficult thought. They could recognize the authentically Christian nature of what he said but it seemed to be meant for a wider, non-Jewish audience. So, Paul was sent into the Hellenistic world.

Most of the followers of the Greek and Roman philosophers popular at the time rejected Paul. The Stoics, Cynics, Epicureans, and Platonists whom he met in the market squares of the Greek towns to which he traveled—Athens, Thessalonica, Ephesus, Corinth—could not accept his teaching of the crucified and risen Christ who Paul insisted is the *Logos* of the universe, the firstborn of the invisible God. They listened to him for a while. And what was most interesting to me, Paul spoke *to* them. He dignified philosophy, which Jesus probably knew nothing about, with a direct appeal to its categories and arguments. In the end, he saw that philosophy was a doomed effort: anyone relying on reason alone would never get the point. Still, reason can admit that the truth is beyond its natural grasp. Perhaps the most reasonable of all judgments is to admit the transcendence of truth. Stop deceiving yourselves, Paul told the philosophers. If you think you are wise by this world's standards, you need to become a fool to be truly wise. For the wisdom of this world is foolishness to God (1 Cor. 3:18–19).

I read on and on until the bell for morning prayer rang through the woods, wrenching me away from my desk to more mundane tasks. The next morning, I found myself back at the book as soon as I opened my eyes. I needed to know more. Who was this man? Why was he so sure that Jesus, whom he had never met, was the Son of God? And why did he believe that Jesus's death and resurrection signified that love triumphed over everything?

Paul was a man on fire with love. He could not rest. He had to tell the world about what he had found. He was afraid of nothing, neither suffering nor pleasure and spurned no one, poor or wealthy, slave or aristocrat. In his own words, he becomes "all things to all people so that by all possible means I might save some" (1 Cor. 9:22).

As a Roman citizen and an official representative of the Jewish faith, Paul at first was possessed by an intense hatred for Christianity and even helped the Romans and Jews persecute the fledgling movement. But one day he had an experience on the road to Damascus that changed everything. The resurrected Christ appeared to him in a flash of light and revealed to him His divine identity. Jesus preached conversion (the Greek word was "metanoia," literally "being turned around"); Paul shows us what it means: to have your life turned upside down. The event is carefully recounted in the Book of Acts:

> As he neared Damascus on his journey, suddenly a light from heaven flashed around him. He fell to the ground and heard a voice say to him, "Saul, Saul, why do you persecute me?" "Who are you, Lord?" Saul asked. "I am Jesus, whom you are persecuting," he replied. "Now get up and go into the city, and you will be told what you must do." The men traveling with Saul stood there speechless; they heard the sound but did not see anyone. Saul got up from the ground, but when he opened his eyes he could see nothing. So they led him by the hand into Damascus. For three days he was blind and did not eat or drink anything. (Acts 9:3–9)

In Damascus, a Christian named Ananias had a vision in which he was commanded by Christ to visit the blind Paul, whom he did not know, in a house on "Straight Street" and restore his eyesight. Ananias did not want to do this. He had heard of the ruthless enemy of Christianity. But he obeyed the vision and found the blinded Paul lying in the house indicated. Ananias laid his hands on him and miraculously restored his sight.

It was at this point that Paul's training began. He was baptized and headed to Arabia for three years. What he was doing there, we do not know, but we can assume he was visiting with Christians, perhaps living alone for some time in the desert, as was the practice of some Jewish contemplatives. He then visited the apostles in Jerusalem, learning all he could from them, for Paul had not known Jesus personally.

Before the Damascus event, Paul believed Christianity to be the worst distortion of the Jewish faith. He believed "the Law," the moral code given to the Jews by Moses that prescribed everything from rules governing eating to the prohibition of murder, to be the highest truth. The Damascus event reversed this: Christ and Christianity were revealed to be the absolute truth. Paul came to understand the Law as a merely provisional truth that was, after the coming of the Christ, no longer necessary. It is love, not rule-following, that redeems the world. In Christ, the transcendent lawgiver of Judaism had shown himself bodily, and personally, and relieved us of the burden of the Law. All that was needed was a full and honest response of faith. The death and resurrection of the Christ justify us (render us innocent before God). The personal relation to Christ saves us. God wants nothing more than our flourishing, beyond the veil of tears, the natural suffering and injustice of life. Christ will become our second nature if we let him. He shall do for us what we cannot do for ourselves. He shall bring us into the intimacy with the Father which is his birthright. If he could do this for Paul, the most unworthy of apostles, the erstwhile enemy of the Church, he could do it for anyone.

Paul traveled for the rest of his life throughout the Roman Empire spreading the gospel of love everywhere until he was imprisoned by the Romans. He kept up his missionary activity even in his prison cell, writing several of his most famous letters in chains, until the authorities silenced him by cutting off his head. In bringing Christianity to the non-Jewish world (his special mission among the apostles), Paul created most of what we recognize today as Christian theology. His letters are alive with his unstoppable faith, which laid the foundation stones for world Christianity. Without Paul, Christianity would have been forgotten as another minor sect of Judaism. Paul universalized the Gospel.

Paul was the first to give the Christian community an interpretive framework for understanding the meaning of the Christ event. His main move was his integration of three concepts or figures into a narrative that has underwritten Western ethics for the better part of two millennia: original sin, the revelation of the Law, and the redemptive power of the crucified and resurrected Christ. Because Adam and Eve fell and brought the whole of creation crashing down with them, the Law of Moses, a moral code to keep people, now chronically prone to sin (the primary effect of the Fall), on the straight and narrow, was needed for a time. But the moral code was never enough; it only reminded us of how far from the good we are.[2]

Paul describes the situation of fallen humanity in powerfully psychological terms: "For the good which I desire, I don't do; but the evil which I don't desire, that I practice" (Rom. 7:20). Even if I wanted to do good, my intention is not enough because an unconscious compulsion to sin always overtakes me. Adam and Eve did not need a Law: their basic natural impulses were moral. When they misused their freedom, however, human nature changed. Death entered the world and the human being fell under the influence of evil. "Therefore as sin entered into the world through one man, and death through sin; and so death passed to all men, because all sinned" (Rom. 5:13).

The Law was needed as a corrective but there was something exclusive, even tragic about it. It prescribed the basic pattern of a good Jewish life and the minimum requirements for holiness. To fail to obey the Law was to condemn oneself. And since no one could keep the Law—not just externally, by following all the rules, but internally, by wanting nothing but the good—all were condemned. For Paul, the religion of the Law stands as an endless approximation to an ideal that escapes the reach of even the most virtuous Jews. The only way out was the Christ. One man who represents all—as Adam represented all human beings—needed to reverse Adam's fateful decision and obey God entirely, with the full assent of his freedom.

Paul never thinks of human beings as separate individuals: all belong together and constitute one spiritual being. All of humanity sinned when Adam sinned, losing its power to obey. Humankind fell as a whole; it could only be redeemed as a whole. The reconstitution of human nature into one obedient and faithful man who could stand for all people, as Adam had stood for all, was the only solution. Christ reversed Adam's sin. Where Adam's disobedience damned us all, Christ's obedience redeems us all.

But it would not have been enough for Christ to do what Adam could not, to remain faithful to God under temptation; Christ also had to suffer the penalty for Adam's disobedience. He had to suffer from the evil and death Adam brought into the world. Sin in Paul's conception is not something subjective or psychological, but a cosmic structure. It has real-world consequences. As in Hindu and Buddhist teachings about karma, the effects of sin must become manifest. Someone has to suffer. Since no ordinary human being could do these two things—obey and suffer on behalf of all—and since only a human being could reverse the effects of sin and satisfy the Law, Christ, the Son of God came. He freely and fully obeyed and took on the suffering, the consequences, of sin on behalf of all who live, all who have died, and all who are still to come. "For as through the one man's disobedience many were made sinners, even so through the obedience of the one, many will be made righteous" (Rom. 5:20). Christ is the cosmic God-man, the new Adam. We are all now "members" of his resurrected body.

Paul's understanding of sin as a cosmic condition might remind us of Plato's cave. But sin in Paul's sense of the word is a much worse situation than the ignorance suffered by Plato's cave dwellers. For Paul, there is no possibility of self-redemption. Paul says that no human being on their own can even begin to understand the things of God, let alone overcome sin. The truth must be revealed; grace must descend; no human can make herself holy by adhering to a set of moral principles. Where we see holiness, we see one who has been gifted with something that she did not earn or achieve through ability and effort. Paul makes the point repeatedly: salvation is a pure gift, not an achievement. This could be his central teaching, the one idea that animates all his thought. Having exhausted himself in a religious practice of self-achievement, Paul discovers that human effort amounts to nothing: everything is grace. "God's love has been poured into our hearts through the Holy Spirit who has been given to us" (Rom. 5:5). On his own, he was running headlong in the opposite direction, away from love. But he was turned around by a power greater than his own and after the event boasted only of the grace that supports and guides him. "I can do all things through Christ who strengthens me" (Phil. 4:13).

The new religion Paul proclaimed was in a sense the end of all religion, for in its light the Jewish Law was no longer needed. Neither was Greek religion or philosophy needed. The pagan priests with their hopeless endeavors to placate tyrannical divinities through sacrifice and ritual were no more necessary to true religion than were the Greek philosophers with their questions and intellectual puzzles that most people could not understand, and which led those who did into dead ends. Until Christ, Paul taught, the world lived in fear of the gods (whom Paul calls cosmic "principalities and powers," Col 1:16) and ignorance of the truth. Christ dispelled fear and showed us that God is love. In a very real way, nature for Paul is now emptied of divinity. Nature that was once full of gods, both charming and terrifying, is now finite. It is *creation,* a being that depends entirely upon the infinite creator. That much the Jews understood and always insisted upon against pagan polytheism. In Christ, the one God of the universe is fully revealed as a human being. With this event, everything is changed. Christ is not like Zeus disguised as a human being (a regular trope in Greek mythology). Nor is he like an angel in the Hebrew Bible, a physical manifestation or messenger of God, like the pillar of cloud that led the Hebrews through the desert. Christ is God *incarnate,* God singularly and uniquely embodied and living among us. Human nature in Christ is singularly and uniquely divinized. It is not possible to extol creation and humanity more highly than this. Creation is now absolutely affirmed as not only of God but sufficient for God. Paganism divinized nature but this was different. Nature is not God; it is *of* God. A divinized nature demotes God to the level of a natural thing, a force, or a spirit of nature. God remains for Paul unimaginably beyond creation and from this place of transcendence descends into creation to be born of a woman and live and die as a man. In the Christ event, both the Jewish and the Greek view of humanity are challenged. The human being Jesus is not one creature among many, and not only the image of God in the Old Testament sense in which each of us is an image of God; Jesus is God among us. No one understood the paradoxicality and poetry of this thought better than the

English writer and poet G.K. Chesterton. "The gods lie dead where the leaves lie red, / For the flame of the sun has flown, / The gods lie cold where the leaves lie gold, / And a Child comes forth alone (G.K. Chesterton, *A Child of the Snows*).

It is not enough simply to know this second hand. According to Paul, something more was required—direct apprehension: "The light of the knowledge of the glory of God in the face of Christ" (2 Cor. 4:6). Early Christianity was not propagated through the communication of a set of propositions. It spread like wildfire through the Greek world because it promised and delivered an *experience* of truth. To become a Christian, one needed to be converted. That meant one's whole life had to be "turned around." Only a direct experience of the Christ event could affect this about-face. Paul did not transform from a self-righteous Pharisee to an inexhaustible preacher of love because he changed his opinions. Paul experienced Christ, and his experience transformed his whole life.

The early Christian martyrs, who were inspired by Paul's writing, allowed themselves to be tortured and put to death because they had also experienced life-changing revelations of the truth of Christ. There is in a sense an "enlightenment experience" in Christianity, a direct apprehension of the truth that cannot be put into words but that shows itself in deeds, in how one lives one's life. Paul calls this experience of Christ "gnosis," which we might translate as direct knowledge or intuition (Phil 3:8). Gnosis is the experience of knowing Christ himself and, through this knowledge, knowing that in this one man, the whole of the divinity stands revealed. The Gnostic Christians picked up this dimension of Paul's teachings and ran with it in directions that Paul himself would not have condoned. But there is a kernel of authentic Pauline doctrine in Gnostic Christianity: faith is an *experience of knowledge,* not simply the assertion of a set of propositions received from authority.

The more I learned about Pauline Christianity, the more convinced I became that this was *the* way for me. It was Sheilagh's way to which she had been led through suffering. I would be led to it through study.

Fully Human/Fully Divine

When they make their vows, monks take a religious name. I chose the name "Sean of Jesus." I was devoted to the humanity of Jesus. Whatever wonders he worked—and I came to believe most of what I read about him in the Gospels—Jesus was, for me, entirely human. My Jesus had a real childhood, with skinned knees and reprimands for bad behavior. He went through puberty and had a genuine young adulthood, with frustration, infatuations, and perhaps even love affairs. And he had all these experiences before discovering his vocation. What else could it mean to say he was human?

That Jesus discovered his vocation, that he was on a quest when he met John by the River Jordan (what else would he have been doing there?), meant to me that he suffered existential uncertainty and questioned his most basic beliefs as well as the beliefs of his culture. I interpreted the baptism scene, in which Jesus is initiated by John the Baptist in the Jordan and a heavenly voice is heard saying, "This is my beloved son" (Matt. 3:13–17), to signify that even he, the incarnate God, went through a crisis of identity before embarking on his three-year mission. This made Jesus more like me, the young man deeply unsure of who he was and what he ought to do, and on a quest for self-knowledge. The mainstream interpretation of the baptism of Jesus is otherwise. The heavenly voice on this line was for John the Baptist to hear and whoever else was nearby. Jesus did not need to hear it; he always knew he was the beloved son. I read the scene in exactly the opposite way. The voice was *for Jesus* to hear *in the presence of the others,* I believed. The Father publicly recognized

Jesus in the revelation in a way that he had not yet, at least not overtly, and perhaps not yet enough to assuage Jesus's nagging doubts, that he was not the one and suffered from delusion. The voice dispelled Jesus's doubts in a moment of life-changing recognition in the presence of John the Baptist, who also wondered whether Jesus, his cousin, was the one or not (Matt. 11:2–3). Many Christians assume that for Jesus to have *discovered* his identity as the Son of the Father in this moment would indicate an imperfection on his part. Jesus is perfect from birth, they assume; he would never have doubted his divine inheritance.[3]

But this is to emphasize Jesus's divinity at the expense of his humanity. We forget that he was "like us in all things except sin" (Heb. 4:15). This vague statement cannot mean that doubt, uncertainty, and fantasy, were not part of his humanity. We know he was tempted. After the voice from heaven declares his divinity, he is driven by the spirit into the desert for forty days where the devil tempts him. How could he be tempted without doubting himself and his vocation? Was this not in essence the one temptation? Jesus, my brother, was like me, struggling with himself and his vocation, and yet divine, and so could redeem me.

It was a game changer in my journey into the history of Christianity to discover that my conviction was anything but heresy. In the year AD 451, the Council of Chalcedon defined the orthodox conception of Christ for the Western and Eastern Churches, resolving disputes among various factions by maintaining a paradox, one the Church fathers believed could alone make sense of the scriptural accounts: Jesus was fully divine and fully human. The dual nature of Christ is a genuine paradox, a seeming contradiction that indicates not an absurdity but an inevitable gap in our understanding. In the face of the mystery of the Christ, it is revealed that we do not truly understand either divinity or humanity.[4]

Nestorius, the fifth-century heretic, pushed the duality of Christ to a breaking point. I'd like to think that Nestorius's intention was not so much to deny the divinity of Christ as to unconditionally affirm the far more difficult thought of his full humanity. That the Nestorian controversy centered around Mary underscores the central paradox of Christianity referred to in the Chestertonian epigram of this chapter: the heart of the Christian Gospel is the scandalous claim that the omnipotent God made himself weak to save us. God became a baby, a helpless infant, to render the human reality—sexual reproduction, motherhood, and babies all—supercharged with grace.

Nestorius's solution, to distinguish two persons in Christ, is unsatisfying. One gets the image of an individual with a split personality, as though two subjects were dialoguing with one another in Jesus. The other side of the paradox had to be affirmed as well. If Christ were not fully divine, we could not have been redeemed. The orthodox formula that won the day at the Council of Chalcedon stipulated that there is only one person in Jesus but that one person possesses two "natures": one divine, eternal, and infinite, the other human, temporal, and finite. The Chalcedonian formula is a koan: it does not so much give us something to understand as deny us various false ways to think of the Christ.

Committed to the humanity of the fully divine Christ, I read everything I could about Jesus: the classic Catholic accounts, the modern biblical scholars, and the infamous Jesus Seminar. This last group of scholars was dedicated to using the most "scientific methods" of historical criticism to ascertain what of the Jesus traditions is historical, accurately depicting the life, teaching, and death of Yeshua ben-Yosef, and what amounts to fabrication by his followers. The results of their historical-critical reduction were pretty thin. Apparently, all we can attribute with certainty to the historical Jesus are the first two words of the "Our Father." No Jew would call Yahweh "Abba" (literally

"Papa"), so this must be authentic, the scholars reasoned. But the beatitudes, the famous parables, the founding of the Church, and the theological teachings were, so we are told, invented by the first generation of Christians trying to justify their way of life.

The results of the Jesus seminar are not so much a coherent reconstruction of the historical Jesus as a torso, a story gutted of what made it significant in the first place. What is left of the biblical accounts when skepticism subtracts everything to which it cannot assent (miracles, divine births, resurrection, etc.)? Not much of interest. The scholars assume that the early writers of the New Testament constructed the figure of Jesus to suit their political and theological needs. Some argue that the most authentic material is the moral teaching. One cannot but suspect that this so-called scientific conclusion is made based on an undefended presupposition about who Jesus was, or at least who he could not be. Since it is assumed that God does not exist, or at least did not incarnate in a carpenter Jew, and since dead people do not come back to life, the scholars conclude that Jesus was primarily a moral teacher whose disciples inflated him into a supernatural figure to cope with their disappointment over his death. There are still many who, deceived by such "scholarship," doubt that Jesus even existed.

The "findings" of the Jesus Seminar did not impress me. Their criterion of historicity ("This could have been made up so it cannot be regarded as historical") would discredit our accounts of most historical figures. We have better historical reasons to believe that Jesus lived than we do for most other historical figures whom it would never occur to us to doubt. The synoptic Gospels (Matthew, Mark, and Luke) are replete with accurate references to historical figures, such as the Roman Prefect in Judea at the time, Pontius Pilate, the Tetrarch in Galilee, Herod Antipas, the Jewish prophet executed by Herod, John the Baptist, and the High Priest of the Temple in Jerusalem from AD 18–36, Caiaphas. Even the Gospel which was written latest (perhaps as late as the beginning of the second century), and which is regarded as the least historical, the Gospel of John, is full of accurate details about the geography of Judaea and the architecture of the major buildings in Jerusalem prior to the destruction of the Temple in AD 70.[5] From a careful, critical study of the New Testament, distinguishing historically plausible material from passages that could have been constructed by the Gospel writers after the fact, we can be certain that during the reign of Caesar Augustus a Jewish religious reformer named Yeshua was born among the working class in Palestine. He earned a reputation as a miracle worker, a healer, and a teacher in the small towns around his native Galilee. He was particularly popular among peasants and rural tradesmen and preferred the company of the lower classes and outcasts of Jewish society. He taught a radical eschatological reform of Judaism and developed a big enough following among the Jews to alarm High Priest Caiaphas, who was expressly charged with maintaining peace in the city. The Jesus of history preached the imminent end of the world and the coming of "the Kingdom of God." Most disturbing to pious Jews, Jesus insisted that he was singularly sent by God to call sinners and that those among them who believed in him and his message were in some sense absolved of observing all details of repentance required by the Jewish Law. "Jesus regarded himself as having the right to say who would be in the kingdom" (Sanders 1993, 236). Even more disturbingly to pious Jews, Jesus predicted the destruction of the Temple, which was the center of Jewish life and the pride of Jerusalem. He declared in no uncertain terms that he himself would somehow have a hand in the destruction, not by physically attacking it but by invoking the wrath of God on apostate Jerusalem (Mk. 14: 57–9). Jesus was for the most part an observant Jew and a type of Jewish miracle worker and prophet who was not unknown in ancient Jewry. But he deviated from the mold by holding himself to be in some ways higher than the Law (Lk. 16:16). Upon interrogation by the High Priest, Jesus refused to cease in this confrontational behavior and was handed over to be flogged and crucified by the Romans, who preferred another martyred Jewish prophet to a riot in the city.

In addition to the four Gospels, we possess accounts of external, non-Christian authorities that verify his life and death: a statement in a letter from an administrator named Pliny to the Emperor; an account by a Roman historian named Tacitus; a reference by the Jewish historian Josephus.[6]

We know from these accounts that Jesus's disciples believed the most extraordinary things about him and were willing to die for those beliefs. They believed that Jesus was the Messiah, the Christ; that he died for all; and that after three days, he was resurrected. In this resurrection, they said, all was changed. The gap between God and creation, opened by Adam and Eve's sin, was closed once and for all. Now God was as close to us as our neighbor and present in the most mundane human experiences. There was no need to climb out of our human nature to reach the divine, for God had descended into our humanity and transformed it from within.

The more I looked into the historical figure of Jesus, the more the figure multiplied into a bewildering number of different kinds of saviors. Which Jesus was I following? The Jesus of Roman Catholicism, a miracle worker born of a virgin whose death satisfies the divine Father's demand for justice? The Jesus of liberal Protestantism, who is no more than a moral teacher, if also the nicest guy who ever lived? The Jesus of biblical scholarship, variously characterized as a misunderstood prophet, a Jewish revolutionary, or a first-century Middle Eastern shaman? Or the Jesus of the Gnostic Gospels, a teacher of inner illumination who talked more like a Buddha than a Jew?[7]

Even as he became increasingly real to me in my prayer life—I spoke with him regularly as though he were sitting beside me in the chapel—the identity of Jesus was anything but precise in my mind. Jesus was an overdetermined figure for me, a man who lived and died as more than a man. The historical Jesus seemed to have inspired the highest aspirations of the human heart, embodying a moral ideal and redemption of suffering that exceeded anything found in other religions. Without Jesus, could we have conceived such things as the triumph of failure through suffering or the ennoblement of the lowly?

There was something in Jesus to offend everyone. It was as difficult for a Greek as it was for a Hebrew to fathom how a carpenter from Galilee could be God. For the Greek philosopher, it was scandalous to say, "Jesus is God but his neighbor is not." The Greek sense of universalism would stipulate that either every human is God or no human is. Greek philosophy had no trouble with the claim that all people are divine in some way. What Greek philosophers for the most part could not accept was the claim that one person could be divine in a preeminent and singular sense.

For the ancient Hebrews, the problem was different. How could Yahweh, the transcendent God of Abraham, become incarnate in the carpenter Jesus, whose career as a preacher and teacher ended in failure? Yahweh was infinite and therefore unimaginably transcendent. What blasphemy was this that collapsed Him into the poor man from Nazareth? Moreover, Jesus was not much of a rabbi. He criticized (among other things) the parochialism of the Hebrews, and rubbed many of the Pharisees the wrong way when he claimed that the salvation that had been revealed through Abraham and Moses was not meant for the Jews alone but for everyone. Jesus went too far. He claimed that to live a holy life was not to follow a set of laws but to follow him. Who did he think he was?

Much as Socrates's message signified the end of a certain form of Greek religion, so did Jesus's message signify the end of a certain form of Hebrew religion. But Jesus did not simply abandon Jewish particularism (the claim of one group of humans to have been chosen as a people by the God of the universe): he radicalized it to the point of reversal. God's choice becomes even more arbitrary, contracted from the choice of a people to the choice of a single individual. It is as though the God of the Hebrews moves from one scandalous move to another. First, he arbitrarily chooses one ethnic culture community among countless others and exclusively reveals his Law to them. Then, from among all the ordinary people, prophets, priests, and rulers of that community, he chooses one man and reveals himself exclusively through him. And it gets worse. Through the death and resurrection of this individual, God's grace is poured out on all people equally and without exception. Just as the Greeks, whose culture and religion were threatened by philosophy, put Socrates to death, so did the ancient Hebrews demand that the Romans put Jesus to death for blaspheming their religion. Still, some of the Jews followed him and spread his word, his Gospel (literally "good news"), to the wider world. We would do well to remember that without the Jew Peter, his brother Andrew, and the other nine faithful Jewish followers of Jesus, the Pharisee Paul of Tarsus, and countless other anonymous first-century Jewish Christians, there would be no Christianity. It was never the Jews versus the Christians; it was rather some Jews, who rejected Jesus, versus other Jews, who revered him.

The divinity claimed of Jesus by the Hebrews who were the first Christians brought about a paradigm shift in the Jewish understanding of the relationship between God and humankind. On the one hand, Yahweh could no longer be regarded as a remote and fearsome Creator. He was the Father, indwelling the human soul and nearest to those who suffered for His name. But even more radically, the human being could no longer be regarded as beneath the divine; humanity, already an image of God in the Book of Genesis, was revealed in the Christ as the physical form most adequate to the manifestation of the divine. This goes much further than Socrates or Plato. Socrates says there is a divine spark in the human being, a spark he calls reason. In Jesus, humanity itself is divinized.

The New Testament pulses with the personality of this figure. Jesus is in every way an individual in the Gospels, instantly recognizable and full of character. He is hardly an archetype, as C.G. Jung would have it. He is at once tender and fierce, full of compassion for the suffering of others and bristling with acrimony for bigotry, pseudo-piety, and self-righteousness. He is indiscriminately generous. He has as much time and patience for the powerful Pharisee Nicodemus as for his beloved poor. He is beloved by women, whom he boldly includes among his disciples (scandalizing the patriarchal society in which he lived), but he also earns the admiration of hardworking manual laborers like the fishermen, Peter, Andrew, John, and James. He delights in talking to children but has no hesitation in going head-to-head with the priests and the scribes, whom he routinely impresses with his knowledge of scripture and insight into its meaning. He is quick to forgive a genuine display of compunction, slow to anger, and slow to judge. But when righteous indignation overtakes him—for example, when he feels "his father's house," the temple, blasphemed by the moneychangers—he explodes into rage (Matt. 21:12–13). He weeps openly over the death of his friends, for he loves the company of others, but needs copious amounts of solitude. He is the man for others and the one alone with God at the same time.

Like ancient Buddhism and medieval Hinduism, Western philosophy tends to regard infinity as incompatible with personality. It is thought that the infinite, which is by definition beyond all limitations, must be impersonal, since having a discrete intellect and will, and being related to others is a limitation. The Christian theologians who first laid out the notion of the person in order to explain how Jesus could be God and yet distinct from the Father (they are two persons in one being—another paradox), explained that personality is no limitation but a perfection, and to deny it of God would be to deny that which is highest and noblest in creation of the divine—plainly an error. They concluded that the essence of the personal is not the limited form it takes in the historically singular human relating to others outside him. The essence of the person is relationality. To be a person is to be related to other persons such that those relations constitute one's identity. The divine personality, the theologians argued, *subsists* in a community of love. This community is unique in that it is composed of three equally divine persons—the Father, the Son, and the Holy Spirit—who exist only in relation to each other.

It is often pointed out that the idea of the Trinity does not appear—except indirectly—in the New Testament. Usually, the point is taken to mean that Christianity ought to have remained with the biblical narrative and avoided all of that theology. But the biblical narrative does not explain itself. It leaves us with too many questions to be settled. Jesus claims equality with the Father in many places (for example, Jn. 14: 8–9; Matt. 11:27). The first Christians worship him; they not only revere him as Messiah, they pray to him as Lord (Acts 7:59). If he had been simply a moral teacher, as the skeptics would have it, Jesus would never have provoked the righteous anger of conservative Jews. The accusation against him is that he claims to be divine, a claim he never in fact denies (Jn. 18: 37). If he was only a moral teacher, he would hardly have caused such a fuss. Much of his moral teachings can be found in the Hebrew Bible. There was something profoundly different about this man, and the difference compelled the early Church to create the discipline of systematic or dogmatic theology in order to explain not only who Christ is but also to explain what kind of creation we live in which has Christ as its *Logos*. This was something more than telling the tale of the life, death, and resurrection of Jesus. Nor was it the same as philosophy, although it borrowed heavily from philosophy and entered into competition with it. The revelation must include its theological interpretation, the first Christian thinkers argued; if the original texts are inspired, so too must be the *genuine* theological interpretations of the text. Not all of the interpretations are deemed equal, of course. Theological hermeneutics has wrestled with the question of discerning true interpretations from false ones since the first century. We may never arrive at certainty on some theological questions. But we never arrive at certainty in natural science either and no one takes this to mean that we should abandon the whole effort. The question of how theology makes progress—which it has, more so than philosophy—is too technical to concern us.

It is false, however, to suggest that theology is a theoretical overlay on the true story of Jesus's life which distorts its meaning. It was not the stories that came first, at least not in terms of written texts, it was the theology. The Gospels were only composed after the first generation of apostles and eyewitnesses had passed away. True, the oral practices of the ancient world, the capacity to remember things verbatim without a written text and across generations, were astounding. It is agreed that the core of the Gospels is composed of stories and sayings of Jesus that had been preserved orally by the first Christians and date back to his time. Nevertheless, the first *writings* in the New Testament, which we can with certainty trace back to the time of Jesus, are the letters of Paul.

Contemporary Christians are vulnerable to a theological confusion that narrows and impoverishes their understanding of Christ and eclipses the great traditions of contemplative Christianity. The confusion has given rise to religious intolerance among Christians which is so antithetical to the New Testament. The error arises from the false assumption that the true proposition, which is older than the oldest Gospel,

"Jesus is the Christ," can be reversed. Christians sometimes falsely assume that the claim not only means that Jesus is the Son of God, the incarnation of the Second Person of the Trinity; it also means that Christ is entirely and without remainder Jesus.[8] Contemporary Christianity is Jesus-fixated; like all things modern, it is reductionist. God is entirely over there, in the man Jesus. Nothing is left of God for us or anyone else. The *Logos* through whom all things are created and who is the light of every person who has ever lived (Jn. 1: 1–6) is reduced to the crucified and resurrected Galilean carpenter. On the basis of this reduction, contemporary Christianity denies that there is salvation outside the visible Church. Not only does it miss the boat on mystical or contemplative Christianity; it denies that other paths can be followed to the one God who calls to each of us in different ways.

Christ and Jesus are not simply identical such that the one can be substituted for the other, like two names for the same being. The Christ is identical with the Father. He is the mind of the Father and so is infinite and therefore *more* than the human, Jesus. Christ is the pre-existing Word of God, the mind of God eternally reflected back to God and accompanying humankind from the beginning of creation, visiting holy men and women, sages and philosophers, whether they lived in Babylon two millennia before the birth of Jesus, or in India in the second century, and enlightening them with the wisdom of the infinite God. This cosmic principle of creation, co-eternal with God and sent into the world at the beginning of time as the light of all people, becomes incarnate in Jesus.[9] And not only does the Christ inhabit the *human* reality through Jesus; the Christ indwells all of nature as its original light and source of life. "All things came into being through him, and without him, not one thing came into being" (Jn 1: 4). In the incarnation, the Christ enters directly into natural history and changes it as a whole. The event is both futural and retroactive. If the human being is rendered super-charged with grace by the Christ event, so too are our paleolithic ancestors. Homo erectus, who walked the earth for a million years, walked in the light of the grace of the Christ event. The natural environment without which the human being could not exist is as full of grace as Mary was. So too is the DNA that the human shares with every other living being on the planet. Christians are not pantheists, true; but they are or should be panentheists.[10]

Where the cosmic Christ is forgotten, contemplative life deteriorates and the mechanistic attitude to nature, to culture, and to ourselves predominates. The early digital age (our time) is particularly gripped by a return of mechanism. If a previous generation dehumanized us by trying to convince us that we are just animals, the digital age dehumanizes us by trying to convince us that we are just machines. What a computer does when it follows a rule in processing a, for us, incalculable complexity of 0s and 1s (but still a finite quantity that is eminently calculable) is assumed to be what we are doing in our brains when we experience anything at all. The human is a beta version of the computer, we are told. Such dehumanizing thinking is not possible in contemplative Christianity. Where the Christ is still genuinely worshiped, the dignity of the human will never be denied.

But here is the crux of the problem: what is "genuine" worship? A Christ who is simply a mythic image, a fable of an external power directing everything for the best, a Christ who is always up there, looking down on us like Zeus, cannot help us shelter the dignity of the still-evolving human form in an age that fetishizes machines. The remembering of Christian contemplation is much more than an act of personal deepening: it has ecological and political significance, which I pursued in another work (McGrath 2019). Christians too often forget that we are not merely to "imitate" Jesus, to carry out his commandments, to love one another—not to say there is anything trivial or easy about love. But we are called to more than morality. We are each of us in our utterly unique and unrepeatable way to become a Christ for our times and in our place. To know Jesus as God and savior is to become identified with the divine mystery that pervaded his historical existence. It is to be able to say, with Paul, "I live now not I, but Christ lives in me" (Gal. 2:20). The Spirit that opens our eyes to the Christ does not leave us gaping at the revelation from a distance. The point is not to stop at the confession of faith, gazing upon divinity somewhere up there. The Christ revealed to us in Jesus is not a spectacle to be enjoyed. We are offered mystical identity: "That they may all be one. As you, Father, are in me and I am in you, may they also be in us" (Jn 17:21). The Eastern Orthodox Church never forgot this and to this day, the doctrine of *theosis*—becoming God through Christ—is mainstream teaching in Eastern Orthodox theology (Lossky 1976). As in other matters, Eastern Orthodoxy remains firmly rooted in Greek Christianity. "For the Son of God became man so that we might become God" (Athanasius, *De inc.* 54, 3: PG 25, 192B). The forgetting of contemplation is one of the most grievous casualties of the sundering of the churches. Union, with everything, through the Christ through whom everything was created—this is the goal of genuinely contemplative Christian worship.

Conclusion to Part One: The No and the Yes to Life

With this plea to remember the Christ nature that is in everything and everyone, I come to the end of Part One of this book. A little like Augustine's *Confessions*, this first part aimed only at touching upon a few key events in my life without which I would never have found my way to the lost road. The two key figures in the story of my search, my cousin John and my twin sister, Sheilagh, are a pair of opposites, the suicide and the saint, but like all opposites, they are two of a kind. They share something in common which sets them apart from everyone I have ever known. Both John and Sheilagh faced first-hand the fundamental problem of life, what Zen calls "the great matter." Both suffered the problem to the point of death. But here, at the point of suffering the cross of life unto death, John and Sheilagh responded in opposite ways. John said No to life. He returned the entrance ticket and said, "It would be better if I had never lived." Every suicide speaks for the whole human community in their suicide. John not only said No to *his* life, he said No to *all* life. If not consciously, in effect he said, "It would be better if nothing had ever lived." Sheilagh said the opposite. She said Yes. And she said Yes not just to her own life but to all life. Despite the physical tragedy of her own life, despite all that she was denied—health, career, marriage—she said Yes. Life is a gift. This is not to judge John, quite the contrary. It is rather to recognize the depth of his suffering and the integrity of his honesty. He at least refused to repress the great matter. He could not in all honesty to himself ride along with his pleasure-seeking generation, acting as though there was not something trivial and dishonest about the life of consumer distraction. He met Sheilagh where she spent most of her short life, in personal tragedy. And yet she said Yes, and in that Yes, the tragedy became a comedy. In her Yes, life becomes gloriously, uproariously worth it. Life is revealed in the Yes to be unimaginably precious, good, true, and beautiful.

When I left the monastery and enrolled in graduate studies in philosophy and theology at the University of Toronto, I thought I was finally, after the false start of young adulthood, entering the world. I had done my retreat. I was ready. I realized with some discomfort that my path was a reversal of the stages of life prescribed by Hinduism. The Hindu ascetical and contemplative vocation is the crown of a life lived in the world. Having exhausted the world and given oneself wholeheartedly to marriage, childrearing, and career, the older man retires to the forest to meditate, takes a begging bowl, and becomes a wandering sadhu. In this way, the Hindus wisely preclude the young man's flight from the responsibilities necessary for the future of his society. One should not run away from what one does not know. One does not run *away* to the absolute, but *towards* it. I had done the opposite of what the Hindus recommended. Inspecting sex, marriage, child-rearing, and career from a safe distance, I concluded that they were dubious goods and withdrew to the wilderness.

The monastery could not contain that much untried youth for long: it spat me out like an indigestible pit. I reappeared, dazed and damaged in my twenty-eighth year, standing on the corner of Yonge and St. Clair. I was adrift in a crowd of people from every culture in the world and wondering what to do next. The hard facts of the city, the grim reality of my times, the wisdom of the flesh—this is what I anticipated experiencing in the world. And certainly, I would. But not right away. The spirit had a gentler introduction planned for me. I landed at Saint Michael's College at the University of Toronto, probably the closest thing to a medieval monastery one could find in the city of Toronto.

The college system at the University of Toronto is a gem from another age that has somehow, inexplicably, survived the centralizing, downsizing, profit-maximizing strategies of the modern university. The college system is what remains of the original federation of theological schools that had united to form the University of Toronto in the mid-nineteenth century. At the time, meadows and thriving copses on the margins of the city framed the stately neo-Gothic buildings of the university. The first University of Toronto was a city of scholarship in a Romantic paradise. Today the colleges are fortress islands in a sea of traffic and modern glass and steel brutalism.

As the rapidly expanding university struggled to tame their ever-expanding curricula by closing down duplicate programs and centralizing, the colleges fought fiercely to maintain something of their autonomy. By the time I arrived at U of T, the colleges had lost most of their independent programs and in some instances their degree-granting status. But still, there they stand: Emmanuel, Victoria, Knox, Trinity, University College, and on the corner of Bay Street, the college that would be my home for seven years, Saint Michael's. These neo-Gothic monuments to another century still function as student residences and faculty offices, with the odd eccentric college program permitted to continue because nothing like it is found anywhere else. Each college has its own distinct identity, bound up with its illustrious history. At Trinity, students wear gowns to dinner and sip sherry in the wood-paneled common room. At Vic, they sprawl on leather couches in the huge foyer and talk about Northrop Frye, the history of science, and English literature. At Saint Michael's, they study medieval philosophy and attend Mass.

The initiation into tradition that the colleges offer their students is nothing compared to the haven of scholarly peace they offer their faculty. Once tenured, it is possible to literally disappear into a college, even taking rooms there (as my doctoral supervisor did) and organize seminars on whatever interests you. In my time, there was the Kierkegaard circle, the medieval music group, the McLuhan culture and technology crowd, the liberation theology enclave, and so on. Here capitalism and utilitarianism are stopped at the door by the porter. Here older rules apply to the pursuit and dissemination of knowledge. Nothing is too esoteric, nothing so obscure that one cannot find someone in some corner of a college working on it with all of his life-energy.

I took a room in the men's residence. Saint Mike's campus is a quadrangle of neo-Gothic buildings and ramshackle Victorian houses around a green lawn. The college was originally founded as a junior seminary by the Basilian fathers—a Roman Catholic order of priests dedicated to teaching and scholarship—and is home to the Pontifical Institute for Medieval Studies, founded by the industrious French Thomist Etienne Gilson. The Institute had once been a hive of black-clad clerics convinced that all contemporary problems in philosophy and science could be answered by correctly interpreting the texts of Thomas Aquinas. By the time I got there, the glory had departed. Most of what the Pontifical Institute does now is manuscript work on the college's significant holdings of medieval texts.

But at the turn of this century, there was still no shortage of characters around. Father Neil ruled over the men's residence like a cardinal. He was one of those zealous young priests who preferred their liturgy in Latin and suspected everyone of heresy. Father Neil's theology was of that fierce and fighting quality frequently encountered in contemporary seminaries. The few that still enter the parochial priesthood typically judge the secular world to be under the reign of the whore of Babylon. Father Neil sneered at what most of us were studying and especially despised the liberalism of Saint Mike's Faculty of Theology.

In the other corner, as it were, sat Father Andrzej, the Polish philosopher priest who was fluent in several European languages and as eccentric as Father Neil but in the opposite way. Andrzej had spent a decade as a visiting scholar in some of the most prestigious universities in the world. He was in his thirties when I met him. He dressed impeccably, but never in a Roman collar. He appeared at dinner in silk shirts with diamond cufflinks. When they first met, Father Neil and Father Andrzej had their only conversation, a heated exchange that went on long after the cafeteria had emptied. They avoided each other thereafter, like two alpha dogs knowing better than to scrap again.

Father Andrzej introduced a welcome note of European *savoir-faire* into the life of Saint Mike's Men's Residence, which, like most of the institutions of contemporary Catholicism, tend towards the frumpy and the tasteless. He was a fellow at the Pontifical Institute and a specialist in contemporary German Thomism. He is also a well-published poet. When I met him, Father Andrzej was spending the better part of his days translating his poetry into English and German. Several graduate students would meet in his room in the evenings to assist him with his scholarly enterprises. In exchange, Andrzej, as we called him, plied us with all the drinks we could stomach. The closet in his office was renovated into an exceptionally well-stocked bar. It was in Andrzej's office, arguing late into the night over words and concepts until both began to fail me, that I discovered my interest in German metaphysics and my appetite for whiskey.

I have always believed that the greatest feature of the Catholic Church is its internal plurality. Critics of Catholicism frequently make the mistake of assuming that Catholicism is a closed system. The Catholic Church has many vices, to be sure, but this is not one of them. My go-to argument on this point is the example of Thomas Aquinas and Duns Scotus. Both are undisputed heroes of the Church. Both are unquestionably Catholic and have made major contributions to Catholic theology. The older of the two medieval theologians, Aquinas, is a saint; Scotus is "blessed," which is only one step away from sanctity. And yet the two disagree on fundamental philosophical and theological questions: on the nature of the human being, on the reason for the incarnation, on the structure of reality itself. The Church can include both Aquinas and Scotus without self-contradiction precisely because the Church is not a closed system. It does not demand uniformity of its members.

Father Neil and Father Andrzej dramatized the plurality of contemporary Catholicism. In clerical black sat Father Neil, the image of the cleric (I never saw him without a Roman collar), learned, inflexible, intolerant of most things outside the Church, fiercely critical of the secular age, and quite sure that the Roman Catholic Church possessed the answers to all the basic questions. And in a white silk shirt with diamond cufflinks sat his exact opposite, Father Andrzej: worldly, equally learned, left-leaning in ethics, right-leaning in systematic theology, which he knew backward and forwards, a defender of appearances, open to all that he deemed worthy of his attention, especially in matters philosophical and artistic, relativistic, ambivalent on most points, a lover of discussion and multiple points of view, but just as much as Father Neil, convinced that Catholicism is the true way. My monastic Father, William McNamara, represented yet another aspect of the world that is Catholicism: the contemplative who is neither left nor right. Somewhere among these three fathers, I found a home in the Church. All three priests identified the Church that Christ founded with Roman Catholicism. My view on the matter has always been a little ambivalent. The true Church is invisible, the mystical body of Christ, and "subsists" wherever Christ is revealed and received and in whatever way. The lost road is not a royal road, lined with statues of popes, leading directly to the Vatican: it leads back to that extraordinary moment of cultural fusion when the ancient Greek mind found its Jewish heart, and vice versa. The fusion of Athens and Jerusalem subsists in the Catholic Church, no doubt. The resilience of Catholicism in protecting the synthesis at the heart of the West never ceases to amaze me. Catholicism is a flame of the ancients which never seems to go out. But the invisible Church which began on the first Pentecost in Jerusalem, and was named shortly after in the near Eastern city of Antioch (where they first used the word "Christian"), includes Catholics, Eastern Orthodox Christians, Protestants, and many others: contemplative Jews, Sufis, esoteric Christians, followers of Jakob Boehme, Rudolf Steiner, Jungians who, with their founder, cannot shake the fascination, however confused, with the so-called Christ archetype, and the countless un-churched lovers of beauty. Membership in the invisible Church is always hidden from view. One never knows who is in and who is not. One cannot even be sure of oneself in this matter. The point is not to smugly identify with the saved and let the world hang itself but to forget oneself in Christ and help all the others, the lost, the confused, the hopeless, and the deceived.

I was home again at St. Mikes, where I felt most myself, firmly installed in the Middle Ages. But I was not entirely happy. All stops in this life are temporary (2 Cor. 5:1). The great matter was still unresolved. The departure from the monastery had been difficult, to say the least. Everyone had wanted me to stay but only on the condition that I really wanted the monastic life. I was torn right down the middle: I wanted it and didn't want it at the same time. I wanted to live in the woods *and* to work at a major university at the same time. I wanted a hermitage *and* a wife. I wanted to be nobody *and* somebody.

At St. Mike's I became a professional philosopher and theologian but to some degree at the expense of my soul. Not that I killed the flame that had burned so brightly in me in my early youth. But I did not feed it either. In the interest of gaining a profession, I neglected for a decade or so the most important part of me, my drive for truth. Very early on in my education (I think I was no more than 22 at the time) I realized that the drive for truth is not all that compatible with the desire for scholarship and academic knowledge. These worthwhile things can dilute the purity of the drive. They sneak in as false substitutes for "the one thing necessary" (Lk. 10: 42). They lull the soul, which is first awakened to the truth by suffering, back to sleep. The drive that cannot be killed in us, only repressed, aims at truth in the strong sense of the word, the truth for which one is willing to live and die.

I graduated from the University of Toronto, got my first teaching job at a mediocre Catholic college in the southern US, got married, moved to a better teaching post at Mount Allison University, and had a child. The worldly life I was missing in the monastery fell into my lap. None of it was all that difficult to secure. And right on cue, the repressed returned. I was successful—and desperately unhappy.

It was not any one element in my life that bothered me. Everything was on the surface perfect and therein lay the difficulty: everything was on the surface. It was a bit early for a mid-life crisis—I was only in my late thirties—but in hindsight that is exactly what it was. Jung found mid-lifers to be the most fertile demographic for his psychological work. In mid-life, the ideals of youth give way to the realities of adulthood. What seemed most worth pursuing in one's twenties is now achieved and no longer appears quite so interesting. The persona, what Jung describes as the mask one assumes for the sake of getting along in the world, no longer suits. Deeper needs, for authenticity, for the depths, for meaning, cause the soul to become irritated with the role-playing and social conformity that had been so crucial to early successes. Many men take mistresses at this point and buy a Ferrari or a sailboat. I went into analysis.

The story of my Jungian analysis and the five years I spent as a training candidate at the C.G. Jung Institute in Zurich do not belong in this book. It was in analysis that I came to understand something about my own personality. Indeed, I discovered for the first time that I had one, and that, like everyone else's personality, it is different from every other one. I also discovered how much fantasy and projection distorted my early search for truth. But at no point did I reject the search. At no point did the lost road become for me nothing but a fantasy. On the contrary, Jung taught me that the road is indeed lost and the recovery of it is the secret to the mental health of many. Most psychological problems, Jung argues, are at root religious problems. All vital human civilizations are rooted in myth and symbol, Jung insists against Freud; the West has lost its myth and so is in crisis (Jung 1933). The West has disenchanted the world and is now vulnerable to dangerous collective neuroses like populism or unbounded consumerism at the expense of the biosphere every living thing depends upon. Post-secular Westerners subsist without a symbolic narrative to psychologically sustain them. We all too easily succumb to right or left-wing extremism, climate-change denialism, conspiracy theories, and New Age ideology. If these extreme positions fail to allure, we default to mindless consumption. If we question ourselves and our life choices, we end up in the psychiatrist's consulting room, unhappy, confronted by our neurotic patterns, and struggling to find meaning in our lives. In my view, the psychological health of the West depends not on "re-enchantment" (too imprecise a term and too susceptible to ideology) but upon the sober recovery of our religious heritage, a secular recapitulation of Christendom that re-actualizes the Christian symbols in a new way. The point is not to return to the past—that is not possible. Rather, the point is to *recognize* the past, to own it as the ground upon which we stand. Only then can our traditions become life-giving again.

I have described the lost road as *I* found it. Others have found their way to the road, and each of their stories is different. Still, the road remains one road, whether one finds it through Buddhism or medieval and mystical Christianity, through personal suffering or study, or both. In the second part of this book, I will endeavor to reconstruct the history of Western thinking by looking closely at its sources in Greek philosophy and Jewish theology. After many years of teaching the history of Western thought at various universities, I am convinced that we can only understand our contemporary political and ecological crises—which are one crisis—by re-examining the philosophical and religious roots of Western civilization. I remain hopeful that some seed of the ecological civilization to come—of which we are the firstborn, the primitives—remains buried in this past, awaiting the opportune conditions to sprout into new life.

The second part is more academic than the first. This shift in gear may pose a challenge to some readers. It is not for a writer to tell a reader how to read their book. One could close the book at this point, for the story of my early religious life has come to its conclusion. On the other hand, a philosophically inclined reader might skip the first part and jump directly to Part Two to see what exactly my argument is. Nevertheless, these two parts of the book belong together and were written to be read consecutively. The road is lost because we have forgotten the religious history that I shall attempt to narrate in the next two chapters. If we are to find a way to it again, we will need to reckon with this history in one way or another.

Not for a moment do I presume to have the final word on these matters. But this is the candle I have been given and I offer its meager light to the reader in all modesty and with the sole intention of helping her find her own way.

Endnotes

1. Paul's authorship of Ephesians and Colossians is disputed among scholars, with one group arguing that the cosmological Christology and the doctrine of the Church belong to a later stage of Christianity—Paul could not have written these letters—and the other group holding the more traditional view that these letters were written when Paul was at the end of his career when Paul was imprisoned in Rome, and thus reflect his more mature Christology. I am in no position to weigh in on this debate. Suffice it to say neither view disturbs my argument. If it was an older Paul writing these letters, all the better. But if it was a disciple of Paul, that's fine too. Christianity is rapidly evolving in the first century and to try to freeze one iteration of it and say, this is the authentic one, is folly. With Karl Barth, I think it is more important to focus on what is written rather than obsess about when it was written.
2. This reading of Paul, which was maintained by Augustine and Luther, is disputed today. The most contemporary Pauline scholarship argues that Paul never denied Law-keeping as a legitimate path to salvation. He only argued that it was a path for Jews alone; the rest of the world needed other paths. I am not sure about this argument as it seems to contradict key passages in Paul, let alone take all the energy from his struggle. See Boccaccini (2020).
3. The question of Christ's ignorance is a disputed one. The view that Jesus's divinity meant he was omniscient is associated with the early Christian heresy of monophysitism (meaning "of one nature," i.e., divine). I was always more prone to the opposite heresy, Nestorianism, the idea that there were two persons active in the life of Jesus, one divine, the other human. On the Nestorian view, Jesus is visited by the *Logos* at a certain point in his human life,

which then fuses with his personality, and he becomes consciously divine, a little like the Buddha awakening to his Buddha nature under the Bodhi tree. The question of Christ's psychological suffering, which means the question of Jesus fully experiencing the human situation—ignorance, despair, weakness, temptation, moments of clarity, and moments of obscurity—was a flash point in the Christological debates of the fifth century. Only humans suffer in this way, it was assumed; God, being eternal, infinite, and immovable, is not subject to any suffering. The Antiochian school based in the Middle Eastern city of Antioch, where Christianity was first named as such, insisted on the full humanity of Jesus: his human birth, his ignorance, suffering, and death. Nestorius was a chief representative of the Antiochian school and argued that there were *two* persons in the Christ, one human and one divine. Nestorius's position provoked its opposite, the monophysite heresy which erred in the direction of the other extreme. Christ was divinity among us, the monophysites insisted. He had one nature, and it was fully divine. Some monophysites concluded therefore that Christ could not genuinely suffer. The debate continued well into the Byzantine period, with major figures like Maximus the Confessor holding that Jesus only pretended to be ignorant for our sake, a little like Socrates and his ironic stance of knowing nothing. Nicephorus the Patriarch of Constantinople (806–815) rejected this view. "He willingly acted, desired, was ignorant, and suffered as man" (Nicephorus cited in Meyendorff 1974, p. 49). The orthodox solution was to distinguish not two persons in Jesus but two wills, one human, the other divine. This led to another still disputed question. Does the human will in Jesus vacillate and deliberate? I won't weigh in on this. I will say only that if Jesus Christ suffered human ignorance, which I believe he did, it was for our sake. The *Logos,* who is the one person in Christ, assumed human nature for us; this assumption could mean that the second person of the Trinity limits himself for our redemption, just as in the Kabbalistic doctrine of creation, the infinite God limits Godself to create the space for something other than God.

4. The council of Chalcedon of 451 was convened to resolve the dispute between Nestorians and Monophysites. It produced the Christological definition that remains binding on all Catholics, most mainline Protestant denominations, and Eastern Orthodoxy. Christ is one person with two natures, human and divine. The one person in Jesus is the *Logos,* the second person of the Trinity who becomes incarnate for our redemption. In him, human nature is united with divine nature, without confusion or diminution of either. Christ is fully human—born of a woman, tempted, suffering—and fully divine, eternally begotten of the Father, and capable of redeeming us. The Chalcedonian definition is difficult to conceive, indeed, ultimately inconceivable. It stipulates that the two opposites, divinity and humanity, coincide in Christ. The definition is a rule for thinking, not an explanation. We must never emphasize the divinity of Christ at the expense of his humanity or vice versa, but neither must we confuse the two. Because of the subtlety and paradoxical nature of the Chalcedonian position, most lay Christians end up being monophysites, if they think about these issues at all. God walked among us; he looked like one of us, but he was really God. Most lapsed Christians end up being Nestorians or Arians, denying Jesus's divinity. He was just a really good guy, they prefer to think, failing to see that such a view does not match the Gospel accounts in the least.

5. On the question of the historicity of the Gospel of John, see Shanks (2005).
6. These historical records have been gathered together into a critical edition by James Stephenson in *A New Eusebius: Documents Illustrative of the History of the Church to AD 337* (Stephenson 1983). For anyone interested in the extra-biblical historical account of the Jesus movement and early Christianity, this is the place to turn (not Dan Brown novels).
7. To dispel more Dan Brown nonsense ("Jesus married Mary Magdalen and started a feminist movement which was crushed by the patriarchy who destroyed the historical evidence for it and labeled it gnosticism"), a study of the Gnostic Gospels is a good idea. Gnostic Christianity was an early competitor with orthodox Christianity. The Gnostic Christians produced their own Gospels, some of which were clearly works of fiction. But the point for the Gnostics was never the historical Jesus but rather the cosmic Christ of Paul who selects some of us for inward illumination or gnosis and so rescues us from the curse of life in the body. The Gospel of Thomas is as old as the four canonical Gospels and undoubtedly contains historical Jesus material not included in the other Gospels. It is well worth reading. Most interesting is the Thomas Gospel's image of Jesus as a teacher of enlightenment by distinction from the crucified-risen savior of the orthodox traditions.
8. The reduction of the Christ to Jesus is the logical fallacy of affirming the consequent. If Jesus, then the Christ does not mean, if the Christ then Jesus. The Christ is the *principle* of Jesus's divinity, which does not preclude the Christ pre-existing the human Jesus (which Paul, John, and the early fathers all maintained). I would add that by the same argument we can say that the Christ exceeds the human Jesus in also the present and the future. The Christ is the

light of all great seers and practitioners of love. But we must be careful not to make Jesus one among many Christs. That is not my point. Jesus was the unique incarnation of the Christ, but the work of the Christ extends beyond the historical incarnation in the man Jesus. It seems to me the only way for a Christian to make sense of non-Christian holiness is by recognizing that wherever people break through to the light and the love which are the origin of everything, they do so with, in and through the Christ, whether or not they recognize Jesus as the Christ.

9. We touch here on the Pauline and Johannine identification of Jesus Christ with the Old Testament figure of Sophia, the eternal (and female) partner of Yahweh. See Proverbs 8:22–31; Wisdom 7:22–27. Here we enter into a field of theological speculation that is at the moment blooming, that of Sophiology. There is no time or space to go into it in depth. Sophia is the divine feminine in Judaism and more, the presence of the Creator in his creation. In Christian Sophiology, Sophia is sometimes described as the soul (*anima*) of Christ. According to Jakob Boehme, Sophia was Adam's first wife, his significant other before the first Fall, which was caused by Adam's envy for the sexual partnership granted to the animals. God makes Adam a human partner, Eve, as a result of his craving for sexuation, and Adam loses Sophia as a result. She was the intimate presence of the divine in Adam's soul, a presence and fullness that rendered Adam androgynous, i.e., complete in himself. She does not forsake humankind after the Fall, however. She visits holy men and women and elevates their minds and hearts to God. Sophia is particularly associated with the divine in nature, with mysticism, especially that of a visionary quality, with inspiration, and therefore with art. For a survey see Martin (2016).

10. Where pantheists believe that nature is God, panentheists believe that nature is *of* God; therefore God interpenetrates nature as the origin of its goodness, truth, and beauty, but God also transcends nature. See Culp (2023).

Part Two
The End of the West

We are experiencing an unprecedented convergence of peoples and cultures. We are finally reckoning with the shadow side of Christendom, with the tyranny and racism of medieval and modern Europeans, who, for the greater part, misunderstood themselves to be the pinnacle of natural, cultural, and religious evolution. We in the West have become the best critics of ourselves. This is as it should be: critique is most effective if it is immanent. I would only add that we must understand that discourse from which we wish to be freed, or what amounts to the same thing, with which we wish to freely engage. For reasons such as these, I remain committed to the Western tradition, to its critique and recreation.

I am skeptical about the "spiritual but not religious" (SBNR) trend. I affirm the persistence of religion in the secular age, which, many have noted, is not an age in which religion withers away, as naive secularists once expected, but rather an age in which religion explodes into an unmappable plurality. At the same time, it seems to me that the final move of consumerism, its checkmating Western culture, is to turn religion and politics (two last holdouts for counter-consumerist critique) into consumer products. We see this happening politically in the echo-chamber news phenomenon, wherein people are free to curate their media to watch and listen to only that which confirms their opinions. Religiously, we now have any number of online options to explore. Whole libraries of hitherto hidden and suppressed heterodoxies are at our fingertips. The Nag Hammadi gnostic scriptures, which were buried in the Egyptian sand for fifteen hundred years, are now ours to peruse on our desktops. But while we may be free to shop for our symbols, what we will be choosing remain *historical* symbols, however uprooted from their contexts. No matter how abstracted, decontextualized, and deracinated, traditional symbols always carry with them some trace of their historical and cultural origins.

In the second part of this book, I will walk the reader through a political theology of the West, beginning with the fusion of Greek thought and Jewish theology in early Christianity, rising to a high point in the mystical theology of the Latin Middle Ages, wherein the seeds of the secular age were planted, and ending with the unraveling of Christendom in secular humanism and consumerism, both of which continue to live from a disavowed, unconscious theological heritage. I have no nostalgia for what has passed. I am quite sure that I would not be happier in a time when the Church dominated all aspects of society. It seems to me an improvement when religion becomes an expression of freedom rather than a social default. Nevertheless, the story to be told is one of decline, as the once-religious civilization of the West deteriorates into its anti-Christian and ecologically violent opposite.

The decline I describe is contingent. It need not have happened. And therefore, I stand by the cautious hope that it can be undone. I am holding out for a new way of being secular, a religious secularism, which, if for no other reasons than environmental ones, will put a lid on consumerism as the work of the devil.

"Hebraism and Hellenism, — between these two points of influence moves our world."

Matthew Arnold

Chapter Four

A Greek Mind, a Jewish Heart

A Coincidence of Opposites

At the origins of the West is the fusion of two very different ancient cultures, Greek and Hebrew. The Greeks were contemplatives; their aim was knowledge. The Hebrews were activists; their aim was justice. The differences between these two are best illustrated through a comparison of the teachings of Socrates (466–399 BC), the Greek philosopher memorialized in a collection of written dialogues by his most famous pupil, Plato, and Jesus (4 BC to 29 AD), the Jewish miracle worker whom Christians believe to be the incarnate God. Socrates and Jesus are a pair of opposites. Both taught a radical doctrine of moral and spiritual reform. Both attracted a large following and came into conflict with the religious authorities of the time. Neither wrote anything down. Both were executed by the state. The similarities between them end with these external facts. When one looks at their teachings, the creative tension at the heart of the West becomes visible.

Socrates is, in the view of many, the first Western philosopher. He is the champion of reason, the defender of skepticism and the power of logical critique. Jesus places no stock in human knowledge and wisdom; he commands moral perfection, a perfection that he recognizes is only possible through divine grace. Socrates encourages his disciples to think for themselves; Jesus tells them to have faith in what is unreachably beyond them. Socrates believes in an immanent order in nature; Jesus believes in the rule of the one God who made nature and is not bound by its laws. Reason for Socrates is the final court of appeal. If you cannot give reasons for what you believe, you ought to abandon it. For Jesus, by contrast, reason has no authority in things divine. One sees, hears, and experiences the power and goodness of the Father and obeys.[1]

For many academic philosophers, the differences between the worldviews of Socrates and Jesus force a choice upon the thinker: either Socrates and the path of reason or Jesus and the path of faith. One cannot coherently follow both, the argument goes. From my earliest forays into philosophy and theology, I rejected this argument. Socrates and Jesus may be opposites, but life thrives in the living tension between opposites.

In some ways, the comparison is not fair. Socrates is a mere mortal, and Jesus is believed to be God. But let us consider Jesus as "fully man," which, in addition to being "fully divine," orthodoxy always insisted he was. Had they lived at the same time and known each other, Socrates and Jesus could only have conflicted, no doubt peacefully and with plenty of brilliant repartees. Let us imagine an exchange between them. Perhaps Jesus goes back in time a few centuries and gets on a boat that takes him from Palestine to Athens, as his follower Paul did. He meets Socrates in the Agora, the public square at the center of the city. Jesus starts preaching the coming of the Kingdom of God to any who cares to listen, and Socrates gets interested. Socrates starts the conversation with a penetrating question. "So Jesus, you say all things depend upon the Father. But what does the Father depend upon?" Such questions were devastating to Socrates's Greek interlocutors. They do not trouble Jesus. He answers with a parable. "The wind blows where it chooses, and you hear the sound of it, but you do not know where it comes from or where it goes" (Jn. 3:8). Socrates responds with more questions. "What do you mean, Jesus? Do you mean that the wind is God?" Jesus then turns the table on Socrates. "It is not the wind that is God but God who sends the wind and every good thing. You do not understand where you yourself come from. Why then do you presume to understand God?" As he did Nicodemus, or the Samaritan woman at the well (Jn. 3:1–21; Jn

4: 1–26), Jesus tries to compel Socrates to question himself, and in such a way as to foreclose any quick rational answers. Jesus wants to save Socrates from rationalism; Socrates thinks Jesus a bit of a fanatic, but a clever one, not to be trifled with. They part from one another perplexed.

Behind these two opposed figures are the two opposed ancient cultures of Greece and Jerusalem. The two cultures clashed on fundamentals: what divinity is, the meaning of life, and the nature of time itself. And yet their fusion in Christianity produced modernity. For the ancient Greeks, divinity is intellect or *nous*. Hellenic wisdom consists in perfecting the human being's mind so that it becomes more like the divine intellect: immaterial, eternal, and unmoved. For the ancient Hebrews, divinity is the personal Creator of the universe. Nothing good could happen without his will. Hebraic wisdom is fidelity to the law of God. It is not so much the human perfection of the intellect as it is moral discernment: knowing God's will and doing it. The point is powerfully made in the Book of Proverbs:

> If you indeed cry out for insight
> and raise your voice for understanding,
> If you seek it like silver
> and search for it as for hidden treasures—
> then you will understand the fear of the Lord
> and find the knowledge of God.
> For the Lord gives wisdom;
> from his mouth come knowledge and understanding.
> (Proverbs 2: 3–6)

Hebraic wisdom is not a human virtue but a gift of God. Hence the ancient Hebrews valued faith above all other virtues, faith in the God of Israel who had chosen the Jews to receive his self-revelation. Jewish faith is an act of the will or "the heart," which is, in Hebrew thought, the essence of the human being.

Hellenic wisdom, by contrast, is a natural capacity of the human being. Knowledge in the Greek tradition is not so much fidelity to God as it is understanding nature, how things fit together and show forth an eternal order. Wisdom leads to the self-control that allows for a beautiful and ordered life. The goal of reason is to rule the passions so that the mind is free to contemplate the truth.

Much of the tension between the Hellenic and the Hebraic view of life involves conflicting attitudes toward the body. The ancient Greeks tend to see the body as a prison for the immortal soul and an impediment to thought. There is no body/soul dualism in ancient Judaism. The body is alive by virtue of the breath (*ruah*) of God. It is God's creation, the instrument of his will, and something to be revered.

That said, the ancient Hebrews were hardly irrationalists. A thorough reading of the Hebrew Bible proves that the people who wrote these texts possessed immense intellectual talent. However, for the Hebrew prophets, in contrast to the Greek philosophers, reason has an ambiguous, even duplicitous quality: it leads to multiple and divergent interpretations from which one must, in the end, make a choice based not so much on reason as on faith. Reason is a gift of God, to be sure, but it only pretends to be in charge. The human will is driven by much darker and more mysterious forces than logic. It is the heart, not reason, that determines the moral course of one's life. "Out of the heart comes evil thoughts" (Mt 15:19).

The distinctive quality of the Hebrew intellectual tradition has been preserved in the history of interpretations of the Law of Moses, that is, the Torah (the first five books of the Hebrew Bible and the history of commentaries upon them). The interpretation of the Law is the special responsibility of the Rabbis. This kind of intellectual work begins with a revealed text, one believed to be of divine rather than human origin and then works out the applications of the text in changing circumstances, producing a wealth of new meanings and never settling with a final result. What many Greek thinkers avoid at all costs, a plurality of equally plausible possibilities for interpretation, the Hebrews affirm. Time leaves nothing standing still, and no intellectual resting place is to be found on earth. The word of God is our only guide. Hebraic reasoning is thus pluralizing rather than universalizing. It is more playfully skeptical than systematic, sensitive to the ambiguities and exceptions that render every theory provisional at best. In the end, it confesses the folly of human ignorance and our absolute dependence on God.

The author of the Letter to the Hebrews, a late addition to the New Testament but undoubtedly of Jewish origin, writes: "The word of God is alive and active. Sharper than any double-edged sword, it penetrates even to dividing soul and spirit, joints and marrow; it judges the thoughts and attitudes of the heart" (Heb. 4:12). Scripture is not just a text for us to interpret as we choose; it is the living divine word, and it illuminates our reason, not the other way around. The diversity of interpretations that emerge from scripture makes the personal decision of the interpreter inescapable. Every genuine decision reveals "the thoughts and the attitudes of the heart."

It would be incorrect to suggest that the ancient Greeks were not emotional or had no sense for the irrational. A brief survey of the cult surrounding Dionysus, the god of ecstasy, clearly illustrates the falsity of such a claim.[2] Socrates himself hears voices, consults oracles, and writes myths. He celebrates "divine madness" as better than merely human self-control (Plato, *Phaedrus* 265b). But the point of religious ecstasy in Plato is to liberate us from the passion-ruled body and to emancipate the mind from mere opinions so that we can know and affirm the eternal truth. Only through transcending the body can the truth be known.

At the center of ancient Greek thought is the assumption that the universe is a rule-bound cosmos, an eternal system of interrelated elements, spirits, metals, and planets that determines an endless cycle of recurring forms. The task for the mind is to understand how it all hangs together. The world is a "moving image of eternity," Plato writes (*Timaeus* 37d). If we can rise above our ordinary, passion-ruled mind, we will see that all things make manifest a divine logic. In the Hebrew Bible, on the other hand, the world is created by a free act of God. It is not eternal but has a beginning in time and an ending when God will declare history to be over. Things are what they are because God wills them so, not because they express an eternal order that the mind can know by perfecting its reasoning capacities.

If the Greeks gave us our sense for the eternal order of things, it is from the Jews that we get our sense for the spiritual reality of the person, the free human being who somehow slips out of the system of causes that rule nature. The concept of the person might be the most significant gift of the Jews to our secular age.[3] It is closely connected to the Hebraic understanding of divinity. One looks in vain for a concept of the person in Plato. This is because Hellenic thought is essentially deterministic: it has no sense for freedom. We find lyrical discussions of the soul in Plato, of course, but the soul is something different from the person. The soul has something cosmological and universal about it, as one sees clearly from a reading of Plato's *Timaeus* or Aristotle's treatise, *On the Soul*. It is something we share with other beings, perhaps with the world itself, even if we are responsible for our own souls in a special way. The person, by contrast, is never merely an instance of a class. Personhood is singular, an invisible center of thought and action; as the Scholastics used to say, it is incommunicable, that is, while it can be expressed, as it is in the words and deeds of the individual, it cannot be shared. *My* personhood is utterly distinct from *yours*.

From ancient Judaism, the concept of the living, human soul (*nephesh*) was passed to early Christianity where it received a more precise definition as "person." The Church Fathers argue that if the three persons of the Trinity are distinct from one another (as they must be if the story of Christ's sacrifice is to make sense), it is not by possessing separate beings, for the Trinity is one God, not three. Rather, the three divine persons are distinct in their relations to one another. Only the Father is related to the Son and the Spirit as *unbegotten*; only the Son is related to the Father and the Spirit as *begotten*; only the Spirit is related to the Father and the Son as *proceeding* from the Father through the Son (Aquinas 1948, First Part, Q. 28). Relationality, which in Aristotle, is an accidental attribute of things, is in Trinitarian theology an essential quality of persons (Balthasar 1986). In accidental relationality, the relations of a being to other beings do not make it what it is. The book on the table is not changed in its essence by being on the table rather than on the shelf, or by being my book rather than yours. In essential relationality, the relations constitute the being as such. My identity is essentially bound up with my relations to others. You make me who I am to some degree. And with other people, I am someone different than I am with you. It is not that I have multiple, pathologically dissociated selves but rather that each of my personal relations actualizes something different in me. The modern Jewish philosopher Martin Buber ran with this idea, and argued in his justly famous book *I and Thou* that a person can say "I" because he stands in essential relation to another "I," one to whom he can say "You" (Buber 1958).

In short, a person is the person they are because of their relations to other persons. Not many secular people today believe otherwise, although they might profess to do so. Even the most hardened determinist holds his relations with others, his love for his partner and family, as most dear to him and most determinative of his identity. He might think that such attachments are philosophically meaningless but in all that he does he acts as though he believes otherwise. His life itself attests to his belief in the supreme value of the personal.

There is no more powerful example of ancient Jewish personalism than Psalm 139. In this psalm, which Jesus himself would have prayed, the psalmist experiences himself as a mystery of interior experience, of subjectivity we would say today, an abyss of personal freedom which is fathomed only by the infinite person, the Creator God. The psalmist stands in direct relation to God, whose mind exceeds his comprehension and from whose gaze he cannot escape:

O Lord, you have searched me and known me.
You know when I sit down and when I rise up;
you discern my thoughts from far away.
You search out my path and my lying down
and are acquainted with all my ways.
Even before a word is on my tongue,
O Lord, you know it completely.
You hem me in, behind and before,
and lay your hand upon me.
Such knowledge is too wonderful for me;
it is so high that I cannot attain it.
Where can I go from your spirit?
Or where can I flee from your presence?
If I ascend to heaven, you are there;
if I make my bed in Sheol, you are there.
If I take the wings of the morning
and settle at the farthest limits of the sea,
even there your hand shall lead me,
and your right hand shall hold me fast.
If I say, "Surely the darkness shall cover me,
and night wraps itself around me,"
even the darkness is not dark to you;
the night is as bright as the day,
for darkness is as light to you.
For it was you who formed my inward parts;

you knit me together in my mother's womb.
I praise you, for I am fearfully and wonderfully made.
Wonderful are your works; that I know very well.
My frame was not hidden from you,
when I was being made in secret,
intricately woven in the depths of the Earth.
Your eyes beheld my unformed substance.
In your book were written
all the days that were formed for me,
when none of them as yet existed.
How weighty to me are your thoughts, O God!
How vast is the sum of them!
I try to count them—they are more than the sand;
I come to the end—I am still with you.

The psalmist can travel to the furthest ends of creation and still, God will be there, watching him. This is simultaneously comforting and terrifying. No matter where he goes, to the distant stars or into the depths of the ocean, the psalmist cannot get away from God. But since God is a loving Father, this is not necessarily unwelcome attention. He can count on God to watch over him and to be there for him. The psalmist's experience of himself as a person, as a free center of agency and incommunicable interiority, is mediated by his relation to the absolute subjectivity of God.

Personhood is at the core of the Christian religion. It is one of the places where Christianity conflicts with Asian religions, which tend towards the impersonal. For some versions of Buddhism, personhood is illusory: the doctrine of no self (*Anattā*) according to some interpretations of Buddhism means that our relations to one another are deceptions. They bind us to the illusory world by tricking us into believing that our identities are more real than they appear. There is no God above us. Buddhist eternity (*Nirvana*) is close to the Greek

Neoplatonist "One" beyond being: an impersonal unity of all things. By contrast, the divinity Jesus represents is infinitely personal, and the relation of the believer to Jesus intensifies the believer's experience of herself as a person. Jesus touches the most intimate depths of the believer's heart, forging a link between these depths (which at their deepest point are unknown even to the believer) and the ultimate source of all that is. It is for this reason that Christianity is not a religion of trans-human states of consciousness and solitary acts of ineffable communion with the divine (even if these do sometimes appear in Christian mysticism); it is a religion of love in the most concrete, interpersonal, and human senses of the term. To deny personality of God, according to Christian theology, is to undervalue personal relations in general and to refuse the highest perfection we know of the divine.

At the inception of the Western tradition, we have Greek impersonal cosmology facing off with Jewish personalism, the former emphasizing contemplation, the latter calling for righteous action. The opposing tendencies were eventually blended by Christianity over the course of a millennium. In the Middle Ages, the two became one homogenous tradition. The Hellenic is the root of the impersonal and objectifying way that Westerners map out the contours of the world—a mode of thinking that has been enormously successful at unraveling the inner workings of nature. The Hebraic is the root of the Western sense for social justice, for the will to change the world, to make it more just for all people. It is the root of the irrepressible Western faith in the possibility of a better, human future.

Ancient Greeks and Jews lived alongside one another for centuries and influenced each other in countless ways. There were natural places of convergence between the two traditions. The Greek philosophical tradition from its beginnings in the mystical speculation of the pre-Socratic philosophers, to its end in the great Neoplatonic systems of the first five centuries of the common era, argues for the philosophical advantages of monotheism over mythological polytheism—even though the latter is more traditionally Hellenic. The Jews, from their beginnings in Abraham's prophetic mission, to follow the unknown God into the promised land, assert the one God of the universe over the idols of the pagans. The Greeks get to monotheism through argument. If all the gods are divine by sharing in the same divine nature, then the divine nature must be one and higher than any particular god. It is better to be ruled by one than by many. Such arguments, the first from Plato, and the second from Aristotle, are strewn throughout the Greek philosophical tradition. The Jews worship the one God because the one God had been revealed to them through their often painful and carefully archived history as a marginalized Middle Eastern community, continually quashed, occupied, and enslaved by the empires encircling them. The rational monotheism of the Greeks and the religious monotheism of the Jews blend in much Roman Catholic theology.

As in a good marriage, it is the differences between the partners that make the union lively. If the West has a Greek mind, that allows it to think methodically about all things, from politics to nature, science to theology, it comes to the task with a Jewish heart, which insists on loving action.

The Beginning of Western Thought

According to Socrates, what makes us particular, individual—different from others—is not the essential element of our being. It is how we are alike that matters. That which is universally present in all humans and in no other animal—reason—makes us human. A human being, Socrates assumes, is human by virtue of his rational powers, which are a spark of divinity within him and a light to guide his way in this realm of shadows. But this light must be cultivated. Reason requires training; that is, it requires philosophy, which Socrates understands as a special kind of discourse (not a private affair at all). The philosopher practices the art of questioning. She is the enemy of ideology, superstition, and dogmatism. This puts philosophy in conflict with the three great powers that ruled Greek society at the time: politics, mythology, and religion.

Ancient Greek culture before Socrates had its share of divine revelations. The mythic stories about the gods—told and retold over and again by the poets—laid out the moral and civic standards for Greek society. Nature was animated by divinities. As one of Socrates's predecessors Thales of Miletus put it, "All things are full of gods." Like the ancient Hebrews, ancient Greeks believed that what a god revealed, either directly in person or indirectly in nature or through an oracle, was not to be measured by human standards. The gods were to be obeyed, not questioned. Socrates caused a revolution in thought when he argued otherwise. Using our rational powers, he claims that we ought to be able to discern the logic and sense of a divine command—or the lack thereof. Obedience to authority is not enough. We must use our native reason to decide, before anything else, whether the gods' commands are moral, which ultimately means, whether the command is from a god in the first place. Not everything the poets tell us that the gods command can be trusted.

The gods squabble in the stories. They do not agree on what is best. How can we decide which of them is right? We must think about these things ourselves. We must critique myth using our reason, for the power of reasoning, a power that can separate the true from the false, the good from the bad, is something that each one of us possesses. We demonstrate our capacity to reason about morality in the most ordinary judgments. "Euthyphro is not a good man." "Athens is the greatest of cities." "Socrates is a bad influence on the young." Regardless of the truth or falsity of these claims, each of them presupposes the possibility of an individual intuition of the good that depends on reason alone.

What Socrates objects to is not the telling of stories for the sake of illustrating moral and spiritual truths—he does that sort of thing often. He objects to an *unreflective* allegiance to examples drawn from myths. He sees it as dangerous that the Greeks justify their actions with dogmatic references to Homeric myths. Stories can be used to justify all manner of acts, even acts that contradict each other. The spin doctors of ancient Athens, the Sophists, used stories and imagery to justify whatever position was most in their interest. It seems to Socrates that moral judgment cannot depend on external authority.

With arguments like these, Socrates scandalized his contemporaries and threatened the social structure of ancient Athens, which depended on conceding to the authority of a special class of people who spoke on behalf of the gods. Socrates challenged the elites and encouraged the youth not to blindly obey them but to rationally test what they said. There exists a higher authority, Socrates argues, an authority to which even the gods are answerable: the good. Knowledge of the good is not the special privilege of priests, poets, or oracles, but an achievement of human reason. The elites were not impressed. They put him to death on a charge of atheism.

Accused of treason, blasphemy, and corrupting the youth, Socrates was found guilty by a jury, and executed by the Athenian democracy in 399 BC. He was ordered to drink poison hemlock, which he did in the company of his friends and disciples, philosophizing until the poison took effect and killed him. In his last dialogue, the *Phaedo,* Socrates is portrayed as entirely unafraid of death. To philosophize, he insists to his disciples, who were utterly distraught that they were losing him forever, is too long for the final answers to the most important questions, and only death shall reveal them. Why should we fear that which might be the highest blessing? Philosophy is "training for dying" (*Phaedo* 67e), the work of freeing the mind in this life from merely bodily self-interest and raising it to the eternal. We prepare ourselves for the transition to the next life, in which Socrates had an unwavering belief, by practicing philosophy.

In his critique of the function of mythology in Greek society, Socrates articulated for the first time in Western history what we have come to know as the principle of conscience. It was difficult for his contemporaries to accept this because it was such a new idea. The Athenian establishment saw Socrates's appeal to reason over myth as blasphemous. They intuited that Socratic philosophy, should it become popular, would bring about the demise of their ancient religion, which was in fact what happened. For if the ordinary Greek possessed a nearly divine capacity to discern true from false, good from bad, what need was there for stories of gods or the priests hired to placate the gods? If the ordinary human being already knew, or at least was capable of knowing, the truth about ultimate things, reason rather than revelation was the final court of appeal.

But we must be careful not to project modern rationalism onto Socrates. Socrates never says that human reason is self-sufficient and has no need of revelation. He consults the gods, the oracles, and even his dreams for guidance in his thinking and acting. He only insists that we should bring our critical reasoning abilities to these trans-rational experiences. When accused of presuming to know more than others, he defends himself by insisting that unlike many others in Athenian society, he does not claim to have any special knowledge that sets him above others. Unlike the elites, who manifestly do not know what they are talking about most of the time, Socrates at least knows that he does not know anything. The highest human wisdom, he proclaims at his trial, is to know the limits of human wisdom (*Apology* 23a).

One of my first undergraduate classes in philosophy was a course on Plato. I was totally taken with Socrates and his subversive questions. I walked home one day after the class, deep in thought. It struck me that my reasoning powers were not free-floating or arbitrary. Reason rested on unspoken assumptions, tacit commitments, and innate ideas, which reason itself could neither justify nor reject. Consider the first law of logic, the law of identity: everything that can be thought is identical to itself. This might strike some as obscure, but the irrefutability of it is plain if you try to think the opposite: try to imagine something that is non-identical to itself, an apple that is not an apple, a place that is here and not here, an object that can both be and not be at the same time in the same respect. One contradicts oneself before the thought is even mentally expressed. We simply cannot think such things because such things cannot exist. The law of identity is, as we like to say in the digital age, "hard-wired into us." It is an operational presupposition of reason, as near to an absolute truth as you are going to find. "A equals A," I repeated to myself, as though in a trance, as I walked home that day. "Being is being. Being is not non-being."

"But so what?" I asked myself, stopping by a brook and watching the little trout dart amidst the brown rocks. "What can we conclude based on this? Nothing whatsoever." It seemed to me impossible to build a system of knowledge on the basis of the laws of logic. Logic could not tell us whether the soul was immortal, whether God existed, or whether, as my cousin John had wondered, life was any good. Logic does not decide anything. The thinker who would come to exert the greatest influence on my thinking, F.W.J. Schelling (1775–1854) points out that logic deals only with *possibility*; it knows nothing of *actuality* (Schelling 2007b). But even at the beginning of my philosophical education, I grasped that the logical part of our minds is curiously out of synch with the world of existence. It cannot explain why anything exists in the first place. Logic is not enough. Once the mind is set in order, it still needs something to think. It needs revelation in the most general sense of the term, the unveiling of things hidden, if it is to take the first step.

But revelation in this general sense must have already occurred. If being had remained unrevealed, we would not only remain ignorant, but we would also be ignorant of our ignorance. The very fact that Socrates knows that he does not know proves that something more than logic is at work in his thought. Socrates is shaken into the knowledge of his ignorance by the revelation of being. He exists and is immersed in being, and neither his existence nor the existence of anything else explains itself. In this way, Socratic skepticism did not lead me away from revealed religion, quite the opposite. It showed me not only the plausibility of revelation but helped me see the factuality of it.

The Good Beyond Being

The centerpiece of Plato's philosophy, at least insofar as the figure of Socrates in the dialogues can be regarded as its spokesman, is the doctrine of form. Socrates introduces the theory of form at various places in the dialogues to explain the puzzle of the one and the many. How can things be both different and the same? If I have three apples and two oranges in my basket, what is it that makes the apples different from the oranges? And if the answer is that all the apples are the same kind of thing and all the oranges are another kind of thing, what makes the apples three and the oranges two? How do we differentiate things that are essentially the same? What is a kind? Is it just a manner of speaking or is it something real that allows us to recognize and order things together? Socrates argues that the forms of things, the principle of sameness, or in more technical terms, universality, is that which makes three *different* things the *same kind* of thing.

Aristotle, Plato's student, adds that the form of a collection of the same kind of things must be distinguished from the matter which makes each member of the collection different. The form is known by the mind, which abstracts it from the experience of particular things of the same kind. There are forms for all of the kinds of things that exist or could exist: a form for all apples, a form for all fruits, a form for all plants, a form for all humans, a form for all just acts, a form for all beautiful things. It is in the light of form that we are able to say, this is an apple, that is not, this is beautiful, that is not. Form is what is knowable in things. It is what we name when we speak of things. It is what we seek to define when we endeavor to define a thing. And yet this most familiar of all phenomena is the most mysterious. For where does form reside? In the thing itself? In language? In the mind of the one who knows the thing? Or in some other realm beyond both matter and mind?

Forms cannot just be a manner of speaking, Socrates argues against the relativists of his day, who held just that. If form were merely a human convention, a way of organizing things that really don't belong together into convenient groups there would be no connection between words and things. But at the same time, a form cannot be one of the things counted in a collection. Form is the principle of counting, not a countable thing. It must transcend matter, Socrates insists (and here Aristotle disagreed), and therefore it transcends time itself.

The forms of things are not known by us in this life, Socrates says over and over again. And if the forms of things converge in the highest form, the form of forms, the good, which they logically must according to Socrates, the Good is not known by us in this life either. If the good is God—and what else could it be—this amounts to a statement of agnosticism. We have no clear and distinct knowledge of God in this life. We no doubt have a dim presentiment of divinity, for the world does not explain itself and seems to require divinity to make sense of it. But of the divine, of the good, like the forms which are its symbols, we have no certain knowledge.

This agnostic turn in Plato's thought had immense repercussions for the development of mysticism in medieval Islam and Christendom. The two great monotheistic traditions of the Middle Ages, stemming in one way or another from Hebraic religion, agree on at least one thing, that knowledge of divinity is revealed not deduced. We do not possess revelation; we are granted it or denied it. God shows and God hides Godself when God wills to.

To understand Plato's agnosticism, we need to be clear that despite his defense of critical thinking against authoritarianism and mythology, Socrates never says that he *knows* the good. He insists that knowledge of the good is a work of the solitary mind; no one, no priest, poet, or philosopher could achieve it for you. But he never says that we are in a position to achieve it now, in this bodily life, nor does he boast of it himself. The symbols of the good are everywhere. But these forms are not seen by us or experienced bodily. They are rather "recollected." We have a vague sense of having once experienced them, but we cannot clearly remember where, when, or how. The forms haunt our daily experience like fragments of a half-remembered dream. This recollection is hardly knowledge. It is rather an indication of the opposite: if we, at some forgotten point in our past, possessed knowledge of the forms of the good, we have since lost it and now toil in a place of ignorance.

In the following passage from the dialogue recounting the death of Socrates, the *Phaedo,* notice how Socrates and his interlocutor, his disciple Simmias, are at once certain that the forms exist and equally certain that they have no clear knowledge of them.

> "Well, but there is another thing, Simmias: Is there or is there not an absolute justice?"
>
> "Assuredly there is."
>
> "And an absolute beauty and absolute good?"
>
> "Of course."
>
> "But did you ever behold any of them with your eyes?"

"Certainly not."

"Or did you ever reach them with any other bodily sense? (and I speak not of these alone, but of absolute greatness, and health, and strength, and of the essence or true nature of everything). Has the reality of them ever been perceived by you through the bodily organs? Or rather, is not the nearest approach to the knowledge of their several natures made by him who so orders his intellectual vision as to have the most exact conception of the essence of that which he considers?"

"Certainly."

"Would not that man do this most perfectly who approaches each thing, so far as possible, with the reason alone, not introducing sight into his reasoning nor dragging in any of the other senses along with his thinking, but who employs pure, absolute reason in his attempt to search out the pure, absolute essence of things, and who removes himself, so far as possible, from eyes and ears, and, in a word, from his whole body, because he feels that its companionship disturbs the soul and hinders it from attaining truth and wisdom? Is not this the man, Simmias, if anyone, to attain to the knowledge of reality?"

"That is true as true can be, Socrates," said Simmias. (*Phaedo* 65d–66a)

I have highlighted phrases in this passage where Socrates speaks of the approximation to knowledge, not its achievement, an approximation that is hindered at every turn by the conditions of our corporeal existence. Our eyes and ears are not only of no help, but they also hinder our approach to the forms. The best we can do is find "the nearest approach" by using our mind "so far as possible" independently of eyes and ears. And since we can never pull this off so long as we live in the world, philosophy is doomed to fail. To be sure, we can hope that this failure is not final. If we have a sense of having known the forms prior to this bodily life we have reason to believe that in a future life, we shall be liberated from the body, perfected, and rendered more adequate to the task of knowing the good.

The Neoplatonists went even further than Plato in stressing agnosticism. They argue that not only is the good beyond our reach so long as our mind is attached to the body; they say that the good is beyond reason itself, even if reason leads ineluctably to it. Their point is not to restore mythological irrationalism but rather to insist upon the supra-rational nature of the origin and goal of all that is. Reason brings us to a threshold that reason itself cannot pass.

Neoplatonism was a natural fit for the theologies of revelation of Islam and Christianity and thus became the predominant philosophy of the two great civilizations of the Middle Ages. It flourished in Europe and the Middle East for a thousand years—longer if we include the Renaissance Neoplatonists in the tradition. The first Christian philosophy, which emerged in Alexandria (now Egypt) in the third century, was a brand of Neoplatonism. The greatest thinkers of Islam's Golden Age (AD 622–1258)—Al Farabi, Ibn Sina, Al Ghazali—were Neoplatonic. If the Hellenic and the Hebraic are the two opposed forces that animate the Western tradition, the fusion of the two is first ventured in Neoplatonism. Where Neoplatonism succeeded, the Western balance of the tension between its Greek mind and its Jewish heart became productive, extraordinarily so, as in the monumental works of theology of the Church Fathers or the sublime architecture of the high Gothic.

A brief history of the movement: Plato founded a school and wrote the dialogues which are widely regarded as the most influential Western philosophical texts ever written. The focus of his philosophical work was on the transcendent element in the teaching of Socrates. Plato's student Aristotle differed from Plato on key points, especially on the question of the transcendence of the good. He introduced certain distinctions that solved several problems in Plato's thought and founded a different school, producing an equally voluminous body of literature with an equally immeasurable influence. Some of the followers of Plato and Aristotle produced a synthesis of their teaching, which we know as Neoplatonism. Aristotle was given his due, but Plato's transcendence trumped Aristotle's naturalism. The first Christian theologians in Rome and Constantinople developed Neoplatonism as the philosophical position best suited to explaining the Christian revelation. When Rome crumbled, Muslim scholars in medieval Bagdad carried the torch and fused Neoplatonism with the Qur'an. But even in the so-called European Dark Ages, small schools of Neoplatonic Christian theology continued to transmit and expand the tradition without interruption: especially in Ireland, where Celtic monks like Eriugena (AD 815–877) mastered Greek so that he could read Plato, Plotinus, and the Church Fathers. Then in the fourteenth century, the Renaissance humanists of Europe, beginning with Dante (AD 1265–1321) and coming to a crescendo in Cusa (AD 1401–1464), Pico della Mirandola (AD 1463–1494), and Ficino (1433–1499), revived Neoplatonism and expanded it further until it became the predominant philosophical position in Europe on the cusp of the scientific revolution.[4]

While all the Neoplatonists returned to Plato and his philosophy of transcendence they incorporated key aspects of Aristotle's philosophy, especially Aristotle's distinction between potency and act, his notion of final cause (that towards which a living thing tends in its growth and development) and his related theory of nature as something that is ever coming to be and passing away. They added that nature is always in process because it is striving to return to the good from whence it has come. They called this process the *exitus et reditus* (the emergence and the return) of the many to the one.

Without any contradiction of the Socratic agnosticism at its core, Neoplatonism, pagan, Christian, and Muslim, advances a monotheistic cosmology that explains the world as the joyous expression of the superabundant goodness of the good, or in a biblical register, the creator God. Like the sun which magnanimously pours forth its light, God streams forth being spontaneously, for it is the nature of the good to diffuse itself and give itself away. All that exists is bathed in the light of the good. Our minds can only know the little that they do because of the uncreated light shining upon it from the Creator. But the light itself is too bright for us and appears as darkness when we try to apprehend it directly. Only the transformation of the mind through death will render us *capax Dei*, capable of seeing God.

The key text for Neoplatonism is Plato's *Republic* Book VI. This famous passage concerns the relationship of the form of the good to all the good things that exist. Socrates concludes not only that the good cannot exist like a thing, for then it would need to be subordinated to something better by virtue of which it is called good; he argues that the good is *beyond* being as such, higher than being, and therefore beyond the logical rules that govern all that exists. Of it, nothing accurate can be said. We cannot even coherently say it exists. But neither can we deny it, for everything that exists depends upon it.

> What gives truth to the things known and the power to the knower is the form of the good. And though it is the cause of knowledge and truth, it is also an object of knowledge. Both knowledge and truth are beautiful things, but the good is other and more beautiful than they. In the visible realm, light and sight are rightly considered sunlike, but it is wrong to think they are the sun, so here it is right to think of knowledge and truth as goodlike but wrong to think that either of them is the good—for the good is yet

> more prized... You'll be willing to say, I think, that the sun not only provides visible things with the power to be seen but also with coming to be, growth and nourishment, although it is not itself coming to be ... Therefore, you should also say that not only do objects of knowledge owe their being known to the good, but their being is also due to it, although the good is not being, but superior to it in rank and power. (*Republic*, 508e–509c)

This is a profound passage upon which heaps of scholarship have been lavished. I will never forget watching John Rist struggle to interpret it for us in a graduate seminar at the University of Toronto in 1995. His head of wild white hair was bent over a Greek copy of the Republic, which was covered with his handwritten notes. His knobby finger was on the lines as he translated them for us. *The good is not being, but greater than it*. Upon finishing the passage, he looked up at us, somewhat baffled, and exclaimed, "That's what the passage says. That's the line that inspired all the Neoplatonists." Upon the foundation of this notion of an absolutely unknowable origin of everything, the Neoplatonists construct elaborate systems, the pinnacle of which is not knowledge but mysticism. Science, by which they understand knowledge of things that could be known with unaided human reason, things that could to some degree be defined and put into relation to one another and so spoken of coherently, science could only take us so far in scaling these heights. At the summit of philosophy, science must be abandoned, but not in a fit of irrationalism, quite the contrary: conceptual reasoning must let go of its concepts if it is to remain reasonable. The Good is absolute infinity, beyond concepts, and of it nothing definite can be said. Pagan Neoplatonists call it "the One," for it is absolutely simple, without parts, opposed to nothing, without an origin, and without relations. Christian Neoplatonists call it "Father." By making the origin of everything inscrutable, things become understandable. Chesterton loved paradox, especially this one which lies at the heart of the Western tradition. "The whole secret of mysticism is this: that man can understand everything by the help of what he does not understand. The morbid logician seeks to make everything lucid, and succeeds in making everything mysterious. The mystic allows one thing to be mysterious, and everything else becomes lucid" (Chesterton 1908, 34).

Neoplatonic systems are various, but they all have a common structure that gives an account of the beginning and the end of all things. The countless creatures that stream forth from the good in the *exitus* are ordered in a hierarchy from the most simple (the divine ideas, the angels, and the souls of human beings), to the most complex, the animals and material beings, with each animated by love for the good, and each in their way seeking their way back to the good from whence they have emanated. For Islamic and Christian Neoplatonists, the word "emanate" is not quite right. They speak rather of creation, which is a free act of the Father, who produces beings that image him. All of creation is a great showing of the infinite depths of the divine mind.

To the degree appropriate to their mode of existence, creatures find their way back to the good/the Father, not by resisting their natures but by more fully being what they are. Everything that comes forth from God seeks to return to God by being the best kind of thing that it is. The *reditus* is instinctive and unconscious in the non-human. The ant seeks God by being an ant; the fox that eats the ant seeks God by being a fox. The human seeks God too in all that she does; she seeks God in seeking to consciously actualize all of her human potential at the pinnacle of which lies the potential for wisdom.

If "the ecological thought" is interdependence (Morton 2012), Neoplatonism is one of the first ecological philosophies. Everything is related to everything else in Neoplatonism, everything depends upon everything else, for everything emerges from a common ineffable origin. But unlike many forms of ecological metaphysics, Neoplatonism is never atheist. God indwells everything, and everything can be said in some sense to be in God. But God also transcends everything. At whatever level of being we consider, there is always some transcendent height upon which the lower level depends, which overarches it and which cannot be comprehended in terms of the lower. Even the being of God is transcended by the incomprehensible abyss of the Godhead, argues Eckhart, the great Christian Neoplatonist of the fourteenth century (Eckhart 2009, especially sermon 87). Divine transcendence does not mean divine absence, quite the contrary. Everywhere one turns in nature, one finds symbols of divinity. Wisdom consists in knowing how to read the symbols and gather the multitude together in a single glance. The many things become the multitude of colors streaming forth from the white light of the good. The wise man sees the one in the many, the divine in matter, and in his contemplation, the return to God, the *reditus*, is effected.

In Neoplatonism, forms are essentially immaterial or spiritual; they do not so much inhabit things as illuminate them from beyond. A form is not a thing that one can handle; it is a principle of intelligibility. The form is eternal, even if the particular thing is not. The Christian Neoplatonists add that the eternal forms of things do not float free in some other world but are thoughts in the mind of the Creator. The forms are the archetypes of things and pre-exist the world in the infinite mind of God. God thinks only one thought, and in that thought are contained all that can be thought, as all the colors of the spectrum are contained in white light. The One is pure divinity, and as such precedes and grounds even the Creator God. It is absolute infinity, for it has no boundaries; absolute unity, for it has no parts, and absolute goodness, for it needs nothing. The only way to truly know it is to become like it, to become one in oneself, which means to become a contemplative, selfless and alone with the alone.

The founder of pagan Neoplatonism was Plotinus, a third-century Greco-Roman sage. We do not know a great deal about him, but we do know that he had a school and attracted a large number of devoted followers. He might have traveled to India and learned something from the Buddhists who were flourishing in the north of the subcontinent at that time or from the Hindu Brahmans who wrote the Upanishads. Like the Indian sages, Plotinus believed that unity is more real than multiplicity. Everything is one: our experience of difference, duality, and division is relative, even illusory. Contemplation transforms the soul and makes it capable of seeing and experiencing the eternal in things, the one in the many. The culmination of the philosophical life is mystical experience of the One. He apparently experienced union with the One a few times in his life when he was reported to have been carried away in ecstasy (Plotinus 1962, 1–20). He describes the experience as a blissful loss of all sense of distinctness: he felt not only the oneness of all things but his oneness with everything. The experience left him enraptured and speechless.

It should be clear from this brief account that pagan Neoplatonism was much more than a merely theoretical philosophy. It was a way of life and a mystical practice. It included exercises directed at the cultivation of a habit of mind that allows us to experience the unity of all things. Plotinus was more like an Indian guru than a professor of philosophy. Through spiritually training, the disciple becomes detached from ego-centric desires and comes to know herself as not essentially different from other things and other selves. No longer in competition with others, she becomes selfless and compassionate. At the same time, she overcomes all interior division. No longer riven by multiple desires, she becomes one in herself: willing one thing, thinking one thing, gathered into herself and focused on a single transcendent aim. She is then a spotless mirror reflecting the One back to itself.

Not many of us, however, pull this off. The world is so deliciously seductive. Being midway between the ideal and the material, human souls experience the possibility of going up or down. The soul can move upwards towards unity or dive downwards into multiplicity, chasing after one thing and then another. The latter is what we usually do, according to Plotinus. We find ourselves, for the most part, turning towards material things. We become enraptured by them, and our desires wreak havoc on our souls. Our passions rage and pull us in competing directions. In order to unify the soul, we must turn away from the many and back to the One. This can only be accomplished through a process of asceticism or self-denial. Break the chains of habits that bind us to the multiple, Plotinus advises; turn around, away from the order of multiplicity and back towards unity.

Argumentative philosophy (which Plotinus called dialectic), while perhaps not enough to reach the mystical goal, is still crucial because philosophy draws our attention away from matter towards form. But to move from the multiplicities of forms to the One cannot be accomplished by reason alone. Reason is discursive and operates by distinguishing things from one another. Reason cannot grasp the One that has no other. We cannot rationalize our way into the mystical union. The ascent into the One is brought about by a leap the soul makes by acquiring a new faculty of cognition: intuition. Distinct from discursive reasoning, intuition does not distinguish, does not go from one thing to the next; it has an immediate grasp of being. It sees in a flashing glance that the transcendent is not on the other side of the immanent, not over there, up there, beyond the world, but shines through all things as the innermost structure of everything that is. For Plotinus, the goal of the philosophical life is ultimately contemplative. As one of

Plotinus's greatest modern commentators, Pierre Hadot, writes, the task is to "consent, with as much courage as Plotinus did, to every dimension of human experience, and to everything within it that is mysterious, inexpressible, and transcendent" (Hadot 1993, 113).

The Baptism of Neoplatonism

Neoplatonism was developed in a Christian key under the leadership of philosophically inclined theologians such as Origen and Augustine. This Church sanction is no doubt one of the reasons Neoplatonism survived the collapse of the Roman Empire while other Hellenistic philosophies did not. But there is more to it than that. Something about the revelation needed Neoplatonism to become fully articulate, and something about Neoplatonism needed the revelation if it was to become a universal religious philosophy. The foundational dogmas of Christianity—the doctrines of the Trinity and of the Incarnation—are originally expressed in Neoplatonic language. Every effort to free Christian doctrine from Neoplatonism, to express the dogmas otherwise, from Luther to Barth, has failed. This is because Neoplatonism was not simply grafted onto Christianity from outside. The Christian schools of Neoplatonism grew up alongside the pagan schools and were concurrent with them. No one has been able to disprove the traditional assumption that Plotinus and Origen were pupils of the same philosopher, Ammonias Saccas. There is reason to suppose that Plotinus's triadic thinking was as influenced by Christianity as Christianity was influenced by his doctrine of the one, the logos, and the soul. We deal here with a living, symbiotic relationship between pagan and Christian religious thinkers, intent on re-interpreting Plato in such as a way as to make his monotheism even more explicit than it is in his dialogues, and not with a philosophical neophyte Christian church struggling to accommodate itself to a more sophisticated pagan philosophical culture. That image, whether promoted by Barthians or philosophical skeptics, simply does not match the history.

In the Christian Neoplatonism of Saint Augustine (354–430), the fusion of Greek and Jewish attitudes to life, death, and what lies beyond them was brought to its first stage of completion. Other Christian authors prior to Augustine produced Christian versions of Neoplatonism, but none with nearly the success or influence of Augustine. Origen and Clement of Alexandria were preceded by Justyn Martyr, the first-century philosopher who believed that he had found the true philosophy in Christianity. A generation before him, the Jewish philosopher Philo proved that the Bible had nothing to fear from Greek philosophy; on the contrary, the latter needed the Bible even more than Jewish religion needed Plato. But in Augustine, the integration of the Hellenic and the Hebraic is so seamless that it can be difficult to distinguish them. Above all, it is in Augustine's personality, vividly analyzed in his *Confessions,* that the synthesis of Greek and Jewish culture is most visible. To understand why he was, as a young philosopher, incapable of bringing about the *reditus* and contemplatively resting in God, Augustine scrutinizes his obsessive-compulsive personality and speaks with great frankness of his addictive tendencies, to sex, to the praise of others, even to the gore of the Colosseum where he and his friends enjoyed the spectacle of watching prisoners being torn to pieces by wild animals. His mind might have been reaching towards the One. But his will was directed otherwise, and not simply because it suffered from mistaken judgments. The will in Augustine is independent of the intellect in a deeply Hebraic sense.

Augustine was a well-off, educated Roman citizen living a century after Plotinus in what is now North Africa. His mother was a Christian and his father a pagan. They could not agree to baptize him. They wanted Augustine to be well-educated, so they sent him to a good school where he quickly proved himself adept in the classical fields of arithmetic, geometry, music, and astronomy (the so-called *Quadrivium* of the seven liberal arts of ancient and medieval education), and in grammar, logic, and rhetoric (the *Trivium*). Augustine chose to specialize in rhetoric, which we might think of as the equivalent to the study of public relations. He had access to all of the luxuries and privileges that were available to a wealthy citizen of the Roman Empire. The *Confessions* are laced with references to racy episodes in Augustine's youth that he remembers with great sorrow and compunction. But Augustine was only doing what all pagans thought a young Roman ought to do, as Augustine's father used to point out to his mother, who took a more critical view of her son's hedonistic lifestyle.

The Neoplatonic emphasis on the return to the One through the progressive simplification of love is central to Augustine's thinking. Christ came, according to Augustine, to help us achieve what the philosophers describe as the goal of life. Plotinus counseled that the soul that is first awakened to its love of beauty by the things of this world ought to practice detachment in order to cultivate an even greater passion and an even more intense love for a higher beauty that is not of this world. The *Confessions*, then, is Augustine's recounting of his education in love. Through the influence of Neoplatonism, Augustine comes to see that all of his problems stem from misdirected desire. "The single desire that dominated my search for delight was simply to love and be loved" (Augustine 1991, 24). Augustine's heart is tangled up in the things of this world and incapable of extricating itself. It is not that creatures are not good or beautiful in their own way. But they are each of them limited and fall short of his heart's desire, which is nothing less than God.

Plotinus's dedication to the One is intellectual. Augustine's devotion to God is *personal*. Augustine makes generous use of

Neoplatonic metaphysics in order to understand the nature of being and the relationship of God to creation. But Plotinus never dreams of praying to the One or of confessing his sins to it. Such an activity makes no sense in pagan Neoplatonism because Plotinus's One is not a person. The One is above the personal, free of all duality, including the duality of I and thou that is the heart of personal relations. Augustine's God, however infinite, is most emphatically a person, the Father of Jesus Christ and the beneficent Creator of heaven and earth. That God has a mind and a will means that the love of God is not one-way. Augustine comes to understand that God loved him long before he learned to love God. Even more emphatically, Augustine concludes that the love he feels for God is an *effect* of God's love for him. He can only search for God because God is already searching for him.

On the basis of the Hebrew account of the Fall of Adam and Eve, interpreted through the New Testament, especially Paul's letters to the Romans and the Galatians, Augustine claims, against Plotinus's more optimistic anthropology, that there is something intrinsically flawed about the soul in its present state: it no longer enjoys a living experience of its Creator. If God is indeed everywhere—and how could it be otherwise—it must be the soul that cannot see Him. Attend, therefore, to your desires, Augustine advises, because they directly affect your perception. Attend to your personality and what makes it tick. Care for your soul so that you can become capable of seeing the God who is everywhere. This much is in line with pagan Neoplatonism. Augustine's experience of his own powerlessness to turn back to God, however, is emphatically Hebraic. "Give me chastity," he famously prays, "but not yet" (Augustine 1991, 145). He has a dramatically divided soul: his mind wants God, but his heart wants his mistress. He longs to turn away from his hedonism and sin, yet finds himself repeatedly doing the opposite. The descriptions of his anguish are among the most vivid accounts of addiction ever written. The experience of moral impotence convinces Augustine that the solution cannot be found in philosophy. Without grace, the human is doomed. The philosophers see the good from a great distance, he concludes, but have no clue how to reach it.

Augustine's experience of moral impotence compels him to look into the Bible, much to his mother's delight. There he reads that we are fallen beings and incapable of helping ourselves. God, out of compassion for his wayward creature, has come to meet us where we are and bring us to eternal life. The soul is responsible for its sorry state of emotional disorder. Created free, which means with the capacity for good and evil, the first humans decided against the good, and the consequences of that choice have affected the whole universe. The human being is endowed with a godlike capacity to choose. We might not be able to create being, but we can change it. This, Augustine theorizes (while meditating deeply on the letters of Paul), is precisely what happened, and all of us now suffer the aftermath of original sin.

Notice the striking difference from the Greek tradition. It is not clear from Socrates and Plato whether anything is to be regarded as evil, nor is it clear whether the soul is truly free. Socrates argues that no one does wrong knowingly; wrongdoing is always a product of ignorance. The soul is determined by the good and is always seeking the good in all that it does. Wrongdoing arises from a confusion about what is best for us in any given situation. In his defense before the Athenian court, Socrates protests that a wrongdoer should be educated, not punished. The matter is conceived quite otherwise in the Hebrew Bible. "I have set before you life and death, blessings and curses. Now choose life, so that you and your children may live," says Yahweh (Deut. 30:199). The implication is clear: we are free to choose death over life should we wish to. God does not compel us to choose the good.

When Adam and Eve make the fateful choice to follow the serpent's advice over God's, they do not yet "know" the distinction between good and evil. It is only after the decision, after the eating of the forbidden fruit and the Fall, that their eyes are opened. But then, how can they be held responsible for the bad choice they made *prior* to their knowledge of the distinction between good and evil? Were they not like children, simply making a mistake in judgment because they were ignorant? The Bible implies otherwise. They are deemed culpable for their decision, which means they should have and could have obeyed and remained in paradise. Because they are guilty, God banishes them from the garden and condemns them to a life of hardship. The decision—the first human decision ever made, according to the myth—is an act of pure freedom that precipitates a corruption of character.

There is no easy answer to the question, why would God do that, tempt the two in this way? Why place them in a garden with a deceitful serpent and a tree of delicious fruit which they are forbidden to eat? God does not want Adam and Eve to be good because He made them that way. He does not want to predetermine their goodness. He wants them to be free choosers of goodness. Only the good that is freely chosen is to be regarded as moral. The good that is not freely chosen is not really good, at least not in the moral sense. There is no point in praising someone for something they do simply because they are made that way. We praise our dogs for fetching balls and coming when they are called, but we know that it is one thing to be a good dog, quite another to be a good man.

But here is the catch: for the good to be freely chosen, the chooser must have the possibility of not choosing it. The chooser must have the possibility of saying no to the good. This negation of the good is the core of the Hebraic concept of evil. To be free for Augustine means, first of all, to be free *from* the good so that we can in the end be free, genuinely free, *for* the good.

Augustine's concept of freedom is dramatized in an account of an incident from his youth, the famous pear-stealing scene (Augustine 1991, 29). He was out with his friends doing what boys do—wrecking things—when they broke into a walled garden where pears were ripening on a tree. The boys stole the pears, not to eat, but to smash them against the garden wall. What strikes Augustine about this seemingly trivial event, hardly so bad, is his and his friends' intentions in stealing the pears. They did not steal because they were hungry. That would have fit in nicely with the Socratic theory that evil is a confused quest for the good. They stole because they wanted to destroy something beautiful. They stole the pears simply because they could.

This story of childish theft illustrates the paradoxical and self-destructive nature of evil. For Augustine, the act of vandalism is not essentially different from Lucifer's rebellion against God or Adam and Eve's fateful theft of fruit from the tree of knowledge (after which the scene in the *Confessions* is deliberately modeled). The boys were also in effect saying to God, "I will not serve"—and in the same way, willing their own downfall. The sinful heart negates the good for no good reason and damages itself in doing so. Sin is always at root without positive motive—it does not try to achieve something but rather to destroy what has been or ought to be achieved. A free soul must be capable of resisting the temptation to chaotic acts of self-destructive spontaneity. It must pass through the crucible of the negative if it is to be free for the good. The pear scene from the *Confessions* is the classic expression of the Hebraic doctrine of freedom:

> I wanted to carry out an act of theft and did so, driven by no kind of need other than my inner lack of any sense of, or feeling for, justice... My desire was to enjoy not what I sought by stealing but merely the excitement of

> thieving and the doing of what was wrong. I became evil for no reason. I had no motive for my wickedness, except wickedness itself. It was foul and I loved it. I loved the self-destruction, I loved my fall... I was seeking not to gain anything by shameful means, but shame for its own sake. (Augustine 1991, 29)

The boy Augustine and his friends repeat in a mundane way the act of Lucifer leaping down from the firmament of heaven to his ruin. The highest angel decides to become the first devil not because he wanted something in a positive sense, some good thing he was lacking, for he lacked nothing, nor because he suffered from a misdirected love and a flawed sense of judgment. Lucifer fell because he chose to. He wanted to say No. He freely resisted the order of the universe and committed an absurd act, an act that has no reason, no why, no solid motive, for it could lead to no good thing. In every act of evil, whether Luciferian or childish, love destroys itself. It ceases to be a conduit of the good and becomes a vehicle of death.

Freedom in the Hebraic tradition is founded in a dark ground of being. It is unpredictable, spontaneous, capable of tearing down the whole universe—which it does in the Fall of Man as described in the Book of Genesis. But it is also the power that brings everything good into existence.

Augustine's concept of freedom and his doctrine of radical evil are inseparable from his theory of grace. The three concepts form a triad of interlocking concepts, each one presupposing the other. The main idea is that freedom has a history. The primordial decision for evil that changed the world cannot be revisited and the innocence we lost in the decision cannot be recovered, at least not by our efforts. After the Fall, we are in a state of sin; we are no longer free as we once were. Our freedom is fallen and damaged and we cannot correct the situation we have brought upon ourselves.

We cannot redeem ourselves. Augustine describes the fallen human as one bound in a chain, every link of which he has forged himself. When he began forging the chain, he was free not to do it, but by the time he finishes, he is caught in a trap of his own devising. Hence, we find ourselves, as Augustine did, constricted by sin and incapable of doing the right thing, even when we know clearly that it is the thing to do. Our only hope is grace. But grace does not mechanically determine anything. Rather, grace restores our freedom to its fully operational state. It does not impose something on us; it restores in us a power for goodness that was once natural to us.

Augustine's *Confessions* spoke directly to my own experience. By the time I was twenty-three, I was intellectually convinced by Plotinus's philosophy of unity. The Neoplatonic path was not in essence different from the way of the Brahmans of the Upanishads, the Vedanta of ancient India. At the heart of both was a distinction between appearance and reality, which struck me as eminently sensible. On the surface, we see difference, multiplicity, and change; we feel ourselves to be singular and distinct from all others and are compelled to assert ourselves against the world. In the depths, reality is one and changeless and there is no separation between us and others or between human beings and the divine. To find peace we need only to ween ourselves off appearance and develop a taste for reality. It is simply a matter of curbing the appetites and developing our higher, spiritual faculties. But who can pull this off? Who can raise themselves above their miserable ego-driven, craven, sensual self? I at any rate could not. All my efforts at self-perfection ended in failure and I remained the same desperate and obsessive hedonist I had always been. The Neoplatonic/Vedantic path was too optimistic about human potentiality; it underplayed the reality of evil and the depth of suffering in the world.

Augustine named the problem: I, like everyone else and the world itself, lie in the grip of sin. good and evil have a history and I am caught up in it. We lost the road long ago. There is no hope for the human alone. The good is not only beyond being; it is also beyond our natural reach.

The Jewish Difference

The Jews are, in their own understanding of themselves, the privileged recipients of God's self-revelation. They do not possess a philosophy of God; rather, they have a story to tell, the story of what God has revealed of Godself in their history. Revelation is not one element among many in their history; it is the foundation of the Jewish identity. Inspired by revelation, the ancient Jews thought differently than the Greeks about pretty much everything. They disagreed with the Greeks on the nature of the human being, on what the world is, and especially on the question of time. Where every other major ancient civilization, whether Egyptian, Greek, Roman, Chinese, or Indian, thought of time as a wheel, an eternally moving circle, the ancient Jews thought of time as eschatological. They thought of time as having a beginning and an end. The beginning never returns, and the end cannot be avoided. Time is always once only. It runs down inexorably until God declares the show over.

This idea is the most influential one to have emerged from the Hebrew Bible. Linear time renders human life a constant crisis. We have no time to waste. What we decide to do with ourselves and our world matters. The moment, as Kierkegaard put it, has "decisive significance" (Kierkegaard 1962: 34). It is no exaggeration to say that our Western civilization is scarcely conceivable without Hebraic, linear time. From it comes not only the anxiety of decision but also the hope, so ingrained in the Western mind, in a future that can be better than the past. This hope has been the cause of our greatest achievements (natural science, the abolition of slavery, declarations of human rights) and our greatest follies (the atrocities associated with utopian revolutions from France to Russia).[5]

Jews do not clearly distinguish sacred from profane time. Every moment of the day is sacred time. The most ordinary acts: washing, eating, and working, are accompanied by prayer.[6] The Christian monk immerses himself in this Jewish sense of consecrated time. Every morning and evening, the monk recites the psalms of King David. These are the prayers that the ancient Hebrews sang at the time of Christ in synagogues all over Galilee and Judaea and in the great temple in Jerusalem. Jesus himself sang them. At the start of the day, the monk prays, "O God, you are my God, for you I long, / for you my soul is thirsting. / My body pines for you / like a dry, weary land without water" (Ps 63). Before retiring, he prays the *Shema*, the most sacred prayer of the Jewish religion: "Hear O Israel! The Lord our God, the Lord is one."

Another key difference between Greek and Jewish religion, one essentially connected to the sense of linear time, is that the God of Israel is the one who has revealed Himself in history to be the only God, the God of the universe. Where Greek philosophers believed in a natural knowledge of divinity, a divine essence, accessible always and everywhere through the use of human reason, the Hebrews believed that no one could know God unless God first revealed Godself to them. Not unlike the human personality, which can only be known through speech and actions, expressed freely by the person without exhausting his and her character, Yahweh's nature is only visible in His speech and acts in history. The divine nature, in the ancient Jewish view, cannot be rationally deduced. Time—linear not cyclical—is His theater of revelation.

Because of the emphasis on historical revelation, Hebraic theology is committed to the concrete, the personal, and the singular. Jewish religiosity is replete with practical details concerning the proper attitude and use of material things and individual beings at different times of the year and different moments of the day. Where Greek thought leans towards monism, doubting the reality of the temporal world, there is nothing in the Bible that would suggest that this world is illusory. For the ancient Jews, the world is precisely where we work out our salvation, the arena in which the drama of sin and redemption unfolds.

The Jews recount the story of their history every year at the celebration of the Passover to remind themselves of who they are. History begins with creation and passes through pivotal moments in which God reveals Godself—Abraham, Moses, and the Exodus, culminating in the time of the Kings and the prophets of the Second Temple period. History will end when God intervenes to set right the injustices of humankind (Jews included) in an apocalypse that is vividly described in the books of Daniel and Enoch.

A people shaped by such a story could not think of time as circular, even if every other culture around them did so. The ancient Hebrews invented what the Canadian philosopher George Grant calls "time as history" (Grant 1995). By "history" Grant does not mean the record of things that have happened or the study of the rise and fall of kingdoms and nations. All peoples, in one way or another, have attended to history in this sense. The meaning of history that is peculiarly Jewish and that shapes the Western understanding of time concerns the sense of how time moves. Time does not simply return to what existed previously but is continually interrupted by new events that change everything and bring about the unforeseen and unforeseeable.

The Jewish sense of time is the logical consequence of the belief in divine revelation. History must be real since God is revealed in it. And it must be uni-directional since God was not always revealed. God's revelation is of a promised time to come, a time of justice that has never been before. Since history rather than nature is the theater of divine revelation, Hebraic theology is bound up with a sense of the unrepeatability and singularity of temporal life.

This thinking about time still permeates Western political and metaphysical thought, even in its atheistic and materialistic modes. Think only of the scientific story we tell our children of time as a linear sequence from an unrepeatable beginning (the Big Bang), through a series of unprecedented events (the evolution of life on earth), to an unavoidable end (heat death). Think of the Enlightenment's myth of progress, or Marx's notion of the dialectic of history, which leads inevitably from capitalism through revolution to the communist utopia. Think of the basic presupposition that permeates the self-understanding of the modern university, the seemingly common-sense assumption that human knowledge increases over time, from premodern ignorance to greater and greater knowledge of nature. None of these attitudes would be possible without the Hebrew notion of time as history.

The path of transmission of the Jewish notion of time from the Hebrew Bible to the modern West had to pass first through Christianity, and Christianity in a bewildering variety of forms before it could overturn the ancient paradigm. The first Christians were not content to shelter the revelation granted to them; they had to tell the whole world about it. Although the God of the Jews is the God of all people, ancient Judaism was not, in general, a universalizing religion. But the Jesus movement most emphatically was. One of the things that irritated pious Jews about Jesus was his insistence on including Gentiles in the redemption promised to Abraham. Paul transposes Jesus's universalism into missionary work. It was a huge success: within three hundred years of the death of Christ, Christianity became the official religion of the Roman Empire.

The early Christians are instructed by Paul to live as though "the day of the Lord" would come at any moment, like a "thief in the night" (1 Thess. 5:2). Other sects within Judaism had emphasized the apocalypse but none so persistently and dramatically as this new breakaway group. There was no point getting married or making plans since the end was imminent, Paul writes (1 Cor. 7: 29–35). He admonishes his disciples not to count the minutes or to calculatedly *expect* the end (a way of avoiding the anxiety of the call). They were to live in perpetual readiness and keep vigil in a state of mind Heidegger calls (drawing on Paul) "resolute anticipation" (Heidegger 1962: 357). This living toward the irreversible future changes the experience of the present. The now is experienced not as the reappearance of the same but as a singular and unrepeatable event, the moment of decisive significance, the moment in which the duty of the Christian could not be postponed. Live as though you are already dead, Paul says, as though the Lord were here, now, before you.

The end of the world did not come as quickly as the early Christians believed it would and eschatology was deferred. Paul's point that the chief thing in eschatological religion is not knowledge of the day and the hour but the attitude of the believer was actually supported by the early Christian disappointment that the return of Christ did not happen as expected in the lifetime of the first generation of disciples. Now resolute anticipation of the imminent end became a philosophy of life. After his conversion at the battle of Milvian Bridge in AD 312, the Emperor Constantine institutionalized the Church, which prior to him was a loose network of house churches and made the Jewish-Christian sense for time normative. Medieval Christianity, the heir of Constantinian Christianity, created a new culture of art and architecture, philosophy, and symbol that engraved the Jewish-Christian attitude to time into stone. Through the rise and fall of Christendom, this unique conception of time sank roots deep into the collective imaginary of Europe.

The medieval peasant might not have been able to read, but he had keen eyesight and the brilliant kaleidoscope of images on the stained glass of the cathedrals was for his edification. The medieval cathedral is an architectural picture book illustrating the story of Hebraic/Christian time: creation, Fall, and redemption rushing inexorably to the Last Judgment. Without Christendom, I am convinced, there would have been no sense of progress, no modern science, no capitalism, and no age of revolution, because there would have been no resolve to change the present on the assumption that the future could be different than the past.

It is not difficult to connect this biblical sense of time to the consumer craving for novelty, to be discussed in the next chapter. But the Bible hardly condones the cult of consumption. On the contrary, Hebraic and early Christian theology is also the source of the Western sense, so imperiled in our day, for the goodness of creation, the goodness of *matter*, the goodness of the *particular* and *concrete*. The Greeks tended either to worship matter as a god or to demonize it. They either spurned matter as so much illusion or invested it with diabolical power. The Jews could neither worship matter as divine nor disdain it as a deception for it is in a strict sense of the word *created*. It is finite and temporal, as we are. Nothing of the hatred of the body so typical of many ancient religious philosophies touched the Hebrews. The world, created by a benevolent God, is unquestionably good, and if it is fraught with suffering and pain, that is not God's fault. Judaism is a religion of *this* world. It emphasizes the sacredness of human bodily existence, the holiness of hearth and home, and the goodness of family, food, and work. Most Jews do not practice or praise celibacy (there are exceptions). The ancient Hebrews assumed that sex was natural to us and as such good, even holy. Plotinus, on the other hand, was reported to have been "ashamed of being in the body" (Plotinus, 1962, 1).

Christianity started with an equally healthy affirmation of the body and a commitment to justice on the earth. But over the course of centuries, a Greek other-worldliness crept in, propagating the widespread Christian confusion that our proper home is in heaven. It is not. Heaven is God's home; He made the earth for us. We are, according to Paul, essentially embodied. The Kingdom of God is not in heaven; it is the future of the earth (1 Cor. 15).

Consider the early Christian doctrine of the general resurrection, which the Christians adopted from the Jews. The Jews were divided on whether or not the body would be resurrected. One group believed it would be, while another thought not. But neither group spoke of a heaven that freed us from the body. For the Jews who believed in resurrection, the coming Kingdom was a perfected material order with a body free of sickness, age, and death. For the other group, the Jews that denied the resurrection, the affirmation of the goodness of matter was even more emphatic. This main current of ancient Judaism did not believe in the afterlife and yet, amazingly, did not fall into the nihilism that is most often associated with the denial of immortality. Beatitude is to be found here on earth or nowhere. The happiness that God granted Abraham meant a long life, wealth, and many descendants.

Early Christianity was convinced that the first generation of believers had seen Christ resurrected. Far from entailing the denigration of life in time, resurrection is the decisive affirmation of it. As Mary Magdalene and the apostles realize, the resurrected body is *this* body transformed, this body with its history, healed of flaws and wounds but still bearing the scars (Jn. 20:11–18; Jn. 20:24–31). Whatever we might think about the plausibility of it, there would have been no Christianity without the belief. The first Christians were ready to die for it. The resurrected Jesus in the Gospels does not promise us a life in heaven after death; he promises us a resurrected body at the end of time on a new earth (1 Cor. 15; Rev. 21; 2 Pet. 3: 10–18).[7]

If the Greeks gave us the philosophy of contemplation, the Jews gave us the theology of action. The one stresses timeless, intellectual enjoyment of the divine essence, the other, the divine imperative for justice. The synthesis of these opposites is, to this day, the secret of the persistence of the Catholic system. The deconstruction of the synthesis was the work of the Lutheran Reformation. Insofar as the decline of Protestantism was the cause for the rise of liberal capitalism and consumerism, the restoration of a proper relation between the Greek mind and the Jewish heart of the West could be the key to the ecological transformation of our civilization. But there is no going back to Christendom: the recovery of the synthesis will have to be something new, a form of religion that has never been and a way of being secular that is fundamentally different than the decadent and now collapsed secular humanism that began with eighteenth-century European unbelief.

Protestant Postscript

I discovered the power and legitimacy of Protestantism when I was a graduate student of theology at the University of Toronto. Protestant theology, especially the Germans, Luther, Schleiermacher, and Barth, showed me the problems with the influence of the Greek philosophy on theology, especially, the problem of human self-reliance, whether it be in rationally venturing knowledge of God, in moral life, or in the search for mystical union with the One. No amount of effort, virtue, or practice can close the gap between sinful humanity and divinity, Luther argues, and after my experience in the monastery, I could not but agree. We are saved by "grace alone."

After spending most of his early life as an Augustinian monk, Luther discovered that monastic discipline could not assuage his guilty conscience or help him live by the high moral standards of the Gospels. He was sodden with sin and could not cleanse himself. Even if he made some progress one day, he was sure to relapse the next. The experience of moral impotence filled Luther with despair until he concluded that Jesus was not calling him to monastic perfection, nor was anyone so called. Jesus offered himself as a sacrifice for the sin of the world precisely because we cannot redeem or save ourselves. We cannot better ourselves or lift ourselves out of the dire situation into which we have fallen. The very effort of trying to improve oneself without total reliance on the help of God is for Luther an act of unbelief, tantamount to saying to God, *I don't need your grace, thank you very much. I can do this without you.*

On the basis of this theology of grace, Luther formulates a devastating critique of monasticism, which targets both the Pelagianism within the clergy (naive human self-confidence and self-reliance, named after the fourth-century British heretic Pelagius), and the other side of the matter, the neglected responsibilities of ordinary Christians to personally respond to the universal offer of grace. By outsourcing perfection to a separate class of elite priests, monks, and nuns, the medieval Church absolved ordinary people of the call to discipleship. This critique is still a mainstay of Protestant theology. "In the Gospel, the very first step a man must take is an act which radically affects his whole existence. The Roman Catholic Church demanded this step as an extraordinary possibility which only monks could achieve, while the rest of the faithful must content themselves with an unconditional submission to the Church and its ordinances" (Bonhoeffer 1959, 5).

The false Gospel of self-effort was a pagan infiltration, rooted in Stoicism, Neoplatonism, and Hellenistic humanism. The Reformation Luther initiated sought to purge medieval Christianity of this pagan element, in effect, tearing the Jewish and Greek elements of the Western tradition apart and throwing philosophy out as the work of heathen unbelief. At first, I was astonished by what I read. It was not the theology I had been taught in the monastery. But after my initial enthusiasm for Luther, I concluded that we can no more undo Christian Neoplatonism than we can the Reformation. Even Luther retains certain Neoplatonic elements in his theology, for example, the medieval doctrine of the unknowability of the divine essence (which he calls the *Deus absconditus*), or his devotion to the *Theologia Deutsch,* a fourteenth-century German mystical treatise influenced by Eckhart. Christianity is intrinsically historical and to try to repristinate it is to disfigure it. While Luther's emphasis on grace and the vocation of the ordinary Christian cut me to the core, I never ceased to believe that the Greek element is as essential to Christianity as the Jewish. When it works, the two opposites make up for what is lacking in the other and correct their excesses. The Jewish side of Christianity corrects the other-worldliness of the Greek; the Greek side of Christianity corrects the materialism and uncontemplative pragmatism of Judaism. Any effort to purge Christianity of the Greek element is doomed to fail. We end up with something far worse than paganism. We end up with irreligious secularism.

It is well known that Luther's Reformation set the stage for modernity.[8] His emphasis on the individual, on lay vocations, and his demolition of clerical hierarchy were crucial to the rise of modern secularism.[8] But we must resist the temptation to turn Luther into the villain who destroyed Christendom and secularized the world. His theology is an essential corrective to certain excesses and confusions in medieval Catholicism and much of it has been accepted by most major Catholic theologians. Luther's primary concern was for the Church and for the integrity of the Christian witness. What he has done is irreversible. Contemporary Catholicism, born of the counter-Reformation, has been decisively determined by Luther, much to its benefit.

I wish I could conclude this chapter with a helpful organization of the history of Western religion into a neat Hegelian story of dialectical progress. I wish I could tell a story of how the Greco-Jewish synthesis that produced the West invited its own negation in Protestantism which produces modernity. If I could, I would say that we await the inevitable negation of the negation, the religious secularism that will restore the synthesis but in a modern key, with the Protestant elements canceled and preserved. Unfortunately, the matter is far less logical than such schemes suggest. I am a Schellingian on these matters and refuse to collapse existence into essence.[9] Logic and reality do not neatly align. History is a story of things that need not have happened. The future in part depends on what we will do now, not on the unfolding of an implicit logic of history. The best we can do is save what we can from a past worth preserving, bid adieu to all of that which no one in their right mind wants back, and try to foster the fragile and often hidden shoots of the new forms of life emerging from the devastated landscape.

But I will say this. The past is never gone. It withdraws into hiddenness, and from that hidden place, it supports and makes possible the present and the future. The past is the ground we stand on. We cannot import solutions to our present problems from other cultures. We must look more closely into the past of our troubled society to find clues to what we need to go forward.

Endnotes

1. For a plausible reconstruction of what Jesus believed, see Sanders (1993). The tension between Jewish voluntarism and Greek cosmology is crucial to understanding the paradoxical beliefs of the West. On the one hand, we are willing to die to protect the freedom of the individual; on the other hand, our natural science is based on the assumption that everything, including the individual's actions, is determined by natural laws. As the contemporary

French philosopher Alain Badiou puts it, the opposition at the heart of the West is between Jewish prophetism, with its presupposition of divine revelation, and Greek philosophical wisdom, with its presupposition of an ordered and self-explanatory cosmos. See Badiou (2003: 41–42): "What is Jewish discourse? The subjective figure constituted by it is that of the prophet. But a prophet is one who abides in the requisition of signs, one who signals, testifying to transcendence by exposing the obscure to its deciphering. Thus, Jewish discourse will be held to be, above all, the discourse of the sign. What then is Greek discourse? The subjective figure constituted by it is that of the wise man. But wisdom consists in appropriating the fixed order of the world, in the matching of the logos to being. Greek discourse is cosmic, deploying the subject within the reason of a natural totality. Greek discourse is essentially the discourse of totality, insofar as it upholds the *sophia* (wisdom as internal state) of a knowledge of *phusis* (nature as ordered and accomplished deployment of being). Jewish discourse is a discourse of exception, because the prophetic sign, the miracle, election, designate transcendence as that which lies beyond the natural totality. The Jewish nation itself is at once sign, miracle, and election. It is constitutively exceptional. Greek discourse bases itself on the cosmic order so as to adjust itself to it, while Jewish discourse bases itself on the exception to this order so as to turn divine transcendence into a sign."

2. Devotees of Dionysus, sometimes depicted as the god of wine, but also the god of all ecstatic states, psychotropical, sexual, religious, etc., would run naked through the woods, high on mushrooms, singing and beating drums through the night. Dionysus liberated them from everyday common sense, domesticity, and rationality.

3. The concept of the person was fully worked out in Christian theology in the context of defining the doctrine of the Trinity in the first three centuries of the Church. See Balthasar (1986). The Church Fathers were deeply indebted to the Hebrew Bible, to which they were more devoted than they were to Greek philosophy. They carried forward into dogmatic theology the Jewish emphasis on the dignity of the human individual and its special, direct relationship to the personal God. The implications of Jewish personalism for our understanding of ethics, politics, and the concept of time as history cannot be overestimated. For a modern Jewish philosophy of the person, see Buber (1958). On the political ramifications of Jewish personalism for liberal democracy, see Berman (2008). For a popular treatment of this whole theme, see Cahill (1998).
4. On the influence of Neoplatonism on early modern science, see Cassirer (1963).
5. On the politics of eschatological time, see McGrath (2023).
6. "The most striking point about Jewish law is that it brings the entirety of life, including civil and domestic practices, under the authority of God ... 'Religion' in Judaism was not only festivals and sacrifices, as it was in most of the Greco-Roman world, but rather encompassed all of life. 'Religion governs all our actions and occupations and speech; none of these things did our lawgiver leave unexamined or indeterminate' (Josephus, *Apion* 2. 171)" (Sanders 1993: 37).
7. On these matters see Sanders (1993) and Wright (2003).
8. On the roots of modernity in Protestantism see Weber (1958); Gillespie (2009); and Taylor (2007).
9. The late Schelling constructed a philosophy of history that in some ways aligned with that of his contemporary Hegel, but with a crucial twist. Both Schelling and Hegel

see modernity as the culmination of Christian history. But where Hegel believes this history is necessary, a logical unfolding of a rational pattern, which he calls "the notion" or "the idea," Schelling argues that history is contingent: a series of accidents and free choices of human beings. This leads to strikingly different conclusions: where Hegel affirms modernity as inevitable and right, Schelling argues that we could have modernized differently. For Hegel, nothing genuinely new is to be expected from the future, and history is in a sense over. For Schelling, Christianity is still evolving. What was promised is far better than what has been achieved. We are still waiting for the Kingdom. On these matters see McGrath (2021).

"The modern world is full of the old Christian virtues gone mad."

G.K. Chesterton

Chapter Five

The Decline of Christendom

Liberal democracy, that signature achievement of Western civilization, is collapsing everywhere, especially in the United States; it no longer even believes in itself. Unmoored from its philosophical and theological foundations, liberal democracy now floats free of its history and appears increasingly both to its opponents and its defenders to be built of nothing more than myths. Freedom, equality, the rules-based political order—all the signs of the times indicate that the West has no interest in these foundational liberal democratic concepts. Trumpism indicates that sooner or later, our failing democracies will give way to authoritarianism, as they have before. Populism, so destructive in an era of global crises that can only be solved with international cooperation (pandemic, climate change, nuclear threats), is now present in virtually every democracy. Populism is based on a rejection of the core value of liberalism: political tolerance. The populist comes to power by demonizing those who do not support him and representing his base while suppressing the rest. Parliamentary debate becomes a rhetorical exercise in consolidating the divisions in the populace. The old liberal ideal of achieving a compromise between opposed positions through argument and debate is dead.

The COVID-19 pandemic made it painfully clear that the world cannot agree on concerted international action, even when it is plainly in its best interest. In the face of overwhelming scientific evidence that their own triply vaccinated populations would not be safe while the virus is permitted to run rampant and mutate through the developing world, the West hoarded vaccines while Africa piled up their dead, and the virus evolved into new vaccine-resistant strains. Ten years on, climate change action is far behind the pledges made at the 2015 Paris Accord, with the West, historically the guiltiest emitter, refusing to make the rudimentary changes to its economies essential for getting through this century without a complete ecological collapse. The left and the right in Western democracies are now so divided that they appear to be living in different universes. They watch different news. They believe in different sets of facts. The one thing they both agree on is that the other side feeds on fake news and is morally incompetent, corrupt, and not worth talking to.

Meanwhile, the consumer-capitalist machine runs strong and apparently will only stop when the abused environment can no longer support it, which, if the most pessimistic climatologists are to be believed, will be sometime around the end of the century.

The soul of the West is indeed lost if it is even still alive. I think it *is* alive, but it's clearly unwell. Western religion did not simply disappear in the last century: rather, it secularized badly and became twisted into a reversal of itself. In its perverse form, Western religion continues to exert a mostly bad influence on the world. The process is largely unconscious. Most Westerners would deny that their secular values have anything to do with historical Christianity. Freud tells us that the return of the repressed is rarely pleasant and life-giving. The Christian unconscious is wreaking havoc on the world.

If a spiritual way of looking at life as a *theophany,*[1] as an ongoing and progressive revelation of divinity, is a common heritage of European Judaism, Christianity, and medieval Islam, what happened to it? How did we get from there to the present moment when consumer capitalism appears to have vanquished all other systems of values and remains the one pursuit we can all agree on, even as ecology shows us that it is unsustainable? Why are we dedicated to a form of life that is manifestly at the expense of the health of the planet itself?

Equally distressing is the next question. How did the Christian belief in human dignity give rise to a society that openly promotes new forms of hierarchy and new forms of slavery? The one percent who own more than all the rest combined are the heirs of medieval Christendom. By benefitting from finance capitalism (making money off of money) and the right to charge interest on loans (the sin of usury which was outlawed in the Bible and re-introduced in the Middle Ages by the Roman Catholic Medici[2]), the one percent is a product of certain values firmly rooted in Christendom: the freedom of the individual, the dedication to profit, the reverence for industry and wealth production. On the other side of the planet, a third-world slave labor force, which makes possible the cheap consumer goods that the "developed world" gluts itself on, is paradoxically maintained by the same ideological commitment to the freedom of the individual. According to this creed, I can pursue and possess whatever it is I desire precisely because I am created free. These others are not denied that freedom, so the triumphant neoliberal narrative goes. They are either suffering under tyrannical forms of government which are resisting the leveling flow of capital, or they are getting what they deserve, in either case proving the superiority of the capitalist system. Even the progressives are implicated in this lie. Insofar as Westerners continue to believe that they are entitled to their first-world consumer lifestyle, they implicitly assert that others *deserve* their position at the bottom.

Here is the terrible problem at the heart of the issue: Christianity is not only the source of the wisdom of the West, but it is also at the root of our moral decline. It is not only the inspiration of Western art and philosophy; it is also the cause of social injustice and ecological ruin.

In a seminal article published in the prestigious journal *Science* in 1967, the historian Lynn White Jr. argues that Western Christian attitudes concerning human exceptionalism and the divine right to dominate and use nature as we wish are at the core of the environmental crisis facing us today (White Jr 1967). His argument has been frequently debated since then but never refuted (LeVasseur 2017). Presuppositions that originate in Christian theology, such as the progress of history, the human vocation to dominate and subdue the earth, and above all, the notion of individual freedom, White claims, made possible the scientific and industrial revolutions that led to the technological society and the destruction of natural environments. These same values, even more disavowed than they were fifty years ago, are driving consumer capitalism.

It is crucial to understanding White Jr's argument and much of what I have to say in this chapter that we distinguish Christianity from Christendom. Christianity is a religious philosophy of universal salvation that originated in Jewish-Hellenism and spread among the poorer classes in urban centers of the Roman Empire. Christendom is a form of Christian civilization based on the institutionalization of much of what was left undefined by the early Christians: the relationship of church and state, the care for the sick and the poor, and the state's involvement in spreading the Gospel. With Christendom comes the separation of church and state, the legal defense of equality, the codification of freedom of conscience, property rights, freedom of economic exchange, and the state's duty to expand and disseminate literacy and social-political norms across the globe—the foundations of liberalism. Christianity preceded Christendom and its bastard child, liberalism. There is every reason to assume it will survive it.

The Theological Roots of Ecological Ruin

White's thesis builds on Max Weber's early twentieth-century work on the sociology of religion. Weber exposes the religious roots of the modern economy. Capitalism, in particular, Weber maintains, is deeply connected to the psychology peculiar to

Protestant Christianity (Weber 1958). To understand his point, we need to understand that capitalism is not simply dedicated to the accumulation of wealth; it is primarily committed to *profit*, which is not the same thing as the accumulation of wealth. I may be wealthy, but if my wealth is not producing wealth, if it is buried in a box under my bed, then I can hardly be described as a good capitalist. Capitalism is the use of money to make money. Weber moves from this rudimentary point to the controversial claim that the capitalist dedication to profit is a special kind of economic attitude that is motivated by a specific form of Christian psychology.

Let's reconstruct his argument. Weber argues that the capitalist must constantly work if he is to continue to produce a profit. Leisure costs money. Early capitalism is anything but lazy and self-indulgent. On the contrary, it is the most energetic and diligent economic system history has ever seen. This is because the capitalist must deny himself the enjoyment of the fruits of his labor. The point of profit production is to save and accumulate, not to spend and enjoy. The psychology of the early capitalist, at once dedicated to the accumulation of wealth and ascetic with regard to its enjoyment, presupposes the peculiar view of life unique to Protestant Christianity.

Protestantism produces capitalists because of certain basic theological innovations. Unlike their Catholic forefathers, the Protestant believes in "the priesthood of all believers": everyone is called to the moral perfection of the saints. Moreover, the place to pursue this perfection is not a monastery or cloister but the world. With the Protestant Reformation, the talent and industry that was cloistered in monasteries in the Middle Ages were set loose on the secular world. Rather than renouncing the world, Protestants set to work building it. Since only some are predestined by God to be granted the grace that will deliver them from ingrained sin (according to the Calvinist doctrine of election), Protestants are doomed to live with chronic anxiety, never knowing for certain whether they are counted among the elect. But this anxiety should not produce apathy. On the contrary, the only thing for the Protestant to do is to act as if he is saved and hope to God it's true. The chosen are generous servants of the Lord, not lazy or self-indulgent. If he can never know for sure whether he is saved, he should nevertheless work tirelessly towards the production of profit and the amelioration of the human condition, for that is what God commands.

It is only with such a religious attitude to life, Weber concludes, that the wealth that made technocratic modernity possible could be produced. The capitalism Weber has in mind is old-school "mercantile" capitalism; the factory owner who gets rich by owning the means of production and capitalizing on what Marx called "the surplus value" of his laborers. It has been pointed out that finance capitalism is a different beast altogether (Tanner 2019). Where the merchant earned money through the labor of others, the finance capitalist earns money by exploiting the ebb and flow of capital in the system. The most successful finance capitalists, the banks, credit card companies, and mortgage brokers, neither produce anything nor own the means to produce anything. And yet they earn unimaginable profits simply by moving capital around. Nevertheless, the point remains that capitalism, both early and late, originates in a specific religious-ethical context, and these religious and ethical presuppositions, however perverted, persist and sustain it. The human being is a religious animal, and some form of divinity, in this case the god of profit, will be worshiped.[3]

On the basis of Weber and White and the now fairly uncontroversial connection between capitalism and environmental degradation, it would seem obvious to conclude that the only hope for the world is to root out the last vestiges of Christianity from the modern mind, to find a new way forward that affirms the earth instead of planning for the Kingdom of

God, that builds communities instead of indulging in the fantasy of individual autonomy, and that dedicates itself to humanity instead of dreaming about divinity.

Rather than deny the connections between Christianity, capitalism, and ecological ruin, I think we should think more deeply about them. I certainly do not mean that we should promote Christian consumerism. But neither do I think we should naively assume that we can quickly and easily transcend consumerism. It has us in its grips because it touches us, at least those of us with a Western cultural heritage, in the depths of our souls. Consumerism appeals to our deepest and most hard-won values, to our sense of individual freedom, possibility, transcendence, openness, and love. Like the Anti-Christ in the Book of Revelation, consumerism seduces us through what is best in us. Instead of prescribing a break with Christian attitudes as the solution to the environmental crisis caused by consumerism, I argue for going more deeply into these attitudes to find in the poison that's killing us the medicine that can save us.

Consumerism is not a form of materialism or a denial of the spirit. It is rather a peculiar kind of spirituality. What is it that we shop for? If it were simply the necessities of life—food, clothes, and shelter—then the whole economic system would break down. We would stop shopping when we had what we needed, and the economic growth which everyone in the developed world depends upon would grind to a halt. While the ecological advocates of a steady-state economy think zero growth is good, most economists think it would be very bad. The ever-growing economy, so the argument goes, produces the wealth necessary for raising standards of living, maintaining social security systems, alleviating poverty, and driving technological innovation. Consumer capitalism not only presupposes but *requires* consumers to purchase things beyond their basic needs.

In a breakthrough work on the psychology of consumerism, which builds on Weber's thesis, the sociologist Colin Campbell claims that consumers are hardcore individualists at bottom, dedicated to self-maximization but with a specific conception of the self in mind (Campbell 1987). The consumer self is free to create and re-create himself at will. He is not determined by his past, his ethnic and religious heritage, or his social and economic position in society. The consumer stands before an open future of possibilities from which he can freely choose in an apparently unlimited and endless project of self-making. He has at his disposal whatever material resources he can legally possess.

The notion of freedom at the heart of consumerism is not universal in the history of ideas. Consumer values are as foreign to the non-Christian ancient world as they are to traditional Indian, Chinese, Japanese and Indigenous cultures. They are founded upon Christian ways of conceiving human beings. Consumerism is a Christian aberration, a monster incubated in Christendom, set loose in the twentieth century, and now literally devouring the whole world. To be clear on this crucial point, what is at work in consumerism is a *distortion* of Christian ideas. But this does not change the fact that they are Christian ideas being distorted, not, say, Hindu or Chinese ideas.

To defend this claim, we need to consider how the Bible broke with all ancient systems of ethics, which shared a common cosmocentric assumption. The ancients lived in what philosophers call a "normative" cosmos, a universe of meaning. Knowing what to do was a matter of following nature, whether it was called the *Stoa*, the *Logos*, the *Tao*, or the *Dharma*. Human beings have a limited capacity for self-determination in ancient thought: their actions can be better or worse, more or less in accord with the law of nature. But they do not create values, as moderns do. Nor do they author themselves, as the philosopher Kant insists we do and as most lifestyle advertisers tell us we can. By conceiving the individual as free and the universe as unfinished, a creation that, as St. Paul puts it, groans as in childbirth (Rom. 8:22–24), the Bible introduced a new conception of nature and the purpose of human life on earth. Whatever else Paul meant by this expression, he does not think of creation as Plato and Aristotle thought of it, as a stable and complete reality embodying eternal and unchanging forms. Paul thinks of creation as not only always changing (Plato might agree on that) but as struggling to give birth to something that has never before existed. In this emergent universe, the individual is born with the vocation of deciding for themselves who they will be. Whereas most ancient peoples conceived of time as cyclical, bringing about an ever-recurring manifestation of stable or eternal forms, the Christian, committed to the freedom of the individual, thinks of time as beginning with an act of divine creation and left open, a world not yet complete and left for us to finish.[4]

These paired ideas of an unfinished universe and human freedom are really two aspects of one idea, which we shall call the strong notion of freedom. Freedom is not merely the freedom to choose from a pre-determined set of options; it is rather the capacity to determine oneself completely, that is, to create that which has never been: yourself. Such individual spontaneity and autonomy are only possible in an unfinished or emergent universe, since if the universe was finished and no longer expanding and producing new forms, we would not be free to create ourselves. It is not exactly to the point here to argue whether such freedom exists. Rather the point is that it is *this* notion of freedom and no other which launches modernity. The unfinished universe is also the universe that evolves, which is the assumption of modern science. Darwin's concept of nature emerges into being not by returning to the eternal and archetypal forms of things but by producing endless novelty.

Without us, that is, without freedom, such a universe would be emerging for no one and into nothing. Thus, the complete idea of human freedom is the idea of an individual who can author himself and so *make history* in an emergent universe, that is, in an evolving cosmos in which the ends of things are not already decided.

The strong notion of freedom, either vaguely defended, as in the American constitution, or precisely defined as in the moral philosophy of Kant, is the basic presupposition of our age.[5] While the strong notion of freedom is at the very root of the sickness that is killing us, I have no interest in advocating any view of the world that would seek to deny it. Others, such as the deep ecologist Arne Naess have taken this route (Naess 1977). The human, he argues, is not special, and its numbers should be reduced to what the biosphere can manage, just as we should limit the populations of any environmentally destructive species. Such an environmental ethic is doomed to fail. An ecology that has nothing to offer the great majority of human beings, who are interested in living and flourishing, is hardly going to galvanize political will. No wonder that, after over three decades, deep ecology has had little effect on environmental politics. Indeed, protecting the strong notion of freedom, making it explicit and coherent, might be our best shot toward producing an ecological civilization. If the future cannot be qualitatively different from the past and we can have no significant moral influence on the direction of history, there is no hope.

In the 1967 article White Jr. writes, "Both our present science and our present technology are so tinctured with orthodox Christian arrogance toward nature that no solution for our ecologic crisis can be expected from them alone. Since the roots of our trouble are so largely religious, the remedy must also be essentially religious, whether we call it that or not.

We must rethink and re-feel our nature and destiny" (White Jr. 1967, 1207). At the heart of the environmental crisis, White writes, lies the assumption of the privilege and primacy of the human found in the biblical account of the creation. The Book of Genesis describes how God created Adam and Eve "in his image and likeness" on the sixth day and then subordinated everything else to them. God blessed the first couple, saying, "Be fruitful and multiply, fill the earth and subdue it, and have dominion over the fish of the sea, and over the birds of the sky, and over every living thing that moves upon the earth" (Gen. 1:28). On one reading of this passage, humans are above nature and commanded by the Creator to dominate and subdue the earth and all that lives on it. This presumption of human transcendence is at variance with the wisdom traditions of the East, as it is with the anthropology of the pre-Christian Greeks and of native peoples worldwide. The perennial philosophy of the ancient world *subordinates* the human being to nature and conceives the latter not as meaningless matter in motion but as a great balance of spiritual forces, elements, or divine powers, which are above us and rule us. The human being, on this view, is not a transcendent sovereign but a member of an organic whole, a natural being nested in a harmonious cosmos. By contrast, the Bible conceives of the human being as an exception in nature, transcending it, free from it, and uniquely possessing reason and moral agency. Nature in the Bible is not divine but designed for our use; it is not to be worshiped but worked, at least according to the mainline interpretation of Genesis 1:27–30 that prevailed throughout the Middle Ages and early modernity.

White insists that the biblical assumption of human exceptionalism and the right to dominate nature leads directly to the technological breakthroughs and new economic attitudes that first appeared in seventeenth-century Europe. The biblical is now largely globalized and constitutes a common human inheritance. The argument is clearly controversial, and one can cite a number of objections. In favor of White's point, however, is the fact that modern technology and economics did not drop from the sky but originated in a European Christian context. That much cannot be denied. White concludes that without Christianity and its thesis of human supremacy, we would never have developed technology. We would never have attacked nature with science the way we did. A historian of the Middle Ages, White points out that seventeenth-century science and technology did not break with medieval thinking so much as develop it further. The breakthroughs we associate with modernity—Galileo's invention of the scientific method, Copernicus's discovery of the heliocentric solar system, Newton's formulation of the laws of motion—were preceded by technological advancements in European medieval society, which are, for the most part, forgotten today but which were essential to scientific and technological progress. The path to modern technology, according to White, begins in the Middle Ages with the application of Christian values to the task of dominating nature and transforming it into a properly human world. "Formerly man had been part of nature; now he was the exploiter of nature" (White Jr 1967, 1205). Technology is driven by Christian theology. It is because Europeans conceived themselves as divinely appointed masters of nature that their approach to it varied so dramatically from that of other peoples throughout history.

The repercussions of White's argument are devastating for a certain naive sense of secular progress. Modernity is not the victory of reason and science and religion. Rather modernity begins with the religious attitudes of the scientists and machine makers. Central to the sense of mastery that drove medieval and early modern science is the Christian conception of human freedom in an unfinished universe.

The Hegemony of Calculative Thinking

Western Christians once believed that humans were called by God to master nature and determine themselves. Calculation and control, therefore, became the highest ideals of modern thinking. But calculation and control are only one side of the Western mind and not even the most important side. The other side is contemplative. Nature was not only to be mastered; it was also to be known for its own sake. The highest act of the mind for Western thinkers from Aristotle to Heidegger is contemplation, knowing things as they really are. Knowledge is more than a means to certain ends; it is also, in its highest iteration, an end in itself. Christianity adopted this Greek idea and considered the chief purpose of human life the contemplation of God.

The calculative and controlling mode of thought, which reckons with conditions, measures, and plans for the sake of achieving some end, has been hyper-developed to the point that we have forgotten its complement, the contemplative mode. When we are calculating, we are not contemplating. We are imposing an agenda of our own on things and manipulating them to suit it. The two modes of thinking need not contradict one another, as Heidegger argued in his later works.[6] There is a time and place for each. It is not time to meditate on the meaning of things when the tire is flat on your vehicle. But if life is nothing but a series of tasks to be accomplished with ever greater efficiency, what is the point of it all? The problem is that in the modern age, calculation entered a hyperbolic key and eclipsed contemplation. We have forgotten that meaning is not a human construct but is intrinsic to things because we have stopped paying attention to what things are in themselves. We are too busy pursuing our plans for changing the world to better suit our needs and desires to notice what things are saying to us.

Still, the agenda driving the rise of calculative thinking in modernity is theological, even if that theology has become unconscious. The West strove to finish the universe that God had left unfinished. Many innovators and leaders in early modern science, technology, and colonial expansion believed themselves to be called to bring order to that which was only partially ordered. They were striving to bring justice to a nature that is "red in tooth and claw" and to bring the light of knowledge to non-Western peoples whom they believed to be languishing in ignorance. The road to hell is paved with good intentions, no doubt, and there is no minimizing the destruction and violence and injustice perpetrated by Western colonialism. But before we vilify Western technology, we should remember that the motivation to control nature is not always evil, for nature is not always just. The desire to make nature a world where humans can flourish is not in itself an evil agenda. As George Grant argues, the desire of early modern scientists and thinkers to equalize the relations between human beings, each of whom Christianity proclaimed to be an image of God, was crucial to the rise of modern technology (Grant 1987).

Unlike ancient Greek or Indian philosophy, Christianity rejects the idea that some people are born to be enslaved by others. Christianity, in principle, if not in practice, breaks with slavery, which is the oldest institution in history. Part of what motivates the intense push toward world transformation that overtakes European Christendom in the early modern era is the conviction that new science and technology are needed to liberate people from slavery. Countless million human beings throughout history have lived their whole lives in soul-destroying drudgery as the property of others. Even if many Christians owned slaves and turned an indifferent eye to its practice, this undeniable fact remained from the beginning a problem for Christianity. The world had to be re-made if it was to become a truly human world, a world in which freedom and equality were accorded to all human beings.[7]

The ancient Greeks believed slavery was natural. It was natural that the stronger should rule the weaker. They did not believe that human beings possessed "inalienable" rights and freedoms. The ancients were, with few exceptions, determinists. Human beings are part of a natural order which they cannot change. This was not only bad news. It was also good news if your goal was to contemplate an eternal order of things. Human reason was *reflective* rather than *creative,* mirroring an eternal harmony of being. The pre-Socratic Greek philosopher Heraclitus speaks of the *logos* (small *l,* not the *Logos* of Paul and John) that is at the heart of the changing world (Heraclitus 2001). *Logos* can be translated as "word," "reason," or "order." The flux and flow of time follow the *logos;* the planets obey it, as does the human body. The *logos* shows itself in the blossoming of a flower just as much as in the mind of the human being. The task for the sage is to hearken to the *logos,* to listen to it sounding in everything so as to live in harmony with all things. "All things follow from the *logos*... For wisdom, listen not to me but to the *logos* and know that all is one" (Heraclitus 2001, 3, 5, 13). One hears the resonance of this philosophy with Eastern ways of thinking. In ancient Taoism, the eternal order is called the Tao. Because all things have a pattern and an order, the sage is advised to let go of all thoughts and plans and to let things be. "Do you want to improve the world? I don't think it can be done. The world is sacred. It can't be improved. If you tamper with it, you'll ruin it. If you treat it like an object, you'll lose it." (Lao-tzu 1992, 134, translation altered). Lao-tzu advises a wise passivity in the face of a universe that orders itself: "'Being' and 'nothing' give birth one to the other... And so the wise person settles into his job of not doing... The thousands of things arise and are active—and he rejects none of them" (Lao-tzu 1992, 92).

However uplifting, this attitude is not one that leads to technological breakthroughs. It encourages a kind of holy surrender to reality that is mostly foreign to the West. The human being for Heraclitus and Lao-tzu participates in a great drama of meaning that does not play out for the sake of humanity alone. The universe is, in a certain way, indifferent to humanity. We are privileged to witness the drama and behold the meaning revealed therein, but there is nothing special about us. We are not created in the image of God because there is no transcendent Creator. Such an attitude does not manipulate nature for human interests. It lets nature be.

Much of the esoteric and New Age religious movement revolves around the effort to retrieve this pagan sense of living in harmony with nature. But in a consumerist context, Eastern oneness becomes quickly ideological if not self-contradictory. We are no longer there. We can *pretend* that the world is animated by spirits, but we cannot truly believe it. If we are to live more ecologically, it will have to be in a universe that is mapped and explored by modern science, that is, a disenchanted universe, in which human beings are free to make themselves, not the magical, deterministic cosmos of ancient Greek shamanism or Taoism. Any environmentalism that wants to win the support of modern people will need to appeal to our sense of individual freedom, as if not the highest value, then at least to be protected and fostered.

The Christian notion of freedom was originally balanced by other values that have since been lost to the culture at large: the transcendence of the good, love for community, fidelity to tradition, and self-sacrificial charity. After the seventeenth century, belief in transcendence and religious tradition diminished in Western societies, and human freedom became bare autonomy. Progress became the new religion. The present and the future were thought to be always better than the past. Happiness came to be increasingly identified with material well-being. The self existed only for itself, and its principal occupation was to experiment with itself, to vary its pleasures and tastes and pursue ever-novel forms of entertainment.

Christian freedom was originally bound up with reverence for nature.[8] This feeling should not be confused with the worship of nature. Reverence is born of the feeling of awe we feel in the presence of the majesty, beauty, and intricate order of God's creation. But there is no confusing God with creation: creation is a theophany, a showing of God, since nothing in it has any other origin than God. Creation is God's self-expression, but God infinitely transcends it. Even if the human being is the center point of this theophany, the image of God, everything equally expresses some aspect of the divine mind. We can and should feel reverence for everything that exists, from the stars in the sky to the smallest creatures that crawl on the earth. The Psalmist sings, "The heavens are telling the glory of God; and the firmament proclaims his handiwork" (Ps. 19: 1–2). The Hebrew Bible always combines these two thoughts, the glory of God shining in creation, and the dignity and freedom of the human being. "When I look at your heavens, the work of your fingers, the moon and the stars that you have established; what are human beings that you are mindful of them, mortals that you care for them? Yet you have made them a little lower than a god, and crowned them with glory and honour. You have given them dominion over the works of your hands; you have put all things under their feet" (Ps. 9:2–6).

As Pope Francis makes clear in his encyclical on climate change, the biblical idea of human dominion over creation must be understood in the sense of *stewardship*, not *domination* (Francis I 2015, 67). We are stewards over a creation that is not our own, but which has been entrusted to our care by its true lord. And we are to rule it as God rules the universe, with justice, generosity, and love for the theophanic diversity of the whole, the glory of it all, from the starry sky above to the smallest and the weakest of creatures that crawl upon the earth. In keeping with this Hebraic attitude of reverence for nature, Jesus gestures to the lilies of the field and the birds of the air as proof of God's providence (Matt. 6: 26–28). The author of the Second Letter of Peter looks towards "new heavens and a new Earth, in which righteousness dwells" (2 Pet.: 3: 12–13). Whatever else this means, it refers to the more than human world. Christian redemption includes the non-human creatures with whom we share the earth.[9]

Reverence for nature is the attitude of one who believes that being is a gift. The Christian is called to co-create an unfinished creation and so actualize human freedom, but she is never to lose her sense of reverence for the beauty and mystery of the whole. Creation points to the Creator. The origin of order in the universe is not us, and the success of the human project ultimately depends on grace, not human ingenuity.

The modern attitude of calculation and control sees in nature only problems to be solved. It is not often recognized that hand in hand with this ethos of control, we find what Thoreau described as "quiet desperation" (Thoreau 2004, 8). The controller is not contained by a cosmos that exceeds his comprehension; he is separate from it and looks upon it as though from a great distance. Thus he finds himself without a home in the universe, for he is not part of what he controls, and since there is no structure or meaning other than his own designs, his existence is without sense. The controller is absurd, a Cartesian subject gnawed at by a fear that nothing is genuinely good, true, or beautiful.[10]

With this flattened notion of reality, the world became, as sociologist Max Weber famously put it, disenchanted. The magic and mystery were gone. There was no longer any eternal guarantee of human values. Morality became relative. The feeling of the sacredness of being, which is typical of all ancient peoples, was put out of commission. There were multiple causes of disenchantment: the fact-value distinction, the subjectivization of aesthetics, the rise of natural science, and the rise of the liberal individual who defined himself by his freedom from tradition. What was once revered as a mystery—existence itself—became a problem to be solved.[11]

On the surface, we see order and meaning and value; in the depths, science reveals to us meaningless chaos. No matter how meaningful we believe our lives to be, the observations of science suggest that nothing really means anything. Our world is the result of an unimaginable accident that made the planet momentarily favorable to life. Even if we succeed in holding the chaos at bay for a few millennia more, our destiny is bound up with the fate of the universe: heat death, entropy, the natural tendency for structure to fall apart, which will eventually destroy all possibility not only of life but of material existence as such. According to this view, a human being is, in essence, doomed matter that has become strangely, tragically, self-aware of its fate. Reality is nothing but particles colliding in space, coming together, falling apart, inexplicably combining to form various compounds and substances, and then disappearing again, all without ultimate purpose.

No people have ever lived in such a hopeless world as we late moderns. Even the personality is threatened by science, which promises to find a neurochemical for every meaningful personal experience. As it does so, we are supposed to be cheerfully convinced that we have advanced knowledge to the point of being able to identify the mechanisms responsible for love, joy, or the experience of divinity. Meanwhile, we are reduced to automata, biological machines without freedom or purpose.

The Strange New Worldview of the Consumer[12]

The disenchanted worldview satisfies few of us spiritually. Since we remain spiritual beings, even in this godless age, we need a supplement to science and technology, a new belief system, and a new set of values to replace the old ones. We need a re-enchantment agenda to help us get through the day. This is the function of consumerism, the spirituality of our age. Consumerism is fueled by an unspoken ideal of immanent self-perfection through the acquisition of material goods. We seek to create or re-create ourselves through shopping, through the compulsive upgrading of our clothes, cars, and digital gadgets, and through our steady consumption of media, news, entertainment and self-help books, podcasts and videos. Consumerism is a spirituality without spirit, a futile search for transcendence on an entirely material level. It is the frenetic activity of a being longing for transcendence but who has lost all sense of the divine. To understand the theological origins of consumerism, we need to understand something of the first wave of secularism that swept across Europe in the period known as the Enlightenment. The Thirty Years' War between Catholics and Protestants caused eight million deaths in the seventeenth century and led to the separation of religion from politics and the creation of the modern, secular state. But Christianity hardly disappeared in the Enlightenment. The eighteenth-century European philosophers and political theorists tried to abolish religion from public life. But they did not succeed. At the same time, they secularized Christianity and rendered it the "natural" religion of humankind. They rejected the miracles of Christ, in particular, the miracle of his resurrection as superstition. But they insisted on retaining the Christian teaching of "do unto others as you would have them do unto you," which they held to be the essence of the Gospel. The moral teaching of Jesus was to be regarded not as a divine revelation but as a rationally defensible truth that all people have always known. Kant argued that "the golden rule" was prescribed by reason. It was universally known or at least universally knowable by all, regardless of historical knowledge of Jesus and the Gospel.

It was the moral law of reason itself, and if we all obeyed it, history would usher in an age of "perpetual peace."

Behind the rational ethics of the Enlightenment lies a deeply Christian assumption, the belief found in no other culture of the world, that the individual is radically free. The other side of Kant's idea of a rational moral rule is the presupposition that morality cannot be forced on anyone. If one obeys the golden rule out of fear of punishment or because one is forced to do it by others, it loses its moral value. The rule is only moral to the degree that the individual decides for it herself. This means that she must be free to reject it however reasonable it is. Kant goes further in his last work, *Religion within the Limits of Reason Alone.* Our free decision for the good is no doubt motivated by our character. But what determines character? If our character is *externally* determined, say by upbringing or genes, then the decision for the good is not truly free and not genuinely moral. The only solution, according to Kant, is to assume that moral agents determine their own character. Moral agents are responsible for themselves in the most radical sense. They author themselves in some unimaginable way.

The dominance of the English economic model over all other economies in the nineteenth century disseminated the religious attitudes of the colonizers just as widely as their language, models of government and industry. The colonization of the world by secularized Christian attitudes in the past two centuries has been so profound as to affect virtually every human endeavor, from science and industry to economics and politics, to psychology and sexuality. Explicit allegiance to Christianity may be at an all-time low, at least in Western nations. But the psychological and social attitudes unique to Christianity remain demonically alive. Consumerism itself lives from secular Christian values.

To get a better handle on the Christian essence of consumerism, let us profile it against its religious ancestor:

medieval Christianity. In the Middle Ages, the highest values were codified as the "three theological virtues": faith, hope and love. The ordinary pious medieval Christian aspired to be faithful, hopeful and loving as the New Testament commanded him to be. He believed that Christ had redeemed the world, or at least he believed that he ought to believe so. He hoped that he, too, would be saved in the end. And he felt compelled to help the poor and to treat others as he would have them treat himself, even if he failed to do so. Medieval Christians were just as selfish, violent, and ignorant as we are. I am speaking not of who the medievals actually were but of whom they aspired to be. The faithful, hopeful and loving ideal of the good Christian life in the Middle Ages was rooted in the teaching of Jesus and Paul and filtered down to the common people through the preaching of countless priests and monks. Your average medieval European, for the most part, did not question this morality, just as we do not question our secular values.

When these three theological virtues of faith, hope and love became secularized in the early modern period, they did not disappear. Rather they changed form.

Faith became freedom, the strong sense of freedom outlined by Kant, the freedom of the autonomous, self-creating individual. Faith singularizes the individual and places him in a solitary relation to God. She must decide who she will be, and no one can do it for her. This radical power for self-determination before God, when secularized, becomes the capacity for the self to create itself. Just as no one can believe for you, so too can no one determine your inner essence, your true self, or better, the self that is coming to be in your life.

Hope became optimism, a general sense that the future can be better than the past. The medievals hoped (with fear and trembling, to be sure) for the return of Christ and the final judgment that would bring history to an end and cast evil out forever. Moderns hope for the best in every imaginable context.

Invincible, irrefutable optimism is the secret to the modern cult of progress. Practically everyone believes that the future can be better than the past in early modernity, from the scientist who is trying to crack the code of nature to learn how to make the machines that will improve the human lot, to the socialist who visualizes a day when people shall, at last, be free from political oppression. Optimism on this scale is only possible where time is no longer thought of along ancient lines as a cyclical return of the same but along Jewish-Christian lines as open-ended. Creation in the Bible has a beginning and an end but remains unfinished. The human being is called by God to finish it.

Love became the call to social justice. Jesus commands us to love our enemies and lay our lives down for each other. Consequently, Christianity gives rise to a socially engaged attitude that is anything but universal in human history, a public concern with transforming the present and improving it for everyone. Again, the point is not that either Christians or moderns are particularly good or interested in the welfare of their neighbor. Nevertheless, charity remains an ideal for them. Since most would rather not be bothered, modernity creates the welfare state, the charters of human rights, and countless other institutions for managing the weak and the vulnerable. Before there was a welfare state, there were the institutions of medieval Christianity, outsourcing to the religious orders the charity commanded of us by Christ. Medieval religious orders educated the poor, distributed food, and set up hospitals to care for them.[13]

The values of freedom, optimism and social justice have become so second nature to us that it is hard to imagine that people ever thought differently about these things. But people have not always held these values, as any careful reading of history demonstrates. The modern places a value on the freedom of the individual that would be scarcely comprehensible to an ancient Chinese or Greek philosopher. In the ancient world people were defined by their gender, their family traditions, and their social class and within these parameters, there was no mystery about how they ought to behave or what they must do to get by. No one created themselves before modernity. The modern anticipates the future in a way that would make no sense to Socrates or Lao-tzu. Because he is called to create himself, the modern anticipates a future of limitless possibility. He is not bound by the past, by his gender, family, or position in society. He is free to make of himself what he chooses. Further, the modern has a duty to leave society better than he found it, to improve things for all by designing new technology or generating wealth or contributing through his tax dollars to the education and health of others.

Energized by the freedom, optimism, and hunger for social justice of secular Christianity, modernity set upon the world with an astonishing energy to build, reform and change things for the better. Secular faith in individual freedom, hope in the future and love for the world rendered modern Europeans tirelessly engaged in deconstructing and reconstructing the present. Much good has come of this. Think only of the emancipation of women, the universalization of education, and the abolition of slavery. None of these things would have happened without secular Christianity. Those who do not believe this admittedly surprising claim are invited to look at the history of these movements.

And yet something has been lost in translation. The transmission of these values from Christendom to the secular age has also been their reversal. They have each turned into shadows of themselves. Cut off from their roots in a living sense of the divine, faith, hope, and love have turned into their opposites, into individualism and the ethics and politics of self-maximization. Those who can't compete are institutionalized. The ideal life is one of constant novelty and material upgrades as we continue to endlessly create ourselves and find new avenues for enjoyment. In short, Christendom has become consumerism.

Campbell argues that consumerism is too often confused with generic human attitudes or universal human practices such as hedonism and the hoarding of wealth. To interpret consumerism as merely another expression of age-old human greed misses something essential about its structure and historical lineage. Campbell points out three essential features of consumerism which remain unexplained when consumerism is identified with hedonism. First, consumerism is characterized by the elevation of individual emotional fulfillment above mere sensual pleasure, that is, by an emphasis on subjective enjoyment, whatever that might mean. The consumer shops, travels and entertains himself for the sake of improving *his experience* of life. Second, consumerism is driven by a craving for novelty that is unknown in the ancient world. The consumer does not want the old pleasures endlessly repeated as did the ancient hedonist; he wants new experiences, change and growth. And thirdly, the consumer's desire for emotional fulfillment and novelty is insatiable. She does not anticipate a final end to her fulfillment or a final and ultimate experience that will bring her quest to an end. Indeed, she does not want her quest to end at all and frantically postpones the cessation of desire by buying new things (Campbell 1987).

The key to the endlessness of consumer desire is the absolute futurity of its object. The consumer always projects the desired into the future, for only thus is it safe from the disappointments of reality. It matters little if the object or the experience is genuinely new or not; all that matters is that the imagination of the consumer renders it so. The consumer imagines the desired to be something new, something not yet enjoyed. And the genius of consumerism is that no amount of real-world disappointment can divest the consumer of his dream, for what is sought is not the thing but the way of being which the thing makes possible. What is desired is an imagined experience, not an actual object. Consumer disappointment is part of the equation. The consumer product which the consumer believed would fulfill him in a new way is not, in the end, significantly different from previous acquisitions. The thing you just bought does not quench the fire of consumer desire, it only fuels the flames. The halo of transcendence quickly fades from the new iPhone, but the response is to eagerly await the next upgrade.

Consumerism appeals in countless ways to our sense of freedom, optimism, and hunger for justice. The ideal of the consumer, enacted in countless advertisements, pop songs, and TV shows, is a free and forward-moving individual who enlivens the community around her. The formal structure of Christian faith, hope and love continue to operate in the absence of their content. Christ promised his followers the fullness of life and a thriving individual existence in a just society on a new earth (2 Pet. 3:13). Consumers no longer believe in this promise, but their subjectivity remains unconsciously structured around the hope belief instilled in us. Consumer longing is infinite. It is not merely a desire for this or that. Consumer longing desires endlessly. It is the perfect capitalist machine of perpetual economic growth. In short, consumerism is not a form of materialism but a form of spirituality. It is not primarily concerned with material possessions (they are only the means) but with the self and its endless possibilities for being. Material goods are used as a means for exploring possibilities for the self.

Consumerism is no doubt the height of self-centeredness. But we should not assume that secularized Christian love has no place in it. The consumer is never alone but is always with other consumers, who admire him or judge him, whose approval he craves or whose lives he envies. The consumer desires things that others desire. The consumer fears things that others fear.[14] He longs to be loved by others and yet is tormented by the nagging fear that he is not. The psychology of advertisement capitalizes on these emotions and simultaneously flatters and threatens us. We are flattered by being told that we belong. We are "hot." We are unique and "worth it." Or we aren't. Many ads combine both messages in one ambiguous image. The ad leaves us with a terrible question: are you in, or are you out? The only way to answer the question is to prove that you are in by buying, doing, being, what "the world" regards as "in."

These values were as unknown to the pre-Christian Greeks as they were to the ancient Chinese or Hindus. But where consumer culture has spread, they are instantly recognizable. One can read them off billboards in India, see them in TV shows in Europe, hear them in pop songs in South America, and recognize them in political rhetoric everywhere.

Campbell traces consumerism back to Romanticism, the nineteenth-century movement in European art and culture, which emphasized the emotional, the individual and the non-rational as a counterbalance to Enlightenment rationalism. Feeling, individuality, and an infinite desire for fulfillment are essentially romantic, whether expressed in the poetry of Byron, Keats, and Shelley, or in the religious philosophies of Novalis, Schleiermacher, and Schelling. The first consumers were Romantics, window shopping in the Paris Arcades or blazing hiking trails through the Alps. What I would add to Campbell's excellent analysis is a further history. We should dig a bit deeper and find in the nascent consumer values of Romanticism nineteenth-century expressions of secularized Christian values. If the consumer is the child of the Romantic and the Romantic is the child of the European Christian, then the consumer is the bastard grandchild of the Christian (a bastard because he was neither expected nor desired). Consumerism commercializes the eschaton.[15] The consumer, not the meek, has inherited the earth. No corner of the planet is exempt from or untouched by consumerism. Everything is a consumable, from eco-tourist adventures in the Andes to mystical experiences in Indian ashrams to slow food experiences in Tuscan farmhouses. Nothing is sacred. Everything has its price. It will persist in being available for enjoyment to the degree that it elicits and continues to elicit the interest of consumers.

The consumer has infinite energy to consume because the goal of consumption is not simply pleasure. Pleasure-seeking comes to an end. Once a desire for a particular pleasure is satisfied, further stimulation becomes unpleasant. The consumer is after something greater than pleasure, even if she continually forgets the end for the means. She is not a hedonist or an Epicurean.[16] These ancient lovers of pleasure were far more sensible than us. The Epicurean needed only a garden and a small circle of like-minded friends to pursue his life of pleasure. The consumer is a neurotic, secular Christian. She multiplies the means because she cannot remember the end. It is enough to note how much pleasure she sacrifices for consumption and how hard she works to earn the capital necessary for constant upgrading to draw the conclusion: the consumer does not live for pleasure. Just look at what we have done to Christmas! The twelve days of medieval merry-making, feasting and fun have become a marathon of shopping that few enjoy, pushing our way through dreadful malls, and borrowing money to buy gifts people don't want or need.

The consumer is possessed by the infinite itself. He will not stop until either the world or consumerism is destroyed.

Endnotes

1. The term, "theophany," is derived from an ancient Greek word meaning the showing of God (*phainein*, to show, *theos*, divinity). The sixth-century Greek theologian and the father of Christian Neoplatonism, Pseudo-Dionysus, holds that because the infinite God could not be other than the finite universe but contains it and manifests

himself through it, the universe is a theophany. The idea is found throughout medieval Jewish and Islamic thought as well. It could be regarded as axiomatic for monotheistic mysticism. A God who is other than the universe, an old man in the sky, is not infinite but finite, an object over and against creation. The infinite God contains and permeates the finite creation, as Paul himself is reported to say in the Book of Acts. "In him, we live, move, and have our being" (Acts 17: 28).

2. The Medici were the bankers of the Renaissance. See Niall Ferguson, *The Ascent of Money: A Financial History of the World* (Ferguson 2008).
3. An inscription carved above the door of C.G. Jung's house in Switzerland reads, *Vocatus atque non vocatus deus aderit*, which is Latin for "Called or not called, the god will be there" (Jung 1975, 611). Jung often speaks of the archetype of the divine "self" that directs the traffic in the unconscious, regardless of whether or not we believe in God. See Jung (1989). F.W.J. Schelling was among the first to argue that we are "the God positing beings" and have to do with God, even when we are most deeply alienated from him (Schelling 2007a, 129). The argument is also found in Freudian psychoanalysis. Jacques Lacan argues that there is no getting rid of the fantasy of "the Big Other." Our sanity requires that something, no matter what, justice, nature, or science, remain divine for us. See Fink (1995).
4. Historians of ideas have shown that this Jewish-Christian concept of an unfinished universe was pivotal to the rise of science, just as the concept of a free individual was foundational for modern political liberalism. See Cassirer (1963); Gauchet (1999); Berman (2008).
5. By basic presupposition, I mean what the British twentieth-century philosopher meant by it, the presupposition

that we cannot coherently doubt because our thinking presupposes it. See Collingwood (1940).

6. Heidegger writes that thinking has two opposite modes of operating: "calculative" and "meditative." Calculative thinking is means-end thinking which only considers things in terms of their relationship to the intentions and goals of the calculator. Everything is valuable and meaningful solely as a means to an end that the calculator has determined in advance. Meditative thinking considers things in terms of their intrinsic value and meaning. It is the kind of thinking "that contemplates the meaning which reigns in everything that is" (Heidegger 1966, 49). Heidegger believes that these two modes of thinking are complementary. But in our era, calculative thinking has developed at the expense of meditative thinking. Another way of putting the same point is in terms of the difference between "quality" and "quantity." The chief error of modernity, according to Robert Pirsig's 1974 cult classic, *Zen and the Art of Motorcycle Maintenance* (Pirsig 1974), is that it has divorced these two. For a more erudite approach to the same theme, see René Guégnon's 1945 book, *The Reign of Quantity and the Signs of the Times Guégnon* (Guégnon 2001). The distinction between two kinds of thinking, one calculative and quantifying, the other meditative and qualitative, has recently been traced to the two hemispheres of the brain, with the right hemisphere being contemplatively oriented to the big picture and the left hemisphere more narrowly and analytically setting about to achieve a given task. See McGilchrist (2009).
7. I am not arguing that Christians have never enslaved others: obviously, they have, and they still do. Our consumer lifestyles are only possible through the exploitation of countless wage slaves in the developing world and on the lower rungs of the working class in the developed world.

Christians have been complicit in slavery throughout history, but they have also been instrumental in abolishing it, recognizing that it is contrary to the ethics of the Bible. Aristotle, by distinction, has no moral objection to slavery, for he does not believe that human beings are morally equal. On the history of Christianity and slavery, see (Stark 2003); Belloc (2007).

8. Albert Schweitzer coined the term "reverence for life" while traveling through the Congo in the middle of the twentieth century and searching for a universal ethic that could unite the world on the verge of total war. See Schweitzer (2009, 154–155). But the German terms for reverence have a much older pedigree. Kant speaks of "reverence" or "respect" (*Achtung*) for the moral law and the freedom of other persons. The nineteenth-century Romantic theologian Schleiermacher extends reverence (*Ehrfurcht*) to nature as such. "Are we not overcome with reverence at the thought and sight of the world?" (Schleiermacher 1996, 35).
9. This argument has been made by theologians such as Jürgen Moltmann (1993) and Catherine Keller (2018).
10. On the argument that a purely technological environment leads us to misconceive nature as meaningless without us, see Erazim Kohak's masterpiece *The Embers and the Stars: A Philosophical Inquiry into the Moral Sense of Nature* (Kohak 1984).
11. On the distinction between "problems" and "mysteries," see Marcel (1949, 117): "A problem is something which I meet, which I find completely before me, but which I can therefore lay siege to and reduce. But a mystery is something in which I am myself involved, and it can therefore only be thought of as a sphere where the distinction between what is in me and what is before me loses its meaning and initial validity."

12. For a more detailed version of this argument, see my article, "The Theology of Consumerism" (McGrath 2014), slightly revised and reprinted in McGrath (2023).
13. The creation of the welfare state as a consequence of secularized Christian charity is a perversion of the Gospel according to Ivan Illich. It results in the creation of a new social class, "the poor." See Cayley (2005).
14. Readers of Heidegger will note that I have borrowed from his analysis of the hegemony of the "they," the anonymous "mass man," over the individual. See Heidegger (1927, 118–122).
15. I refer here to the eschatological attitude of early Christianity, which we now know was a pervasive feature of second-temple Judaism and the early Jesus movement. See Boccaccini (2020); McGrath (2023).
16. Epicurus (341–270 BC) was an ancient Greek philosopher who believed pleasure was life's highest good. One needs to avoid and minimize pain, especially pain from addiction and not getting enough pleasure. Paradoxically, the Epicurean practiced self-denial to learn how to satisfy himself with the simplest and easiest to acquire pleasures. Nothing is less Epicurean than consumerism.

"We are just setting out."

Karl Jaspers

Conclusion

Even as it becomes economically marginalized by the sheer momentum of consumer power awakening in China and India, the West still bears the responsibility for perpetrating the greatest problems threatening humanity today. These problems are so familiar that it almost seems unnecessary to name them: the commodification of everything, the technological domination of nature, environmental degradation, and social and economic dehumanization. Motivating this book is a still open question: since the declining West has produced the monsters of consumption, calculation, and control, could the resurrection of the Western soul help a decadent civilization rediscover its center? How to reawaken the ethos of reverence that was so basic to ancient Greek thought and Hebrew faith?

There is no going back to Christendom. Our time is for better or worse a secular age. But a secular age is not necessarily an irreligious age. There may be new forms of religion dawning. The classic theories of secularism spoke of the progressive separation of culture from religion influenced by the spread of wealth and science. The phenomenon is far more complex. Secular society is itself a product of the Christian religion, and in it, Christianity continues to thrive and produce new forms of life.

To understand our time, a distinction must be drawn between naive and mature secularism. Naive secularism is the thing that so annoyed Chesterton at the beginning of the twentieth century. It is the false assumption that religion is a product of poverty and ignorance; as science progresses and capitalism or socialism (depending on your economic theory) distributes wealth and knowledge, religion is supposed to die out. Only it did not. Religion has not died out in the developed world because it was never a symptom of poverty and ignorance.

There are plenty of wealthy Christians in the US or wealthy Muslims in the Middle East to disprove the first part of this assumption and no shortage of great intellectuals and scientists in every major religious tradition to disprove the second. Mature secularism does not identify religion with poverty and ignorance and hence sees no reason why it should disappear with economic development. But religion has indeed changed under the conditions of modernity. If one is generous enough to include movements like New Age, Neopaganism, deep ecology, wellness culture, and Jungianism under the banner of religion (and why shouldn't we?), there are as many people practicing some kind of religion in the West today as there were a hundred years ago.

You could respond cynically, with Žižek and his disciples, that religion never goes away because it is the constitutive ideology of the inescapably neurotic human being, the fantasy of the Big Other we need to get through the day. This position, however powerful, does not question religion; it condemns it.

The major shift in religion in the secular age is in the way religion is transmitted. People no longer necessarily practice the religion their parents practiced. If they go to a church, a temple, a synagogue, a mosque, an ashram, or an eco-retreat, it is because they choose to. Religion, like everything else in consumerism, has become a matter of individual preference. One can be critical of this, but it is not easily denied. We shop for everything now, even our gods.

Mature Western secularism is deteriorated Christianity. It is Christianity hysterically extroverted, in disavowal of itself, and become a non-confessional agenda for everybody. Secularism radiated out from early modern Europe to the colonies and the globe over the past one hundred years, with devastating effects on local cultures and ancient traditions. Still, there is nothing un-Christian about wanting to liberate individuals from ideology, to improve material and ecological conditions for all, or to build a caring, tolerant society. All these secular aims are founded upon Christian virtues (respectively, faith, hope, and love). But like all extroverts, mature secularism is in danger of forgetting its soul. Instead of living in denial of our religious heritage, secular Christians (among whom I include myself) might become contemplatives once again. Recognizing the religious spirit that still animates modernity, secular Christians might realize that modernity itself is a religious enterprise, one that might have evolved otherwise and might still change its course. Religious secularism, if such a thing is possible, would be built explicitly on religious values, values that most moderns readily endorse but without recognition of their Christian roots: human dignity, freedom, and reverence for all of creation. At the same time, religious secularism would not nostalgically pine for another age. Religious secularism would be inherently pluralist and committed to the contemporary moment as yet an age of revelation. It might be essentially Christian in origin, but it would never forbid other traditions from arriving in their distinctive ways at the secular altar, the one common site of the sacred, which is the earth itself.

What we are imagining here is not as far from the religion of Paul as one might assume. Paul's Christianity is not bound to temple or synagogue. It is inclusive and recognizes multiple paths to the one savior of the world (Boccaccini 2020). There were no dedicated churches prior to the conversion of Constantine three centuries after Paul's death. The "way" (which was how they referred to Christianity before it was named at Antioch) was a practice of living together in the world but not of it. There were no priests or institutions. Small groups of like-minded people would live a common life, quietly subverting the injustices of the Roman world in anticipation of a better one to come. Instead of hierarchy, they practiced equality; instead of revering power, they protected the weak; instead of supporting a small aristocracy that hoarded wealth, they shared everything. Most importantly, Paul's Christianity looks to a more just future, a thriving human community on a transfigured earth (Rom. 8:22–24). The point of it all is not to commemorate a past event. The first Christians turned their faces to the East, to the rising sun, in anticipation of something wonderful still to happen. Christ is the midpoint of a three-act drama; the third act is still to come.

Religious secularism would retrieve from the past those forms of life that can still carry us into an unknown future. Monasticism, for example, is not over, even if it is at a nadir of popularity at the moment. It was always a secular movement. As in Judaism, there is no rigid distinction between daily life and religious practice in monasticism—that is the whole point of the monastic rule. The essence of monasticism is not poverty, chastity, and obedience but community. The three "evangelical councils" are too often interpreted concretely, as though a monk must literally own nothing, physically live alone, and obey a superior. The point of these principles, as every monk knows, is spiritual: to live as though you own nothing, to love knowing that you must in the end stand alone before God, to surrender your self-will every day and in countless ways. The one thing a monk cannot do without is community. And the world has never been more in need of genuine, local, and concrete forms of community.

I have no hope in mass movements. But it always matters what each of us does, as Grant once said. I have no hope that our governments will construct the policies needed for the transition to ecological civilization. They are too busy exploiting the earth and pursuing the always lucrative business of war. But change can come from below, where it has always originated, from the countless little communities quietly defecting from the global politics of ecological and social violence and pursuing another way. Many of these groups are organized around an ecological agenda with only a tangential relation to religion. This only confirms that the earth *is* the new site of the sacred for a mature secular age. Nature is becoming, once again but in a new way, an index of the transcendent.

I began this book by suggesting that the quiet desperation of modern Westerners will only be cured when the West recovers its desire for the genuinely transcendent. This rediscovery of the one God of the universe is perhaps the greatest challenge to a secular society. There is too much false transcendence on offer. We are deceived at every turn and prefer to remain so. No one needs God anymore, I am told. We have technology, shopping, and endless travel. But can we genuinely reverence anything without desiring transcendence? Can we love one another and all things appropriately without anticipating the new earth promised to us by Saint Paul? (Rom 8:21–22).

I dare to finish this book on a hopeful note. Nothing is to be gained by critique alone: one simply adds to the cynicism of our time. Without hope, there is no will to change the present. And if hope is to be a vital force for change, it must have no limits placed on it. We must be free to hope without condition, that is, our hope must be theological, in essence, if not in word. Theological hope is to be sharply distinguished from optimism. Optimism naively assumes that we possess the means necessary for bringing about the desired change. Theological hope is much more mysterious than that. It can survive under the bleakest conditions because it never relies on the merely human. It does not remove us from the world, as the critics of Christianity have monotonously and incorrectly claimed. It does not devalue the present but rather so values it as to insist on justice for it.

And so I close with a confession. I hope for a future that will be better than the past, a future that will redeem the past, a future that will restore all the beauty that has been lost and, at the same time, resurrect us into the radically new. Such hope not only clears the way to the lost road. It is the road itself.

References

Augustine, Saint. 1991. *Confessions*. Trans. Henry Chadwick. Oxford University Press.

Aquinas, 1948. *Summa Theologica*. Trans. Fathers of the English Dominican Province. Benzinger Brothers.

Badiou, Alain. 2003. *Saint Paul: The Foundation of Universalism*. Redwood City, CA: Stanford University Press.

Balthasar, Hans Urs von. 1986. "On the Concept of the Person." *Communio* 13: 18–26.

Barth, Karl. 2022. *Spiritual Writings*. Ed. Ashley Cocksworth and W. Travis McMaken. Mahwah, NJ: Paulist Press.

Belloc, Hilaire. 2007. *The Servile State*. New York, NY: Cosimo Books.

Berman, Joshua. 2008. *Created Equal: How the Bible Broke with Ancient Political Thought*. Oxford, UK: Oxford University Press.

Boccaccini, Gabriele. 2020. *Paul's Three Paths to Salvation*. Grand Rapids, MI: Eerdmans.

Bonhoeffer, Dietrich. 1959. *The Cost of Discipleship*. London: SCM Press.

Brown, Peter. 1969. *Augustine: A Biography*. Berkeley, CA: University of California Press.

Buber, Martin. 1958. *I and Thou*. Trans. Ronald Gregor Smith. New York: NY: Charles Scribner's Sons.

Cahill, Thomas. 1998. *The Gift of the Jews. How a Tribe of Desert Nomads Changed the Way Everyone Thinks and Feels*. New York, NY: Anchor Books.

Campbell, Colin. 1987. *The Romantic Ethic and the Spirit of Consumerism*. Oxford, UK: Blackwell.

Cassirer, Ernst. 1963. *The Individual and the Cosmos in Renaissance Philosophy*. Philadelphia, PA: University of Pennsylvania Press.

Cayley, David. 2005. *The Rivers North of the Future: The Testament of Ivan Illich*. Toronto: House of Anansi.

Chesterton, Gilbert K. 1908. *Orthodoxy*. New York, NT: John Lane.

——. 1923. *St. Francis of Assisi*. London: Hodder and Stoughton Ltd.

——. 1933. *St. Thomas Aquinas*. New York, NY: Sheed & Ward.

Collingwood, R.G. 1940. *An Essay on Metaphysics*. Oxford, UK: Oxford University Press.

Copleston, Frederick. 1946–1975. *The History of Philosophy. Nine Volumes*. New York, NY: Doubleday.

Culp, John. 2023."Panentheism," *The Stanford Encyclopedia of Philosophy* (Fall 2023 Edition), Edward N. Zalta & Uri Nodelman (eds.), URL = <https://plato.stanford.edu/archives/fall2023/entries/panentheism/>.

Cusanus, Nicholas. 1954. *Of Learned Ignorance*. Trans. Fr. Germain Heron. London: Routledge & Kegan Paul.

Dodd, C.H. 1920. *The Meaning of Paul for Today*. New York, NY: G. Doran Company.

Dostoevsky, Fyodor. 1914. *Crime and Punishment*. Trans. Constance Garnett. London: William Heinemann.

Daniel-Rops, Henri. 1956. *Jesus and His Times*. Two Volumes. New York, NY: Doubleday.

Eckhart, Meister. 2009. *The Complete Mystical Works of Meister Eckhart*. Translated and edited by Maurice O'C. Walshe. New York, NY: Herder & Herder.

Eliade, Mircea. 1964. *Shamanism: Ancient Techniques of Ecstasy*. Princeton, NJ: Princeton University Press.

Eliot, T.S. 1934. *After Strange Gods: A Primer of Modern Heresy*. New York, NY: Harcourt, Brace & Company.

Ferguson, Niail. 2008. *The Ascent of Money: A Financial History of the World*. New York, NY: Penguin.

Fink, Bruce. 1995. *The Lacanian Subject*. Princeton, NJ: Princeton University Press.

Francis I. 2015. *Encyclical on Climate Change and Inequality: On Care for our Common Home*. Brooklyn, NY: Melville.

Gauchet, Marcel. 1999. *The Disenchantment of the World: A Political History of Religion*. Princeton, NJ: Princeton University Press.

Génon, René. 2001. *The Reign of Quantity and the Signs of the Times*. Hillsdale, MI: Sophia Perennis.

Gillespie, Michael Allen. 2009. *The Theological Origins of Modernity*. University of Chicago Press.

Grant, George. 1987. *Technology and Justice*. Notre Dame, ID: Notre Dame University Press.

——. 1995. *Time as History*. University of Toronto Press.

Haughton, Rosemary. 1979. *The Catholic Thing*. Springfield, Ill: Templegate Publishers.

Heraclitus. 2001. *Fragments: The Collected Wisdom of Heraclitus*. Trans. Brooks Haxton. New York, NY: Viking.

Heidegger, Martin. 1962. *Being and Time*. Trans. John Macquarrie and Edward Robinson. Oxford: Blackwell.

——. 1966. *Discourse on Thinking*. New York, NY: Harper and Row.

Jung, C.G. 1933. *Modern Man in Search of a Soul*. Trans. Cary F. Baynes. London: Kegan Paul.

——. 1970. *Psychological Reflections*. Ed. Jolande Jacobi. Princeton, NJ.: Princeton University
Press.

——. 1975. *Letters: 1951–1961*. Ed. G. Adler, A. Jaffé, and R.F.C. Hull. Princeton, NJ: Princeton University Press, vol. 2.

——. 1989. *Memories, Dreams, Reflections*. Recorded and edited by Anniela Jaffé. Nerw York, NY: Vintage Books.

Kazantzakis, Nikos. 1960. *The Last Temptation of Christ*. Translated by Peter A. Bien. New York: Simon & Schuster.

——. 1962. *Saint Francis*. Translated by Peter A. Bien. New York: Simon & Schuster.

Keller, Catherine. 2018. *Political Theology of the Earth: Our Planetary Emergency and the Struggle for a New Republic*. New York, NY: Colombia University Press.

Kierkegaard, Soren. 1962. *Philosophical Fragments or Fragments of Philosophy by Johannes Climacus*. Princeton, NJ: Princeton University Press.

——. 1983. *Fear and Trembling / Repetition*. Trans. Howard V. Hong and Edna H. Hong. Princeton, NJ: Princeton University Press.

Lao-tzu. 1992. *The Tao of the Tao Te Ching*. A Translation and Commentary. Michael LaFargue. Albany, NY: State University of New York Press.

LeVasseur, Todd, and Anna Peterson, eds. 2017. *Religion and Ecological Crisis: The "Lynn White Thesis" at Fifty*. London: Routledge.

Lewis, C.S. 1952. *Mere Christianity*. London: Geoffrey Bles.

——. 1955. *Surprised by Joy*. London: Geoffrey Bles.

Lossky, Vladimir. 1976. *The Mystical Theology of the Eastern Church*. Crestwood, NY: St. Vladimir's Seminary Press.

Marcel, Gabriel. 1949. *Being and Having*. Trans. Katharine Farrer. Westminster, UK: Dacre Press.

Marsh, James. 2014. *Strange Glory: A Life of Dietrich Bonhoeffer*. New York, NY: Knopf Doubleday.

Martin, Michael, ed. 2016. *The Heavenly Country: An Anthology of Primary Sources, Poetry, and Critical Essays on Sophiology*. Brooklyn, NY: Angelico Press.

McGinn, Bernard. 1991. *The Foundations of Mysticism*. Volume 1 of *The Presence of God: A History of Western Mysticism*. New York, NY: Crossroads.

——. 2003. *The Mystical Thought of Meister Eckhart: The Man from Whom God Hid Nothing*. New York, NY: Herder & Herder.

McGrath, Sean J. 2014. "The Theology of Consumerism." *Analecta Hermeneutica* 6. https://journals.library.mun.ca/ojs/index.php/analecta/article/view/1667

——. 2019. *Thinking Nature: An Essay in Negative Ecology*. Edinburgh, UK: Edinburgh University Press.

——. 2021. *The Philosophical Foundations of the Late Schelling: The Turn the Positive*. Edinburgh, UK: Edinburgh University Press.

——. 2023. *Political Eschatology*. Eugene, OR: Wipf & Stock.

McGilchrist, Iain. 2009. *The Master and his Emissary: The Divided Brain and the Making of the Western World*. New Haven, CT: Yale University Press.

McNamara, William. 1967. *The Art of Being Human*. New York, NY: Doubleday.

——. 1976. *The Human Adventure: Contemplation for Everyman*. New York, NY: Doubleday.

——. 1983. *Earthy Mysticism: Contemplation and the Life of Passionate Presence*. New York, NY: Crossroad.

Merton. Thomas. 1948. *The Seven Storey Mountain*. New York, NY: Harcourt, Inc.

——. 1985. *Disputed Questions*. New York, NY: Houghton Mifflin Harcourt.

Moltmann, Jürgen. 1993. *God in Creation: A New Theology of Creation and the Spirit of God*. Minneapolis, MN: Fortress Press.

Morton, Timothy. 2012. *The Ecological Thought*. Harvard University Press.

Naess, Arne, 1977. "Spinoza and Ecology," *Philosophia*, 7 (1977): 45–54.

Novalis. 1997. *Philosophical Writings*. Translated and edited by Margaret Mahony Stoljar. Albany, NY: State University of New York Press.

Pascal, Blaise. 1995. *Pensées and Other Writings*. Trans. Honor Levi. Oxford, UK: Oxford University Press.

Pirsig, Robert M. 1974. *Zen and the Art of Motorcycle Maintenance: An Inquiry into Values*. New York, NY: William Morrow.

Plato. *Complete Works.* Ed. John M. Cooper and D.S. Hutchinson, Indianapolis, MI: Hackett, 1997.

Plotinus. 1962. *The Enneads.* Trans. Stephen Mackenna. London: Faber & Faber.

Sanders, E.P. 1993. *The Historical Figure of Jesus.* New York, NY: Penguin Books.

Schelling, F.W.J. 2007a. *Historical Critical Introduction to the Philosophy of Mythology.* Albany, NY: State University of New York Press.

——. 2007b. *The Grounding of the Positive Philosophy: The Berlin Lectures.* Trans. Bruce Matthews. Albany, NY: State University of New York Press.

Schweitzer, Albert. 2009. *Out of My Life and Thought: An Autobiography.* Baltimore, MD: John Hopkins University Press.

Shanks, Hershel. 2005. "How Historical is the Gospel of John?" *Biblical Archaeology Review,* September/October vol. 31, n. 5.

Stark, Rodney. 2003. *For the Glory of God: How Monotheism Led to the Reformations, Science, Witch-Hunts, and the End of Slavery.* Princeton NJ: Princeton University Press.

Stephenson, James, ed. 1983. *A New Eusebius: Documents Illustrative of the History of the Church to AD 337.* London: SPCK.

Tanner, Kathryn. 2019. *Christianity and the New Spirit of Capitalism.* New Haven, CT: Yale University Press.

Taylor, Charles. 2007. *A Secular Age.* Harvard University Press.

Teilhard de Chardin, Pierre. 2001. *The Divine Milieu.* New York, NY: Harper Perennial Modern Classics.

Thoreau, Henry David. 2004. *Walden.* Princeton, NJ: Princeton University Press.

Weber, Max, 1958. *The Protestant Ethic and the Spirit of Capitalism.* New York, NY: Charles Scribner's Sons.

Weil, Simone. 2009. *Waiting for God.* New York, NY: HarperCollins.

White Jr., Lynn. 1967. "The Historical Roots of our Environmental Crisis." *Science* 3767: 1203–1207.

Wright, N.T. 2003. *The Resurrection of the Son of God: Christian Origins and the Question of God,* Vol. 3. Fortress Press.

THE NEW OPEN SPACES

Throughout the two thousand years of Christian tradition there have been, and still are, groups and individuals that exist in the margins and upon the edge of faith. But in Christianity's contrapuntal history it has often been these outcasts and pioneers that have forged contemporary orthodoxy out of former radicalism as belief evolves to engage with and encompass the ever-changing social and scientific realities. Real faith lies not in the comfortable certainties of the Orthodox, but somewhere in a half-glimpsed hinterland on the dirt track to Emmaus, where the Death of God meets the Resurrection, where the supernatural Christ meets the historical Jesus, and where the revolution liberates both the oppressed and the oppressors.

Welcome to Christian Alternative … a space at the edge where the light shines through.

If you have enjoyed this book, why not tell other readers by posting a review on your preferred book site.

Recent bestsellers from Christian Alternative are:

Bread Not Stones

The Autobiography of An Eventful Life

Una Kroll

The spiritual autobiography of a truly remarkable woman and a history of the struggle for ordination in the Church of England.

Paperback: 978-1-78279-804-0 ebook: 978-1-78279-805-7

The Quaker Way

A Rediscovery

Rex Ambler

Although fairly well known, Quakerism is not well understood. The purpose of this book is to explain how Quakerism works as a spiritual practice.

Paperback: 978-1-78099-657-8 ebook: 978-1-78099-658-5

Blue Sky God

The Evolution of Science and Christianity

Don MacGregor

Quantum consciousness, morphic fields and blue-sky thinking about God and Jesus the Christ.

Paperback: 978-1-84694-937-1 ebook: 978-1-84694-938-8

Celtic Wheel of the Year

Tess Ward

An original and inspiring selection of prayers combining Christian and Celtic Pagan traditions, and interweaving their calendars into a single pattern of prayer for every morning and night of the year.

Paperback: 978-1-90504-795-6

Christian Atheist

Belonging without Believing

Brian Mountford

Christian Atheists don't believe in God but miss him: especially the transcendent beauty of his music, language, ethics, and community.

Paperback: 978-1-84694-439-0 ebook: 978-1-84694-929-6

Compassion Or Apocalypse?

A Comprehensible Guide to the Thoughts of René Girard

James Warren

How René Girard changes the way we think about God and the Bible, and its relevance for our apocalypse-threatened world.

Paperback: 978-1-78279-073-0 ebook: 978-1-78279-072-3

Diary Of A Gay Priest

The Tightrope Walker

Rev. Dr. Malcolm Johnson

Full of anecdotes and amusing stories, but the Church is still a dangerous place for a gay priest.

Paperback: 978-1-78279-002-0 ebook: 978-1-78099-999-9

Do You Need God?

Exploring Different Paths to Spirituality Even For Atheists

Rory J.Q. Barnes

An unbiased guide to the building blocks of spiritual belief.

Paperback: 978-1-78279-380-9 ebook: 978-1-78279-379-3

Readers of ebooks can buy or view any of these bestsellers by clicking on the live link in the title. Most titles are published in paperback and as an ebook. Paperbacks are available in traditional bookshops. Both print and ebook formats are available online.

Find more titles and sign up to our readers' newsletter at www.collectiveinkbooks.com/christianity
Follow us on Facebook at
https://www.facebook.com/ChristianAlternative

Also in This Series

Quaker Quicks - Practical Mystics
Quaker Faith in Action
Jennifer Kavanagh
ISBN: 978-1-78904-279-5

Quaker Quicks - Hearing the Light
The core of Quaker theology
Rhiannon Grant
ISBN: 978-1-78904-504-8

Quaker Quicks - In STEP with Quaker Testimony
Simplicity, Truth, Equality and Peace - inspired by Margaret Fell's writings
Joanna Godfrey Wood
ISBN: 978-1-78904-577-2

Quaker Quicks - Telling the Truth About God
Quaker approaches to theology
Rhiannon Grant
ISBN: 978-1-78904-081-4

Quaker Quicks - Money and Soul
Quaker Faith and Practice and the Economy
Pamela Haines
ISBN: 978-1-78904-089-0

Quaker Quicks - Hope and Witness in Dangerous Times
Lessons from the Quakers On Blending Faith, Daily Life, and Activism
J. Brent Bill
ISBN: 978-1-78904-619-9

Quaker Quicks - In Search of Stillness
Using a simple meditation to find inner peace
Joanna Godfrey Wood
ISBN: 978-1-78904-707-3